Digital Scholarship in the Tenure, Promotion, and Review Process

History, Humanities, and
New Technology

Series Editors:
David J. Staley, Heidelberg College,
Dennis A. Trinkle, DePauw University,
Jeffrey G. Barlow, Pacific University

Sponsored by
The American Association for History and Computing

COMPUTERS, VISUALIZATION, AND HISTORY
How New Technology Will Tranform Our Understanding of the Past
David J. Staley

TEACHING HISTORY IN THE DIGITAL CLASSROOM
D. Antonio Cantu and Wilson J. Warren

**DIGITAL SCHOLARSHIP IN THE TENURE, PROMOTION,
AND REVIEW PROCESS**
Edited by
Deborah Lines Andersen

Digital Scholarship

in the Tenure, Promotion, and Review Process

Edited by Deborah Lines Andersen

M.E.Sharpe
Armonk, New York
London, England

Library of Congress Cataloging-in-Publication Data

Digital scholarship in the tenure, promotion, and review process / edited by
Deborah Lines Andersen.
    p. cm.—(History, humanities, and new technology)
   Includes bibliographical references and index.
   ISBN 0-7656-1113-9 (cloth: alk. paper) — ISBN 0-7656-1114-7 (pbk.: alk. paper)
   1. College teachers—rating of. 2. College teachers—tenure. 3. Scholarly electronic
publishing. 4. Education, Higher—Effect of technological innovations on. I. Andersen,
Deborah Lines. II. Series.

LB2333.D54 2003
378.1′21—dc21   2003042445

Table of Contents

List of Tables and Figures

Tables

Figures

Acknowledgments

This book started with the American Association for History and Computing. The executive director, Dennis Trinkle, asked if I would like to work on a survey that explored the use of digital history in the tenure, promotion, and review process. Dennis and I developed the survey over several months, sending e-mail between Greencastle and Albany until we had a product we both liked. Dennis put the survey on his server, collected the responses, and presented me with the raw data that eventually became the qualitative and quantitative materials for presentations to the American Historical Association, and the American Association for History and Computing, as well as a paper in the *Journal of the Association for History and Computing*. Chapter 3, which presents the results of a survey of academic historians, relies upon these same data to draw conclusions about digital scholarship in the tenure, promotion, and review process. My first thanks go to Dennis and the association for supporting this endeavor.

Andrew Gyory of M.E. Sharpe approached me about writing a book that would look at digital scholarship across a variety of disciplines. Again working over e-mail, Andrew and I crafted a table of contents that would explore digital scholarship—its definition, evaluation, uses, and future for students, academics, and administrators in the university environment. Thank you, Andrew, for your persistence and insight.

This book is a collaborative effort of large proportions. Tom Mackey and Terry Maxwell have offices down the hall from mine, and wrote their chapters knowing I was just around the corner waiting for their pages. They were also the people who asked how things were going when we had chance encounters in the hall. Thanks to Terry and Tom for taking the time both to write what is here, and to pay attention to the rest.

Jerry Zahavi and Susan McCormick are also University at Albany colleagues, in the history department on a different campus. Their chapter on the *Journal for MultiMedia History* provides key insights into digital scholarship, for it describes the context in which digital scholars publish and are evaluated by their peers in e-journals. My thanks go to both of you.

Daphne Jorgensen and Jessica Lacher-Feldman are former MLS students of mine who have both gone on to jobs and PhD programs. They graciously said they would write chapters based on their work in the field of digital scholarship, despite impossible schedules and workloads. They have put up with my e-mail pestering about deadlines and details that go along with writing a collaborative volume. Thanks to both of them.

Several colleagues from the American Association for History and Computing have been working in the field of digital scholarship and are contributors in this volume. Ian Anderson brings his insights from Scotland, looking at how computers can be used in the history classroom, and, by extension, to a variety of humanities classrooms as well. Lynn Hattendorf Westney has written before on tenure, promotion, and review from her position as an academic reference librarian and bibliographer, and used her chapter as an opportunity to update her research in this arena. Ryan Johnson's chapter presents a critical issue for this book—how universities change their tenure, promotion, and review policies to include digital scholarship. Finally, David Staley has used his gift as futurist to write the final chapter that proposes five scenarios about the possibilities that lie ahead for the digital scholar. This book would not work without all of these chapters in place. Thanks to all.

While doing research for presentations on digital scholarship in the tenure, promotion, and review process I came across several journal articles that were critical to my understanding of the field. I am grateful to the late Rob Kling, Lisa Spector, and Kathleen Carlisle Fountain for agreeing to update previous research to provide chapters for this book.

Books take time. I thank my students for encouragement and understanding when I rambled on about chapters or took extra days to get papers back.

For their support and help in getting my mind off the book for a while each week I thank the members of my book group, and my spinning group, The Squeaky Wheels.

For encouragement and patience in the face of deadlines and decisions, I thank Kate, Beth, and Meg, daughters who have watched and helped while I pursued my research throughout the years.

For David, who makes lists, listens, reads chapters, and finds ways to help on a daily basis, I am continually thankful.

Finally, as a PhD student I was blessed with an adviser who listened, encouraged, corrected, and cheered as I worked my way toward becoming an academic in the field of information science. For a while before he retired we were colleagues in the same department. This book is dedicated to Tom Galvin, friend and mentor.

Digital Scholarship
in the **Tenure,
Promotion,** and
Review Process

Introduction

Deborah Lines Andersen

Defining Digital Scholarship

Computing has become so ubiquitous in today's world that it is hard to imagine an individual who never uses computers.[1] Just going about the functions of life—getting ready to go to work in the morning—puts one in contact with computing components in stoves, dishwashers, microwaves, and radios. Individuals rarely think of themselves as citizens of the digital world when they turn the key in the car's ignition. As long as the car starts, the underlying chips and microprocessors are of little consequence to the driver.

This same underlying computer technology is even more pervasive in the world of academics. Telephones were once only centrally located and then became standard items in every office on campus. Computers, which once resided only on secretaries' desks—after replacing their typewriters—now occupy a prominent place in each professor's office. Whereas once there was a secretarial pool to type up handwritten manuscripts for academics in every department, there is now a printer in every office. Professors have become their own secretaries. These technological changes—innovations diffused through entire universities—have turned everyone into some sort of digital scholar.[2]

The question then, for this discussion, is what constitutes digital scholarship. It is not enough to say that one uses a computer, a scanner, or a digital camera. Promotion committees would laugh at the notion that someone should be given credit for typing a manuscript or taking a picture. This was not the case when cutting-edge technology consisted of typewriters and black-and-white photography. It is not the case now just because the technology has gotten more sophisticated, and arguably takes longer to learn.

The critical issue in academe is what one does with what one has. It is the act of creation that defines the digital scholar. Tools such as computers and software programs are critical to this creation, but they are only the means to this end.

Evaluating Scholarship for Tenure, Promotion, and Review

In the precomputer world of academia as well as today, faculty members are usually judged based upon three standard criteria—research, teaching, and service. There are some institutions in which research is less important than teaching, although the three are usually weighted in the order listed here. These three are the tripod upon which tenure and promotion rest.

Professors coming up for tenure and/or promotion start by updating their résumés and then writing statements about their research programs, philosophies of teaching, and service to the department, the university, and the field. They amass a portfolio of all their published work and reproduce it in as many copies as necessary for internal and external review. Their departments solicit external letters of review, internal letters of support, and evaluations from students. Their chairpersons and deans write letters of recommendation. The department's tenure and promotion committee reviews the documents, writes a letter of evaluation on behalf of the department, and sends the entire portfolio on to the next level of university review. Although the particulars might vary, the process is more or less the same.

The striking part of the tenure, promotion, and review process is the sheer number of individuals who are involved in it. By the time the department solicits feedback from colleagues, students, external reviewers, and university-wide committees, there are tens of people who need to be not only familiar with the work of the individual scholar but also familiar enough with scholarly methods to evaluate how well the work makes a particular contribution to scholarship, teaching, or service. This was no small task in a precomputer age when the products of scholarship were in print format. University-wide tenure, promotion, and review committee members had the imposing task of reading through the life's work of a fellow professor and making a decision about how well that work met the promotion standards of the university.

Enter the Information Age. Nothing has really changed in the above scenario as it relates to tenure, promotion, and review on university campuses. Instead, the technology forms another layer of complexity in the process. A good example is the case of an e-journal article that an assistant professor might include in her portfolio.

The E-Article

This description starts with several assumptions. There is the assumption that the professor in question knows what she is talking about and has done a good job of research in creating the article in question. She has cited appropriate sources, followed usual research methods for her field of inquiry, and had several others in her department read her work before sending it out for review. We assume that she has used a word processing program on her office computer to create the document. We also assume that she could send this out to a standard, paper-based journal for peer review, but instead she chooses to send her paper in digital format to a reputable e-journal in her field. Leaving aside the question of why she would do this, we look at the question of how.

Submission to an e-journal is really not that different from submitting the paper to a paper-based journal. The major difference is that one usually submits the article as an e-mail attachment rather than in multiple paper copies through surface mail. Today it is becoming increasingly more common to submit an e-mailed, digital copy of a paper no matter what the final format. The first skill that the professor must have is the ability to send an e-mail attachment. She must have both the technology (e.g., an Internet service provider) and the expertise to do this.

At this point there are a multitude of "bells and whistles" that she might have added to her paper. Perhaps there are hypertext links to Web sites that serve as footnotes in her paper. The Web master of the e-journal might hyperlink all of her footnotes so that instead of residing at the end of the paper, they are only a click away for the reader. Perhaps she has included other materials that she wants hyperlinked in her paper, thus creating a text that readers can move through in a nonlinear fashion, referring to data displays or documents as needed while reading the main body of the paper. These additions are all brought about by the availability of hypertext in a Web environment, but they do not change the scholarship of the original work.

After the paper arrives in the e-mail box of the editor of a journal, he sends it out for peer review—i.e., digitally sends it out as an e-mail attachment to subject experts in the field. Again, this review is little different from paper-based review except that it is faster than conventional mail and necessitates that the reviewers have the ability to detach documents from e-mail messages, read them, and then send comments back through e-mail. If we assume that the readers positively receive the paper and notify the editor that it should be published, with or without revisions, then the Web master of the journal will assign it a volume and issue number, Web publishing the paper for the journal. The major differences in publication are that it is faster all around, and there has been no paper-based sending of the article from author to publisher to reviewers and back again.

The major difference between this e-article and its paper-based equivalent is access. Critical for this discussion, the topic of access cuts a variety of ways. First, if the article is published in an e-journal that is accessible by the public, then that publication makes the author's work available to anyone who wishes to read it. The issues of copyright and ease of copying digital documents aside, this has to be good for the author, the journal, and the field. At the same time, there are archival issues of access. How long will the e-journal maintain the document on its server? Will the publisher create a backup system that will allow access five, ten, or twenty years from now? How will this happen with changes in delivery technologies (remembering 5-inch disks that can no longer be accessed by today's computers)? The author could, and probably should, print out a copy of the article along with the journal's policies on peer review, just in case the journal has ceased to exist by the time tenure review and promotion come around.

There is a third issue of access that bears attention in relation to tenure and promotion. In what format should the scholar present her digital materials to her departmental and university-wide promotion committees? She could hand the committees disks containing both her paper-based works and URLs to on-line materials. She could, on the other hand, print out everything and present a more traditional dossier to these individuals. Either way requires making materials available in other than their original formats. Presenting both paper and URLs might make the most sense, although it would be redundant and cumbersome for those committee members who are fully conversant with World Wide Web technologies. Furthermore, printing out an article with all its hyperlinks not only defeats the purpose of the technology but also makes reading the entire work extremely difficult. The most pressing question in this particular discussion is that of access for the reviewers. Are they familiar enough with the technologies involved in e-journal production and layout so that they can adequately review the materials presented to them? Do they have compatible technologies on their desktop computers that will allow them access and appropriate viewing of all the materials in question? Do they understand the process so that they can evaluate the product?

The Act of Creation

The first step in creating scholarly digital works, or evaluating them for promotion and tenure, is to know the range of what might be possible. Understanding what has been done in the past is a building block to understanding what is new, creative, and innovative. Creating an article on a word processor might be innovative, but only to the person who has never seen one before. Academics should be credited for creation that is better, cheaper, or faster, but the evaluator needs to know the present state of affairs to make that decision about excellence. In the case of an e-journal article, the scholarship itself should be enough to merit consideration, but in the case of other products of digital scholarship, the act of evaluation becomes more difficult.

There are some criteria that one might use in deciding on the merits of a piece of digital technology. These criteria help to define the digital scholar and digital scholarship and are presented here as a series of questions that the evaluator might ask about a piece of scholarly work.

- *Time*: How much time did it take to create this piece of work? Is that substantially more than would have been the case if the work were presented in a more standard, paper-based format? What would be lost if the format were paper-based instead of digital?

- *Difficulty*: Time aside, how difficult would it be for another scholar to create this work? Did it require skills or knowledge that had to be acquired in classes or through individual study?

- *Originality*: Does this work build on the efforts of others, creating something unique, or is it an example of an application that others have used? There is nothing inappropriate about repeating applications with new materials, but if the evaluator is familiar with the digital technologies in question, then he would know when something unique is presented for evaluation.

- *Transferability*: Does this application, if it is unique, serve as a model that could be used by others to advance the field under study? Does the application advance the knowledge base of digital scholarship in general?

- *Usefulness*: What purpose will this digital scholarship serve? Is it an aid to teaching, an enhancement of service, a presentation of research? In each case, how will the scholarship be used in its specified setting? Is it better than what has come before? Does it make a difference?

Many of these questions could be asked of traditional scholarly endeavors. Perhaps that is the point. In order to understand traditional scholarship and evaluate its contribution to the field, one must know what has come before. The same point holds true for digital scholarship. It is hard to evaluate something one does not know. One critical issue for universities, and one goal of this book, is to educate academics about the nature of digital scholarship—how it is created, structured, and presently evaluated—in order to make informed decisions about its worth in the university setting.

Practice Across Disciplines

Although this volume looks primarily at digital scholarship in the context of the social sciences and humanities, it is important to look at the full spectrum of disciplines when thinking about the digital scholar. The nature of these different disciplines—their research products and modes of communication—makes an enormous difference in the kinds of technologies scholars might use.[3]

The Sciences

Fields such as biology, chemistry, and physics have had a natural advantage in accepting digital scholarship for tenure, promotion, and review. Scientific fields have always been highly quantitative, using mathematics and the notation of their fields to gain insights, test hypotheses, and create theory. Furthermore, private sector corporations and the federal government have sought out this sort of research, bringing substantial funding into research endeavors. Scientists have embraced every digital technology as it appeared, using the power of technology to advance their fields. One needs to look no further than the human genome project to see the power of technology for the sciences. Individuals in mathematics and computer science have been at the cutting edge of creating new technologies that can be used by other academics. These fields expect that their leading researchers will all be digital scholars.

Scientific publishing has benefited equally from the use of technology. Since findings in the sciences build upon each other, it is important to present new research as quickly as possible. The Internet has made publishing of preprints a fast and desirable form of information dissemination. Likewise, e-mail connects scientific communities across geographic borders, making speedy collaboration possible in ways that paper mail never could.

To be a scientist is to be a digital scholar. In the face of tenure and promotion review, scientists might find themselves evaluated by university-wide committees that contain humanists and social scientists not familiar with their methodologies. Several things can happen. The committee members will first rely on other members who are familiar with particular scientific methods. Second, they will rely upon the recommendations and evaluations of the untenured faculty member's department, as well as departmental chairs or deans. Finally, the tenure and promotion committee will rely upon external letters of review to evaluate the contributions that this scholar has made to his field as a whole.

This method of collecting information to make informed decisions about a researcher's scholarship is one model for this book. Tenure, promotion, and review committees are not expected to know every aspect of a researcher's scholarship, but they are expected to know how to gather appropriate, informed evaluations to make those decisions.

The Social Sciences

The social sciences have traditionally been considered hybrid in terms of their use of technology.[4] Sociology, psychology, and geography, for example, all deal with people and with culture, but they also use digital technologies to collect and analyze data. As with the sciences, there is an expectation on the part of departments and university administrations that social scientists are digital scholars, using the power of computers to address social science issues.

Geographers became excellent examples of digital scholars because the power of computing allowed geographic information systems to flourish. We no longer draw maps by hand, but use sophisticated satellite systems to take digital photographs of our world. Geographers take these, and other digitally created maps, and add layers of information to them. City planners look at power, water, sewer, and transportation systems layered on unified maps. Social workers look at the same city but want layers that deal with schools, social services, employment offices, day care, and transportation for their clients. The strength of this scholarship is that it has taken information that existed in paper format, collected it digitally, and created programs that provide information faster and better than ever could have been done before computer technologies existed.

This social science example is a second model for this book. Scholars who work with geographic information systems use those systems to solve information problems. They are rewarded for the creation and use of digital systems that were not possible in a precomputer age. Following the same argument used earlier in this chapter, it is not that they use technology, for example, to type an academic paper, but that they use technology so well that it transforms their field and the kind of work that is possible in it.

The Humanities

The humanities have been the most resistant to digital endeavors.[5] Arts, languages, literature, philosophy, and religion have not naturally embraced digital scholarship in the ways exhibited by scientists and social scientists. There are a variety of very good reasons for this resistance. Foremost among these reasons is the type of material that humanists study. Diaries, plays, music scores, novels, paintings, religious works, and philosophical treatises, to name a few, do not lend themselves to quantification. They are not composed of numbers, or formulas, or spatial data. Second, these documents have traditionally been in nondigital format, created by individuals who used pens, stone, or paint to create works that will in turn be studied by humanistic scholars. Whereas scientists and social scientists tend to create their own data, storing those data in digital forms for digital analysis, humanists look at the creation of others, studying documents and artistic expressions to create interpretation and meaning.

It is no wonder that humanists have been resistant to using digital technologies, and that tenure, promotion, and review committees have been equally resistant to reward digital efforts when they appear. First and foremost, the subject of their inquiries is not in digital format. One must transfer these documents or artistic expressions from the original medium into a digital proxy. Although it might be easier to study Mrs. Norris in Jane Austen's *Mansfield Park* by querying a database about all instances of Mrs. Norris's name, the Jane Austen scholar probably considers such digitization a waste of time. Learning to use a database, scan materials, and query that database all consume time that could be used to write scholarly articles. Why not just read the book and get on with the analysis?

Furthermore, scanned materials are digital proxies. They are not the originals, and in many cases the humanities scholar must see the original to really understand the work that he is studying. The scholar might find it helpful to look at thumbnail pictures of the works in a distant museum, making a decision about whether or not to travel there, but would probably not write an article without doing that traveling.

What is missing in the above discussion about humanists is the act of creation. None of the examples speak to creation as do geographic information systems or the human genome project. The examples speak to working in a different medium, e.g., doing research with technology instead of with paper. A tenure, promotion, and review committee would look to these uses of digitization and discount them.

For this book then, the question is, what does constitute truly interesting, innovative, and scholarly use of digital technologies in the humanities and in other academic fields that have traditionally been paper-based? How can tenure, promotion, and review committees evaluate the act of creation for the humanist who is also a digital scholar? One way of promoting appropriate evaluation is through examples of digital creation. The next section of this chapter looks to a variety of those examples.

Practice Across Applications

As there is a decided difference in the past and present use of digital scholarship across disciplines, so there are distinctions that one might make across various applications of technology in the university setting. These applications fall roughly into the same categories that review committees use to decide upon promotion and tenure. Whereas teaching and research easily lend themselves to digital examples, the relationship of service and technology is more tenuous. The discussion here focuses on teaching, research, and publication in turn.

Teaching

Within the realm of teaching there is a continuum of possibilities for using technology in the process of education. Information presentation methods include the use of PowerPoint slides, posting class notes to the World Wide

Web, or teaching an entire class at a distance. Included in the area of distance education is computer-assisted instruction—using the capacity of computing to present and reinforce materials for students, as well as to administer tests and capture grades from those tests. Communication in teaching can take the form of basic e-mail communications with individual students, class listservs that allow class members and the instructor to post messages to the entire group, or electronic bulletin boards. There are also possibilities for communication in networked computer laboratories, asynchronous group conferencing, and moderated discussion lists.

Implicit in this list of methods, at least from the point of view of educational theory and practice, should be a strong sense of why one would use these digital venues instead of more traditional methods of teaching. Do students learn better (capture new concepts, retain information, or acquire new skills) than they would using traditional methods? Can more students be exposed to these materials because of the technologies? Is this method of instruction more efficient for the professor and for students?

First, the strongest evaluative question is one of the horse and the cart. It would make sense to start with educational goals and then decide if teaching technologies would attain those goals better, cheaper, or faster than in the past. Starting with computing and then figuring out what to do with it probably does put the proverbial cart in the lead. Second, it is nonetheless worth asking if there are educational goals that can be accomplished only as a result of new technologies that were never possible or practical before the computer. Going back to the previous examples, the human genome project could occur only when there was enough computer memory available to analyze an enormous data set. Asking students to draw maps by hand and then overlay them to look at various public works systems was always possible, but it was not particularly practical given the hours of work it would have taken. The digital professor not only knows what technologies he might use, but also knows which ones will best meet the needs of his students and are worth spending his time and the time of students and teaching assistants to learn and apply in educational settings. In the act of deciding how to use digital technologies, by focusing on educational goals, the professor creates both the rationale for using the power of computing and the means of evaluating its worth.

Research

As mentioned previously, when looking at the application of digital scholarship to research, one must look at the discipline within which the researcher works. Of scientists, social scientists, and humanists, scientific scholars were the first to go digital, using the power of the computer to create and store data when computers were extremely large and very expensive. Social scientists were not far behind, using computing to store and analyze the data that they needed to look at the behavior of human beings in their organizations and cultures. Humanists were the last to embrace digital technologies, mostly one would posit because the grist of most of their research was not self-generated data but primary source materials created by others, and it was not often created in digital formats that were easy to manipulate with software programs.

What is common among all disciplines is that they have embraced digital technologies for research at the point at which these technologies made their jobs easier or possible. If one were to ask a geographer why she used geographic information systems, she would probably say that she could not do her job without GIS software. In that answer is the rationale for using computing and for being a digital scholar—I could not do my research without it.

In that answer is also the means to evaluate the use of technologies for research. It is essentially the same rationale as for teaching. The digital scholar focuses on creating new knowledge in whatever discipline he works. When the technology supports his endeavors and makes new endeavors possible, then he can make a strong statement for why computing is critical to his field and to his research. He can be evaluated—by his department, his university, and his discipline—based upon the strength of that statement.

Publication

Why do scholars publish? Based upon the title of this book, one might think that it is to form a résumé that will assure them tenure and promotion! That reasoning will again find the cart before the horse. Instead, one must think of publication as advancing a particular field or discipline. Researchers cannot just do research. They disseminate their findings so that others can learn about and build upon their results. Digital publication can therefore be evaluated based upon how well it disseminates information.

Earlier in this chapter we left aside the question of why a researcher would choose to publish her work electronically, in an e-journal, as opposed to a paper-based, more traditional format. According to the criteria of better, cheaper, or faster, there are a variety of answers to that question.

Faster

For a scientist, the issue of faster is extremely important. Getting important discoveries into the world in a timely manner means that others can quickly go on to the next level of research. Using the World Wide Web for publication saves time. One can self-publish on a Web site and make information available to others instantly and internationally. A researcher can also choose to submit his paper to a peer-reviewed e-journal, guaranteeing that his scholarship has been evaluated by his peers and that his paper will be published more quickly than in a traditional paper-based format that can easily take months to arrive via surface mail at libraries and academic offices.[6] Social scientists can equally feel the need to disseminate their findings in a timely fashion, especially about discoveries that will have a significant impact on their study populations or those associated with them. They have a strong rationale to expedite the publication of their findings.

Humanists have traditionally been in less of a rush to publish their works. They usually support their research hypotheses with primary source documents that have existed for a period of time (e.g., Picasso's paintings, Jane Austen's novels, Abraham Lincoln's diaries) and as a result look at these works in historical context, often prefer monographs to journal articles, and worry less about speedy publication. Perhaps the criterion of "faster" does not create a strong digital rationale for humanists.

Better

The criterion of "better" can apply to humanists, as well as to scientists and social scientists. In many instances there could be no discernible difference between a paper-based and an e-journal article—text is text. Increasingly, however, researchers are starting to think highly creatively about their e-journal publications. Hypertext allows for the creation of links to other sites or to other parts of the text. Hypermedia means that one can embed sound bites, film clips, music, or works of art in "hyperpapers," greatly increasing the researcher's ability to support his hypotheses, and also greatly increasing the reader's ability to see and hear this supporting evidence, without having to go to a library or museum. In cases where motion, sound, or highly complex visual images would enhance the reader's understanding of a piece of research, digital publication has created a much better dissemination medium for that work.

Cheaper

In the academic world there are a variety of costs associated with research publication. The university pays faculty members to teach and to do research. Faculty members write papers, and often sign their copyright ownership over to paper-based journal publishers. These publishers create journals and sell subscriptions to individuals and to university libraries—at costs that are almost universally on the rise. Thus the university can pay several times, first to have the information created, and then to have access to it.

In many cases the e-journal can be a cost-saving option. If the purpose of publication is to make research available to others, and if that publication is evaluated based upon how well it is disseminated, then electronic journals have a lot in their favor. There are those that charge no fees. They exist because of the support of societies, universities, or individuals who believe that it is worth their time and effort to produce them. Other journals have become dual format. Having started in paper-based form, they make articles available to their paying subscribers through password-protected files. Publishers do this because it is convenient for their readers, their authors have already submitted these articles in usable digital form, and the costs of paper publication make a strong case for eventually eliminating paper altogether.

This cost argument is different from that for the first two criteria of better and faster. Unless an author wishes to subscribe to a particular journal, and thus incur a subscription fee, the major cost is to the university, both for supporting the research, and for paying for journal subscriptions. A faculty member or student is less concerned with what the university paid for a journal subscription than with the fact that the information is readily available to him or her. Digital articles mean that one does not need to go to the library. The article is as far away as one's personal computer with an Internet connection. Thus, it would appear that the criterion of "cheaper" is not particularly relevant in the tenure, promotion, and review arena. Digital scholars, it would seem, do not consider whether electronic publication is cheaper when making decisions about publication venue.

Interestingly enough, this last statement is probably false. One could hypothesize that "cheapness" is a very important criterion—for causing junior faculty members to think twice before publishing in digital format. One argument states that e-journals are less good because it is much easier to put materials up on a Web site than to publish them in paper format. Another argument holds that e-journal publication is less academically rigorous than paper publication and should be discounted because of this weakness. These arguments were a critical impetus for creating this book. One can counter the accusation of cheapness only by carefully evaluating the way in which electronic publication is peer reviewed and quality controlled. Just because materials are published in a less costly, more accessible fashion does not mean they are less worthy. It does mean that individuals who are on tenure and promotion committees need to pay close attention to the scholarship, as well as to the dissemination venue, when making decisions about how that scholarship advances a particular field and creatively uses digital technologies to do what could not be done in a paper-based world.

Digital Proxies or Analogs

Perhaps a college professor might decide to publish in an e-journal simply because she has never done so before—a foray into uncharted territory. In this case the e-journal article is a digital analog for the paper that she could have easily published in a top journal in her field. There are many examples of digital analogs, although as the technological medium gets more complicated, and takes longer to learn, there are probably additional reasons for moving there—more than just for the adventure.

CD-ROM and on-line textbooks are examples of digital proxies—materials that have traditionally been paper-based but that are now appearing on-line or as disks either for entire texts or for parts of them. Electronic texts are often cheaper than paper textbooks. This can be a benefit to students, as can accessibility through a personal computer. These digital texts have the additional advantages of other hypertext products in that the writer can add sound, motion, color, and hyperlinks to other portions of the text or the World Wide Web as seems educationally appropriate. The publisher can also make on-line corrections or updates in a way not possible with paper media.

Another interesting digital analog is that of the e-journal editor or peer reviewer. Most faculty at one time or another have been asked to review articles for a peer-reviewed publication. Aside from the speed of communication and the exclusively digital mode of communication among editors, reviewers, and writers, there are few differences between the paper and the electronic forms of a journal. Either the editor or his staff needs to understand the appropriate markup language for creating hypertext. Someone needs to have the appropriate skills to keep a server up and running. Editors, reviewers, and writers must be willing to send and receive e-mail attachments of the papers that will appear in the journal. Editors still work to balance the articles that appear in any given issue. Reviewers still screen articles to make sure that the best scholarship—scholarship that advances their fields—is published in a timely and accurate manner.

A third example of a digital analog has already received some attention here. Listservs, bulletin boards, and moderated discussion lists are all proxies for face-to-face communication. In the small seminar room, face-to-face communication continues to be the best mode of eliciting information from students and faculty and of creating and sharing ideas about scholarship. In other instances the digital mode is preferable. Students can post to bulletin boards at any hour of the day and night. They are not constrained by geography, so that posting from a block or a hundred miles away is the same. Those who have a hard time speaking in front of groups might find this digital proxy far preferable to speaking in front of the class. Just as most individuals would balk at the notion of turning all reading materials into digital texts, so would educators balk at the notion of strictly virtual classrooms and discussions. Each has its place in the university. The advent of digital scholarship has created options that we did not have before.

Evaluating the Digital Scholar

It is the act of creation that defines the digital scholar. The digital scholar can see the options made available to him, his students, and his research by new technologies. He has a rationale for taking the time to learn these technologies and for applying them to his scholarship. If this is true, and the premise of this book is that it is, then the digital scholar—and especially the untenured faculty member—has the ability to inform tenure and promotion committees about his work simply by writing about this rationale. It will make perfect sense that his research is better for the use of technology. He will have clear goals for his students—goals that can best be met by digital technologies. His service, perhaps in the form of maintaining a Web site for the department or editing an e-journal, will also be clearly defined in light of his overall agenda as a professor.

All universities have guidelines that deal with evaluating academics for their contributions in research, teaching, and service. There is a move afoot to add to these guidelines additional attention to digital scholarship in the tenure, promotion, and review process. This book presents research on digital scholarship today, case studies on the use of this scholarship, guidelines that have been developed to deal with digital scholarship in the university setting, and, finally, thoughts on the future of scholarship in a digital environment. For the time being, digital scholars will be their own best advocates, taking the time to clearly state their case for working in nontraditional media. In the future, university policy will make this evaluation easier, creating clear policies that help tenure, promotion, and review committees evaluate digital scholarship. In the meantime, the authors of this book present research, case studies, and examples that bridge the evaluation gap between traditional scholarship and the creative potential of the information age and the digital scholar.

A Systems View of the Academic Universe

It is essential to remember that digital scholars do not stand alone. They function within departments, schools, universities, and academic communities both national and international. Furthermore, within these widening circles of context, they affect and are affected by these players in academe. This is a feedback view of the professorate—a view in which the actions of one individual affect others, and, in turn, the actions of others affect the individual. A feedback view requires that one think not linearly, but in closed loops, looking at the policies and actions that control the behaviors of a system.

Who are the players within the system of tenure, promotion, and review? Using a list that starts with the digital scholar and works outward in larger and larger circles, the players are diffuse and their roles are varied.

Digital Scholars

At the center of the list of players are digital scholars themselves. Not only must they decide whether or not to pursue technology products alone or in concert with fellow academics, they must also gauge the effect that their behavior will have on other academics in their departments. If a digital scholar is given a poor three-year review, due to lack of traditional scholarship in his dossier, the word will quickly get out to other junior faculty members that this is not a good pretenure path to follow. One might expect that the word would also spread to prospective faculty members who are considering applying to a particular department. A newly minted PhD with a strong digital background could very well decide not to apply to a particular school if it were known for not valuing the products of digital scholarship. On the other hand, if a digital scholar received tenure and promotion, word would also spread that this reward system was in place at a particular university.

Departments and Schools

Following directly from the scenario presented in the previous paragraph, one might expect that the word would also spread to students within a department, teaching through example that they should, or should not, value digital scholarship in their studies. If potential digital scholars shy away from work with technology before they are tenured it is probable that they will also not teach about technology or use it in their classrooms because it takes away from traditional research time. The culture of a department within the university is affected by this kind of behavior. The emphasis on particular courses or fields of study can bring in or drive away potential students as well as faculty. These issues drive the perceptions of individuals seeking to gain admission to the department, presenting strong forces for self-inclusion or exclusion.

Universities

The next players in the circle of actors in the tenure, promotion, and review process are universities. It is quite usual for university administrators to be highly in favor of digital scholarship while individual departments struggle with granting tenure and promotion for nontraditional teaching, research, and service. A university's reputation is in part made up of the cutting-edge research in which its professors engage, as well as the kinds of programs that departments offer. There is a tension that exists within universities between these two circles.

Academic Communities

Finally, one must consider communities larger than just the university. These are communities of scholars across the world that interact with one another and are aware of the research that drives particular fields. Their methods of communication are conferences, journals, and, more and more, listservs and electronic discussion lists. In a well-developed field, its members know who the leaders are, who produces the most innovative work, who brings in the largest grants, and who have received awards of recognition for what they have accomplished.

Although the single, untenured professor seems very far away from the upper echelon of the scholarly community, this professor is the future leader, innovator, and award receiver. Decisions he or she makes today, about research, service, and teaching, will affect the work that he or she does in the future. There is no expectation in this book that every untenured professor should be a digital scholar. There is the expectation, nonetheless, that university and departmental policies can have consequences for students, scholars, departments, universities, and scholarly communities that extend years into the future.

These consequences can affect a variety of players in many ways. In fact, it is probable that these effects are linked, like dominoes, so that a policy change or promotion decision at one point in time can have effects over time and across a wide number of players. The feedback view in the next section presents such a linked conception of the forces and players that interact in systems of tenure, promotion, and review.

A Feedback View

The organization of this book, including the selection of its topics and their arrangement into chapters, is predicated on a view of the central role that promotion and tenure plays in the overall emergence of strong and effective digital cultures within units of modern universities (indeed within the culture of the university as a whole). Figure 1 reveals the basic causal assumptions, often forming feedback loops that undergird this organizing framework.

Figure 1　A Feedback View of Digital Scholarship in the Tenure, Promotion, and Review Process

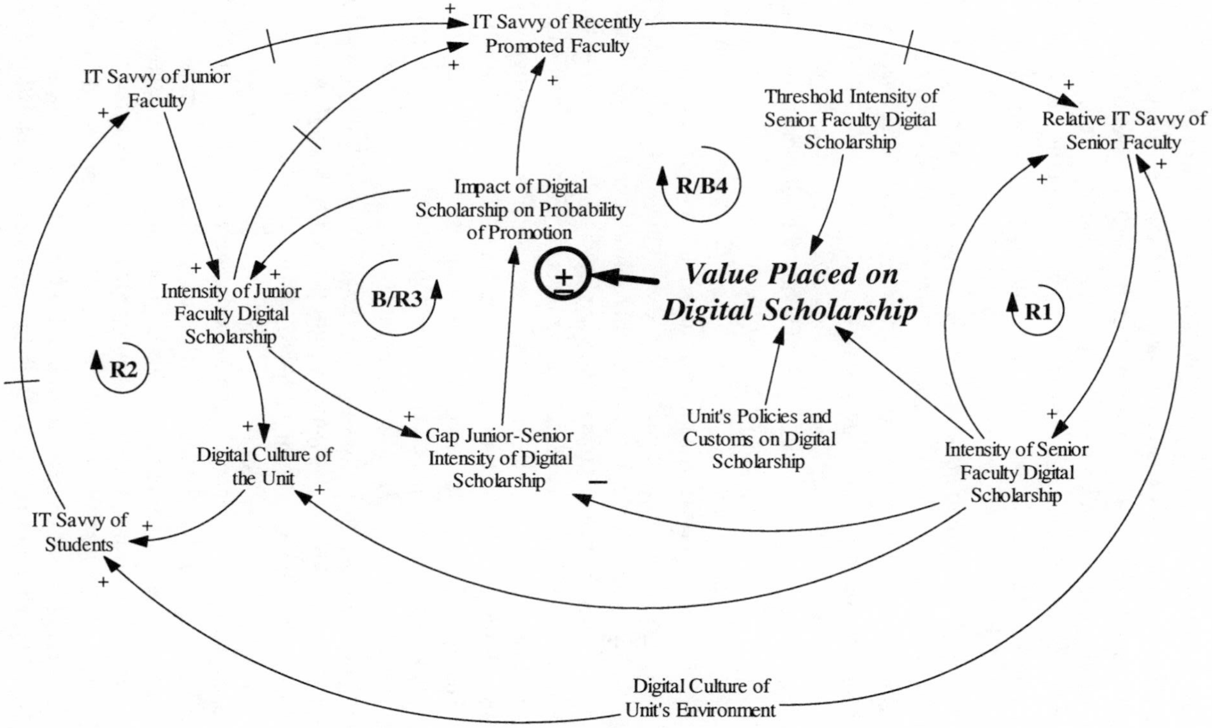

Several conventions common to the systems-thinking field help the reader to make sense out of this diagram.[7] The directed arrows between two phrases represent a causal connection. Hence the arrow connecting *Digital Culture of Unit's Environment*[8] (at the tail of the arrow) to *Relative IT Savvy of Senior Faculty* (at the arrow's head), with a positive sign at the arrow head, indicates that a *higher* level of digital culture in the unit's environment will lead to a *greater* level of IT savvy among senior faculty within the unit. Conversely, a negative sign at the head of the arrow signifies an inverse causal relationship..Hence, the negative arrow connecting *Intensity of Senior Faculty Digital Scholarship* with *Gap Junior-Senior Intensity of Digital Scholarship* indicates that an *increase* in digital scholarship per capita on the part of senior faculty will *decrease* the gap, other things being equal.

Sometimes causal relationships join to form closed feedback loops and the analysis of these closed pathways of mutually reinforcing or balancing causation is an important focus for studying the system as a whole.[9] For example, the closed feedback loop labeled "R1" demonstrates a mutually reinforcing relationship between *Relative IT Savvy of Senior Faculty* and *Intensity of Senior Faculty Digital Scholarship*. Simply put, as senior faculty become more experienced with information technology (IT), the volume of digital scholarship per capita rises. A rise in digital scholarship per capita, in turn and over time, increases the overall IT knowledge and experience among senior faculty. Notice that this reinforcing feedback loop can move in a positive direction leading to ever increasing levels of IT savvy, or it can move in a negative direction as relatively less IT savvy leads to less digital scholarship, creating a powerful trap that inhibits the takeoff of digital scholarship.

The loop "R2" posits a second mechanism that can serve to reinforce IT savvy on campus among faculty and students alike. Begin to look at this loop by assuming that the *IT Savvy of Junior Faculty* starts to rise (not a bad assumption in this era). Increased savvy on the part of junior faculty leads over time to a greater *Intensity of Junior Faculty Digital Scholarship*. In turn, the contributions of junior faculty increase the *Digital Culture of the Unit* ultimately producing greater *IT Savvy of Students*. The dash across the causal link arrow between *IT Savvy of Students* and *IT Savvy of Junior Faculty* represents a delayed causal influence. In this case it means that after some time, students complete graduate school and become future junior professors, bringing their increased IT skills with them. Notice that this same mechanism works as junior faculty become recently promoted faculty with a delay, and ultimately after a further delay become senior faculty.

A central feature of Figure 1 is the assumption that *Value Placed on Digital Scholarship* is an internal system variable that can and does vary over time. As *Intensity of Senior Faculty Digital Scholarship* grows, so does the *Value Placed on Digital Scholarship*. This relationship implies that senior faculty who do not use or produce digital scholarship in their own work, other things being equal, will tend not to value it in the promotion and review process. Conversely, as senior faculty become more productive in the arena of digital scholarship, they will come to place more value on it in the promotion, tenure, and review process.

Not only does the *Value Placed on Digital Scholarship* depend on the per capita production of digital scholarship, over time it also controls that same variable through several direct and indirect feedback effects. The *Value Placed on Digital Scholarship* is so important in this figure because it controls the polarity of the effect (negative, zero, or positive) between the *Gap in Junior-Senior Digital Scholarship* and the *Impact of Digital Scholarship on Probability of Promotion*. When this polarity is zero or negative, junior faculty perceive (correctly) that time that they spend creating digital scholarship will not be valued highly and hence their probability of being promoted will decrease. They should have spent their time creating nondigital products that are more highly valued by senior faculty.

Loop "B/R3" has a sometimes balancing and sometimes reinforcing polarity. When the relationship between the gap and the probability of promotion is negative (that is, when digital scholarship is not valued or is negatively valued) junior faculty's production of digital scholarship seeks to close the gap with their seniors. In a word, seeking to look more and more like their seniors, junior faculty produce more traditional and fewer digital products. At the same time that loop "B/R3" is in its balancing phase, loop "R/B4" is reinforcing. The senior faculty side of the loop is driving the reinforcing growth of digital scholarship. Notice that if *Relative IT Savvy of Senior Faculty* declines (perhaps because the overall digital culture in other units increases), this decline will touch off a downward-spiraling trap that locks senior faculty into a world of nondigital production. In this mode of the system's behavior, senior faculty are caught in a downward spiraling trap of less and less (in relative terms) digital scholarship, and junior faculty are working hard to match their overall pattern of performance in order to get promoted.

However, when the *Value Placed on Digital Scholarship* shifts polarity and moves from zero or even from negative to positive, the whole behavior of the system shifts. Senior professors now value digital scholarship and the gap in such scholarship between juniors and their seniors is a plus, not a negative, at tenure time. Hence, loop "B/R3" shifts to a reinforcing one, with production of digital scholarship per capita by junior faculty racing ahead of that for senior faculty with the gap being rewarded by promotion, creating even further momentum. With a delay, these junior faculty are promoted, becoming senior faculty, further reinforcing the overall growth of digital scholarship in the unit or across campus. When the system is operating in this mode, notice that senior professors are following the lead of junior faculty. This occurs because the polarity of "R/B4" is now balancing, indicating that senior faculty's per capita production of digital scholarship seeks to close the gap with the juniors (who are continuing to race ahead).

Hence, the single structure of feedback relationships in Figure 1 implies two quite distinct regimes of behavior over time. In the first regime, digital scholarship is not highly valued in promotion, tenure, and review, and hence junior faculty work to look like their seniors who are caught in a downward-spiraling trap of relatively less digital scholarship per capita. The second regime occurs when positive value is placed on digital scholarship. In this situation junior faculty take the lead in providing ever-greater productivity in digital scholarship per capita because their relative advantage in this area gets rewarded at promotion time. Senior faculty work to close the digital scholarship gap by cranking up their own rate of per capita production.

Finally, notice that Figure 1 assumes that the overall digital scholarship of faculty and students alike in a given unit is driven exogenously by the *Digital Culture of Unit's Environment*. If we were to think of a "unit" as a department in the humanities or in the social or physical sciences, then that unit's environment would be other departments on campus or even similar departments at other university centers. It is possible and even probable that various units on campus could be operating at different places within this structure. For example, the history department might not place value on digital scholarship, while the sociology department does; and the campus as a whole is indifferent. If we think of the unit under analysis as being the whole university, then the digital culture for the whole university would be that of peer institutions or the social context of the university as a whole.

Since a digital culture is becoming pervasive (at least in North America and Europe), eventually the unit's environment will drive the unit toward the second regime implied by the feedback structure. The assumptions laid out in Figure 1 imply a future where junior faculty take the lead and the gap between junior and senior scholarship is closed by growing per capita production of digital scholarship by senior faculty. The first regime is a transient that will persist for some time, but all units will be placed under increasing pressure to place greater and greater value on digital scholarship in the tenure, promotion, and review process. Hence, Figure 1 has a sort of technological determinism built into its assumptions.[10]

Transitional Strategies

If this transient persists for some time, and if we are indeed moving toward an information culture that values digital scholarship throughout academe, then the purpose of this book is appropriate—to fill the gap while academic culture moves from one state to the next.

There are a variety of foci on which students, scholars, departments, universities, and scholarly communities might concentrate during this transition. These foci will shift depending upon one's status—student through scholarly community. Furthermore, the digital culture of a particular environment as it now stands will make a difference in the response of any player within this arena. Academic departments that have always embraced technology will continue to accept new mediums and methods in digital scholarship. On the other hand, universities that see discrepancies in the behavior of their departments might look toward university-wide policies or guidelines to move gracefully through this transition. Junior faculty members would wisely understand the various roles they might take in relation to digital scholarship, discuss these roles with their department chairs, and have strong rationales for why their nontraditional teaching, service, or research are appropriate credentials for academic promotion.

The chapters that follow present a variety of lenses through which one can look at the benefits, challenges, and behaviors that surround digital scholarship. Part I focuses on research that has created benchmarks for what is being done in various academic cultures today. Part II centers on a series of case studies—presenting actual instances of using digital products for service, teaching, and research. Part III offers guidelines and criteria for evaluating digital media activities and copyright issues, and provides specific examples of how universities might change the wording of their policy statements to incorporate digital scholarship into the culture of their communities, especially as those communities struggle with rewarding faculty for their work in a swiftly changing information age. Part III also looks to the future, exploring the ways in which digital scholarship might change and evolve in the years to come.

Notes

1. This view of the "ubiquitous computer" is troubling. In parts of the world where individuals struggle to find water and food, the notion of a computer inside every appliance is ludicrous. Since the central premise of this book is that digital scholarship should be included in the tenure, promotion, and review process, the reader is asked to forgive the Western nearsightedness of the arguments here. If an academic has access to computing, then it is important that he or she be given appropriate credit for being a digital scholar.

2. See Everett Rogers, *Diffusion of Innovations*, 4th edition (New York: Free Press, 1995), the seminal work in the field.

3. See J.M. Budd, "Research in the Two Cultures: The Nature of Scholarship in Science and in the Humanities," *Collection Management* 11 (1987): 1–21; and Mary-

Hilda Elbert, "Contrasting Patterns of Specialized Library Use," *Drexel Library Quarterly* 1 (1971): 13–27.

4. David Ellis, Deborah Cox, and Katherine Hall, "A Comparison of the Information-Seeking Patterns of Researchers in the Physical and Social Sciences," *Journal of Documentation* 49 (1993): 356–369.

5. Carole L. Palmer and Laura J. Neumann, "The Information Work of Interdisciplinary Humanities Scholars: Exploration and Translation," *Library Quarterly* 72 (2002): 85–117; Stephen S. Wiberley, "Habits of Humanists: Scholarly Behavior and New Information Technologies," *Library Hi Tech* 9 (1991): 17–21; Stephen E. Wiberley and William G. Jones, "Humanists Revisited: A Longitudinal Look at the Adoption of Information Technology," *College & Research Libraries* 55 (1994): 499–509.

6. The *Journal of the Association for History and Computing* has three editors. Two live on the West Coast, one on the East. We do all of our correspondence electronically and can get a paper from the reviewers to the author and back to the journal editors in less than two weeks. If the editor who does hypertext markup drops everything and sees to the paper, it can be published in the next issue of the journal in a matter of days and be available to readers at the moment of Web placement. This speed is just not possible with the page counts, formatting, printing, and surface mail necessary with paper-format journals.

7. See the following texts for additional materials about the field of System Dynamics. Ignacio Martinez and George P. Richardson, "Best Practices in System Dynamics Modeling," *Proceedings of the 19th International Conference of the System Dynamics Society*, Atlanta, GA, 2001; John Morecroft and John D. Sterman, eds., *Modeling for Learning Organizations* (Portland, OR: Productivity Press, 1994); Jorgen Randers, "Guidelines for Model Conceptualization," *Elements of the System Dynamics Method,* ed. J. Randers (Cambridge, MA: MIT Press, 1980), 117–139; and Eric F. Wolstenholme, *System Enquiry: A System Dynamics Approach* (New York: John Wiley & Sons, 1990).

8. In the text that follows, italics indicate reference to a variable name found in Figure 1.

9. See the following texts for discussions of systems thinking for decision making and policy analysis. P. Reagan-Cirincione et al., "Decision Modeling: Tools for Strategic Thinking," *Interfaces* 21: 52–65; John D. Sterman, *Business Dynamics: Systems Thinking and Modeling for a Complex World* (Boston: Irwin/McGraw-Hill, 2000); Jac A.M. Vennix, *Group Model Building: Facilitating Team Learning Using System Dynamics* (Chichester, UK: John Wiley & Sons, 1996); and Jac A.M. Vennix, George P. Richardson, and David F. Andersen, eds. "Group Model Building," special issue of the *System Dynamics Review* 13 (1997).

10. Special thanks to David F. Andersen for model conceptualization. His insights into system structure and feedback were invaluable in this chapter.

Part I

Policies and Procedures

Studies from the Field

Deborah Lines Andersen

Cumulative Research

Digital scholarship can take on a wide variety of faces, from the fairly mundane use of e-mail and listservs to the extremely complicated and time-consuming creation of Web sites, e-journals, or CD-ROM materials. Having defined some broad parameters about what digital scholarship is today, and realizing that developing technologies will quickly change those bounds tomorrow, the chapters in the first section of this book focus on research that addresses both how academics use digital technologies and how those uses have been received in the university setting.

One way to gain knowledge and appreciation about digital scholarship in the tenure, promotion, and review process is to look at examples of large-scale studies that have addressed this issue. These studies are an interesting case of doing research about ourselves. By looking at what others have found, we have a chance to reflect on what has worked and not worked, on practice and best practice, and on how changes in policy could make a difference in the evaluation of scholarship, teaching, and service in the university.

In addition to providing evidence from the field, the first four chapters also provide additional information that the reader can turn to. Across the four, there are more than one hundred citations to other literature. This is truly a wealth of information that can inform administrators, faculty tenure committees, untenured faculty members coming up for tenure, and individuals aspiring to a position in academe. One of the tenets of exhaustive literature research is that it is complete when one can find no additional sources—when the authors refer again and again to the same critical articles in the field. The four chapter bibliographies are not only detailed, but they also overlap in their reference to critical studies that came before them.

Types of Studies—Assessment Issues

There are a variety of methods that one could use to assess the present influences of digital scholarship in the tenure, promotion, and review process. These methods are as varied as the kinds of information science and social science research methods that are used by scholars in the field. Bibliographic studies, surveys, and content analysis are all valid and useful methodologies for uncovering these influences, and, in fact, have all been used by the authors of the chapters in Part I. In order to ground the reading and understanding of these chapters in their respective research methodologies, it is worth looking at each method in turn—its definition, strengths, and limitations.

Bibliographic Studies

The heart of bibliographic analysis lies in conducting exhaustive literature reviews of a given topic. The researcher needs to be trained in the fine points of bibliographic control—in indexing, abstracting, on-line database searching, Boolean logic, and, increasingly today, the additional skills of searching for relevant materials on the World Wide Web. As mentioned earlier, exhaustive searching means that no stone has been left unturned—the researcher is sure that this is *the* literature. The bibliographic researcher also mines the citations of all the articles that he locates, looking for earlier materials that informed the research and thoughts of others.

Bibliographic studies have become stronger research methods as the power of information technology has improved. With Web-based indexing and abstracting services, full-text articles on-line, and international library catalogs available over the World Wide Web, the researcher can access a world of knowledge without leaving his desk. Bibliographic research requires a schooled understanding of the way in which information is stored and retrieved and a knowledge of the indexing practices of the disciplines pertinent to any study.

The limitations of bibliographic research arise from this same wealth and international nature of information today. There might be so much information on a given topic that it would be extremely time consuming to capture all of it and to select the best sources. If the topic is large enough, the researcher will have to make decisions about what to leave in, and out, perhaps limiting the exposure of the eventual reader of an article. The research is also constrained by what others have studied and written about. Rather than creating new data, the bibliographic domain amasses what already exists. Finally, international access also means that language can be a limiting factor, if either the bibliographer or the reader does not work in the language of a particular piece of research.

An example of strong bibliographic research is Chapter 1, a review that specifically looks at teaching, publishing, and technology in the tenure, promotion, and review process. Lynn C. Hattendorf Westney updated her original 2000 study with a second review of more than twenty databases in the social, applied, and health sciences. Her chapter concludes that, although there is a long way to go, teaching with technology is creating a force and dialog in these fields. She does conclude, nonetheless, that, "the creation of formal criteria and guidelines for the assessment and evalua- tion of digital scholarship and teaching with technology for purposes of tenure, promotion, and review remains largely in the discussion stage."

Surveys

Survey research is an important social science tool for collecting and ana- lyzing data in the field. The researchers define the scope of their studies, the questions to be included, the subjects to be queried, and the research problem to be addressed. They also may choose the method of adminis- tration of the survey. Face-to-face interviews and paper-mailed documents have been the most usual methods of conducting survey research. With the advent of information technologies, it is now more common to find surveys e-mailed to respondents. A variety of this electronic method is posting a questionnaire to a Web page and then e-mailing potential re- spondents, asking them to go to that Web page and fill out the survey. With the addition of database software on the Web site, it is possible not only to administer the survey electronically, but also to have the computer store and tabulate responses as they come in.

Surveys are limited to the extent that the researchers cannot go back after the fact to change or clarify a question unless they are involved in a face-to-face administration. There are also issues of response rate. As anyone who has received a survey knows, it is usually easier to throw it away than to take the time to answer it. Surveys suffer from bias of selec- tion when respondents are systematically different from those who decide not to respond. Nonetheless, even with these limitations, surveys have the advantage of reaching a wide range of individuals and collecting far more useful data than might be possible with qualitative, face-to-face in- terviews. Questionnaires lend themselves to quantitative questions, with the potential for sophisticated statistical analyses. These analyses may lead to insights about the population under study or about a sample of that population.

In Chapter 2 on Web projects, Kathleen Carlisle Fountain used two mailed survey administrations to explore the value of World Wide Web projects for 99 teaching faculty and librarians. She selected the original set of these individuals based upon the inclusion of their projects in the

Librarians' Index to the Internet. Her primary concerns were how well these Web projects were regarded, as well as "what institutional and individual factors contributed to acceptance of them as legitimate professional activities." The second administration of additional survey questions was limited to previous respondents who had not yet been granted tenure and promotion, "asking them to discuss their experience within the context of their tenure status." Fountain's chapter includes five recommendations for Web evaluation as well as guidelines for supporting a Web project. This chapter makes an important contribution to the field not only in documenting what librarians and teaching faculty have experienced but also in suggesting what others could do to strengthen their successful submission of digital scholarship in their tenure, promotion, and review portfolios.

In Chapter 3, Deborah Lines Andersen and Dennis A. Trinkle also use survey research to explore how academic historians value digital scholarship in academic advancement. Their survey was announced to every history department chair across the United States in a surface mail letter. The announcement directed the 66 respondents to a Web survey that asked about formal and informal institutional policies and the place that digital scholarship had in the tenure, promotion, and review process, and in institutional support. In particular, the study found that there was an apparent "lack of formal means for dealing with digital history products within departments," and concluded that "the challenge for national associations is to help create broad-based policies that will further scholarship and teaching, providing community-based support for those working in digital scholarship."

Content Analysis

The focus of content analysis is on documents rather than on people. Researchers define an area for review and then use materials, often written, as their analysis units. This method of research is very similar to what one sees in literary or historical analyses, where researchers use primary sources to support their scholarly arguments and interpretations. With the advent of World Wide Web technologies, it is becoming more common to see these analyses focus on Web sites and Web publications, looking for similarities, differences, and, most important, best practice within a particular field. A strength of this research, especially analysis of on-line digital documents, is accessibility. Rather than taking road trips to find material for analysis, the Web researcher uses search engines as aids to finding appropriate materials. The inclusiveness of the research will be as good as the researcher's abilities to use appropriate search engines—engines that are increasing in sophistication and ease of application at an amazing rate of speed.

In Chapter 4, Rob Kling and Lisa B. Spector focus on the area of e-journals in the academic environment. Their extremely thorough chapter, the longest in the book, describes and differentiates various types of e-journals, using a framework that Kling and McKim developed to "assess the strength of publishing within scholarly communication"—a framework that includes trustworthiness, publicity, and accessibility in its application. Kling and Spector describe a variety of e-publications, providing examples of how administrations and tenuring committees can use this framework in their own academic institutions. Central to their thesis and the focus of this book is the topic of scholarly credit. Their main argument is that "e-scripts should not be automatically discounted in academic reviews. . . . Rather, they should be assessed, as are other publications in an academic's corpus under review." Their chapter gives reviewers guidelines and examples that will make this process possible.

There is great importance in a multimethod approach to research. Each type of research has its strengths and its limitations. When multiple methods are brought together they reinforce one another, and the whole is much greater than the sum of its parts. Through literature review, surveys, and content analysis, this section gives the untenured faculty member, and other players in the academic tenuring and promotion arena, a mix of tools and approaches with which to view assessment in the university setting.

Chapter 1

Mutually Exclusive?

Information Technology and the Tenure, Promotion, and Review Process

Lynn C. Hattendorf Westney

Teaching and Technology

Jargon that attempts to capture the character of contemporary scholarship has contributed to the creation of new words that define the essence of information technology (IT) and its role within academe. These new words have become mainstreamed swiftly into the vocabulary of most disciplines and the vocabulary of everyday life. Information technology encompasses all facets of digital and technological instruction and publishing, including distance education, electronic publications, and teaching with technology.

Teaching, per se, is one of the crucial components in the tripartite scholarly mission (research, service, and teaching) of higher education. The incorporation of technology into the teaching process is an integral and vital part of the teaching component within the entire spectrum of postsecondary education. A vast number of institutions require their faculties to integrate technology into their teaching portfolios. The design and implementation of distance education and on-line Web-based courses is becoming standard procedure in a variety of disciplines. Faculty are caught in the middle of this all-pervasive conundrum: they are expected to be familiar with the latest in cutting-edge technology; they are expected to have mastered HTML; they are expected to conduct their classes with and through technology; and they are bewildered by the enormity of these expectations.

College and university faculty have been preoccupied during the past two decades with their concerns about the formal legitimization of information technology within the promotion and tenure processes of their institutions.[1] Although IT is an all-pervasive phenomenon throughout academe, it remains, curiously, relatively new and basically uncharted territory in this serious process. Promotion and tenure review committees are perplexed by the challenges of evaluating and assigning meaningful credit for the enormous amount of time spent by faculty on integrating technology into the teaching component of their positions. External reviewers are reluctant to commit themselves when requested to evaluate appropriately this portion of instruction. More often than not, IT is dismissed, ignored, or at best, given short shrift in formal faculty evaluations.

A major ingredient of scholarship is the discovery of new knowledge. Since the application, integration, and dissemination of new knowledge through text, Web pages, CD-ROM, DVD, videos, and audio constitute another major element of contemporary scholarship, IT must become one of the criteria recognized and assessed in promotion and tenure decisions. Because they are used as vehicles for the dissemination of knowledge, electronic modes of scholarly distribution must be considered serious and legitimate.[2] A monograph with the intriguing title, *Information Technology in Higher Education: Assessing Its Impact and Planning for the Future*, is most disappointing because it ignores totally the role of IT within the tenure, promotion, and review process.[3]

Information technology was first used as an adjunct tool in the teaching process. However, as IT has continued on an upward spiral within all facets of contemporary society, it has become an inherent, necessary, and vital part of formal instruction. This chapter addresses the issues facing faculty who are up for tenure and/or promotion and review and the corresponding issues with which their evaluators must grapple in reviewing their formal tenure, promotion, and review documents.

Literature Review

An interdisciplinary review of the literature on teaching with technology and electronic scholarship, and its place within the tenure, promotion, and review process, was conducted from March 2000 through August 2002. This review was performed to update a previous review by Westney that formed the basis of an article, "A Trivial Pursuit? Information Technology and the Tenure Track," published in 2000.[4] The second review was conducted in more than twenty on-line databases in the applied sciences, health sciences, humanities, and the social sciences in order to obtain an overall depiction of the current status of technological scholarship within this critical process.

The results of the second review indisputably show that the evaluation of the use of IT as an integral part of mainstream instruction is continuing to gain momentum and is generating spirited dialogue within the professional literature of diverse disciplines. However, the creation of formal criteria and guidelines for the assessment and evaluation of digital scholarship and teaching with technology for purposes of tenure, promotion, and review remains largely in the discussion stage.

Promotion and Tenure Considerations

Guidelines for the evaluation of teaching with technology are sparse. The literature of all disciplines is rampant with articles on "how to do it right" and "how to do it better." Conspicuously absent from the literature are concrete examples of how information technology is to be evaluated for purposes of promotion and tenure.

One concrete example has been provided by the Department of English at Bradley University, which took the first tentative steps toward creating new guidelines for evaluating computer-related work in 1996. A member of the committee charged with this formidable task stated that:

> ... to revise evaluation criteria to accommodate computer-related work, we will be threatening traditional practices and will encounter resistance from those who do not understand or perceive the value of computer-related academic work. Most departments have not yet added official language concerning computer-related activity to their evaluation guidelines.[5]

Bradley's guidelines were adopted in October 1996. The guidelines stated, albeit simplistically, "Computer-related work, like other forms of scholarship, teaching, and service, should be evaluated as an integral part of a faculty member's accomplishments."[6]

The Ad hoc Committee on Information Technology in Political Science declared that:

> ... the issue of information technology is increasingly a critically important area of substantive study and scholarship for political scientists. Faculty members who develop computer-based educational applications and scholarly works should be recognized for their curricular, pedagogical, and scholarly contributions.[7]

The Committee recommended that, "Political Science departments should develop evaluation procedures that specifically take into account electronic scholarship."[8]

An alternative viewpoint was expressed within the discipline of management information science:

> IT is primarily used to automate the information delivery function in classrooms. In the absence of fundamental changes to the teaching and learning process, such classrooms may do little but speed up ineffective processes and methods of teaching.[9]

This statement is detrimental in the extreme for those who are engaged in defending information technology as an integral part of the teaching component.

Teaching with technology has been nowhere addressed as vociferously as in the *Chronicle of Higher Education*. Guernsey stated: "College faculty, particularly in the humanities, were finding that their institutions did not always treat substantial work with electronic media as a form of [serious] scholarship or service." Indeed, faculty were finding that involvement with technology posed a serious risk to their careers.[10] Lawson and Pelzer affirmed that "little is known about how technology-based projects are reviewed for promotion and tenure purposes in academic libraries."[11] Their seminal article serves as a literature review in this area for all academic disciplines.

Deans of education schools were surveyed to ascertain the value of technology-based projects for tenure and promotion. A major finding of this 1995 survey was that while faculty and administrators valued technology-based projects for tenure and promotion, their institutions did not.[12] Two years later, in another survey performed on teacher educators, encouraging evidence was found indicating a paradigm shift in considering new forms of scholarship for promotion and tenure.[13]

Thus far, this shift has perhaps been best acknowledged within engineering. A survey reported in the *Journal of Engineering Technology* identified criteria considered important for faculty promotion and tenure. In addition to research and service, creative endeavor was considered most valuable in this process.[14]

The importance of creativity was reiterated by the Computing Research Association, which proclaimed that, "relying on journal articles to evaluate engineering and computer-science professors for promotion and tenure is a mistake and that the fundamental basis for academic achievement is the impact of one's ideas and scholarship on the field."[15] This statement urges academe to place as much weight on the artifacts, such as software and Web sites, as on traditional forms of publication.

The institutional reward systems for distance education were examined by Wolcott at four Carnegie Category I research institutions. Although faculty accomplishment in distance education was acknowledged and credited at the departmental level and during annual performance reviews, at the institutional level, distance education was a low priority. Chief academic officers stated that faculty were placing their careers in jeopardy for engaging in distance education to the detriment of discipline-based research and scholarly publication.[16] In direct contrast to Wolcott's findings, the Kellogg Commission urged colleges and universities to use technology to promote lifelong learning and advised them to invest in new classroom technologies and in faculty development.[17]

"Tenure and Technology: New Values, New Guidelines," was the title of a theme issue in *Kairos: A Journal for Teachers of Writing in Webbed Environments*, containing four pioneering articles on computer-related promotion and tenure concerns in higher education. *Kairos* was the first electronic journal to devote a collective argument against the firmly entrenched traditions of the promotion and tenure process.[18]

The Committee on Computers in Composition and Communication (CCCC), adopted an optimistic and succinctly stated viewpoint of the role of IT. To ensure that candidates' work with IT was explained accurately and evaluated fairly, the CCCC approved a model document in November 1998, which contained specific guidelines for both promotion and tenure committees and for candidates in the promotion and tenure process.[19]

The American Association for History and Computing (AAHC) conducted a survey in the spring of 2000 of current tenure, promotion, and review practices regarding technology-related activities in the history departments of United States colleges and universities. From the results of this effort, AAHC created a draft policy, "AAHC Suggested Guidelines for Evaluating Digital Media Activities."[20] An underlying theme of this survey was the difference between using technology for teaching and using technology for research. Survey results indicated that technology for teaching was not particularly valued for tenure and promotion. Technology for research was seen as inferior to the usual methods of disseminating research through peer-reviewed articles and monographs. Chairpersons questioned whether a peer-reviewed electronic journal article was "as good as" a peer-reviewed print article. The peer review process should be of equal weight whether the format is print or electronic, but this is currently not the norm in most institutions. It is obvious that promotion and tenure committees need to become much better informed about the specific peer review polices in effect for peer-reviewed electronic journals.

In the Lawson and Pelzer survey, tenure-track institutions were asked if technology-based projects (computer software, articles in e-journals, Internet-based materials, videotapes, and audiotapes) alone, without accompanying traditional scholarship, would ever be sufficient evidence of scholarship for the granting of tenure. A somewhat pessimistic viewpoint was reflected in that, ". . . sixty percent of the respondents felt positively that this *could be* the case in the future . . . but also stated that they did not expect a change in the near future."[21] Although there have been some positive steps taken since the Lawson and Pelzer survey, traditional modes of scholarship continue to remain the primary mechanisms by which all faculty in all disciplines are evaluated.

Teaching with Technology

The initial time commitment for faculty members employing technology in teaching is enormous, and other responsibilities (research, publication, and service) may suffer while planning and teaching on-line and distance education courses. The purpose of moving to on-line and distance education courses needs to be identified clearly.[22] It may well be that on-line and distance education involvement is mandated by the institution. If this is the situation, faculty have no choice but to participate fully in teaching with technology activities.

Promotion and tenure review committees demand evidence of everything that faculty have achieved in all three interconnected areas (research, teaching, and service) of their university responsibilities. The assessment component is especially important for the documentation of teaching with technology. Student evaluations are part and parcel of traditional classroom teaching. There is no reason why they should not be part and parcel of distance and on-line course evaluations as well. In fact, there is every reason why they should be. "Evidence-based" is more than just a buzzword in the health science professions. It needs to be extended to the promotion and tenure review process for evaluating the technological components of contemporary teaching, research, and service.

An article in the February 22, 2002, *Chronicle of Higher Education*, "Ever So Slowly, Colleges Start to Count Work with Technology in Tenure Decisions," provides a glimmer of hope that things are changing, albeit slowly. MERLOT, a nationwide project that applies the identical peer-review system used for journal articles to the evaluation of electronic teaching materials, was discussed at length. MERLOT began in 1999 and is currently supported by 22 college consortia and systems.[23]

Publishing with Technology/Digital Scholarship

An electronic journal has been defined as "an edited package of articles that is distributed to most of its subscribers in electronic form and accessed primarily in electronic form," although there may or may not be a print counterpart.[24] Journals routinely distributed in both paper and electronic format are excluded from this definition. The major benefit of publishing in electronic journals is the speed with which articles are accepted and published. Electronic journals, even when they have a strictly defined peer-review process, continue to be less widely perceived by scholars as being of the same scholarly caliber as are traditional paper publications.

Faculty who choose to publish the results of their teaching with technology activities in electronic journals are faced with yet another dilemma—they have now two new venues to defend, explain, and justify to their promotion and tenure review committees. While electronic journals offer many advantages to multiple constituencies, their acceptance by university promotion and tenure committees remains unclear. Concerns about receiving appropriate recognition and formal rewards for publishing in electronic journals were verbalized at the Fourth Symposium on Scholarly Publishing on the Electronic Networks.[25] Scholars who had published electronically believed that there is a widespread perception that electronic publication is less significant than print publication. Their beliefs continue to be reflected in the current practices of promotion and tenure committees and by external evaluators.

Cronin and Overfelt found that any formal analysis of promotion and tenure policies with regard to electronic publication was noticeably absent from the literature. They examined standards and criteria for evaluating electronic publications in the context of the promotion and tenure process. The results of their investigation suggested, unsurprisingly, that there may very well be inconsistencies in interpretation and practice in the academic reward system.[26] Although their study was performed in 1995, their conclusions have not yet been overturned by other research.

Langston examined how scholarly publishing in electronic form affects the academic tenure process. Perceptions of the stability and quality of electronic publications by those who hold academic power, whether or not the publications are refereed, attitudes toward technology within and between academic disciplines, ease of access, and the ability to retrieve electronic works through indexing and abstracting services were her primary recommendations when making decisions on where to publish.[27]

Just as teaching with technology is relatively new territory in the promotion and tenure process, so too is publishing in electronic journals. Promotion and tenure review committees do not view publication in electronic journals as possessing the same value as publication in traditional paper format. Electronic journals are not indexed as well or as often as are print journals by the major indexing and abstracting services, thus hindering access to them. "E-journals have had relatively little impact on the academic community as evidenced by the scarce number of citations emanating from e-journal sources."[28] Indeed, the most significant factor influencing the acceptance of electronic journals as a viable publication is the legitimacy of this outlet from the promotion, tenure, and reward perspective.[29]

Obstacles to determining appropriate recognition and rewards for faculty engaged in on-line research and teaching were discussed at a forum at Indiana University in 2000. Issues of promotion and tenure, especially the lack of tools for evaluating on-line scholarship, were the focus of this forum. Skepticism about the quality and effectiveness of digital research and instruction was seen as discouraging to young faculty members who are using on-line media.[30]

The Florida State University system investigated the perceptions toward electronic publishing held by their university administrators and faculty. It concluded that there is a need to develop formal policies regarding the acknowledgment of electronic scholarly publishing in promotion and tenure decisions for faculty.[31] Unfortunately, this study does not add anything new to the literature because it merely recognizes the lack of formal policies and addresses the need for formal policies and, in effect, says nothing about how and when these formal policies will be created. There is dialogue, but it is just that, dialogue without affirmative action. It is not just teaching with technology that is an issue in promotion and tenure decisions; publishing with technology is an analogous concern for faculty going through the promotion and tenure process.

Library Faculty

College and university librarians are soldiers serving on the front lines of this intellectual dilemma, developing and implementing innovative methods of obtaining, organizing, delivering, and facilitating the use of information. Academic librarians are helping to define the value and significance of using IT in teaching within all disciplines. It is, moreover, within the literature of academic and research librarianship where a significant portion of the groundbreaking articles addressing teaching with technology and the promotion and tenure process are being published. This may be due, in part, to the fact that in those institutions where librarians have full faculty status, they are perceived by the teaching faculty as being different from them because their teaching role is inherently different. Librarians perform bibliographic instruction for the classes of the teaching faculty. This is usually done once or twice a semester per class rather than on an ongoing basis. The nature and frequency of the instruction differ from that of the teaching faculty.

Academic librarians have yet another cross to bear. They must defend the type of teaching they do, which falls under the librarianship component of their positions, and must attempt to make it fit into the teaching guidelines of the promotion and tenure requirements of their universities. This is a difficult challenge, because teaching is only one of the many components of academic librarianship. It is not always the primary component. Langston stated:

> Implications for faculty members going through the tenure process, and thus for academic libraries and for librarians, who work to be integral players in the university community, will depend to what extent contemporary theoretical positions are put into practice, whether as radical change or as assimilated into current practices of the advancement, [tenure], and promotion process.[32]

Neely took Langston's delineations a step farther in her statement that, "Librarians contribute to the electronic environment by developing and contributing to the creation of Web-based tutorials, virtual tours, interactive instructional Web sites, etc. Should these contributions be considered alongside print publications in determining reappointment, promotion, tenure and tenure equivalent?"[33]

There have been no significant developments toward formulating a core set of measures or assessments for promotion decisions affecting academic librarians within the Association of Research Libraries (ARL).[34] This lack of standardization within academic librarianship can be further applied across all disciplines to all faculty who are using their technological expertise within the teaching component of academe while working simultaneously toward tenure and promotion in the research and scholarship component of this process.

Teaching with technology, especially for the novice, is difficult to do on one's own. Faculty must take every advantage offered to them from their computer centers and from their colleagues, in particular, their librarians. Libraries are a major campus resource, as are the librarians who manage and operate them. Librarians are an often overlooked and underutilized institutional resource.

Following the trendsetting example of the University of Iowa Libraries, which created an Information Arcade™ in 1992,[35] many college and university libraries have created similar information arcades, facilities designed to support the use of electronic services in research, teaching, and independent learning. Faculty can consult electronic services and systems librarians for the purpose of learning how to use most efficiently the latest IT for their on-line and distance teaching and multimedia presentations. These arcades have served as springboards for developing collaborative technology-based services. At the University of Iowa, new Technology in the Learning Environment (nTITLE), was the result of a campus-wide initiative involving 96 professors who attended a series of workshops taught by librarians in the arcade classroom.[36]

The Promotion and Tenure Review Process

Faculty preparing for the promotion and tenure review process must make every effort to document thoroughly and impeccably their teaching, research, and publication contributions using information technology. Before they can successfully accomplish this, they should have done some or (preferably) all of the following:[37]

1. Documented formally their teaching with technology activities.
2. Received appointment to campus committees that deal with technology and/or have become involved with technology committees within their professional associations.
3. Served as invited speakers to discuss the development and successful implementation of their teaching with technology projects.
4. Received appointments to editorial advisory boards of print or electronic journals (preferably peer-reviewed journals).
5. Published the results of their teaching with technology activities in peer-reviewed (print or electronic) journals.
6. Obtained teaching assistant or graduate student support. This allows faculty time to concentrate on performing institutionally valued, traditional discipline-based research and scholarship.

When preparing their promotion and tenure papers, faculty should, in addition to describing their technology-based projects, present a strong case for the value of their work.[38] Faculty should describe its impact and explain in what ways and for whom their work has significance. Indicators that will help substantiate the scholarly value of their information technology projects include the following:

1. Projects that have received internal or external funding.
2. Projects that have received an award or other professional recognition.
3. Published reviews of their projects.
4. Publication of their results in peer-reviewed journals (electronic or paper).
5. Citations to their projects and papers within the professional literature of their disciplines or related disciplines.[39]

Conclusion

The Committee on Workforce Issues in Information Technology of the National Research Council held hearings to help Congress decide whether the IT workforce shortage was serious enough to warrant more than the 115,000 H-1B visas granted in 1999. The Information Technology Association of America (ITAA) reported that at least 400,000 IT jobs nationwide would remain unfilled in 1999. The U.S. Department of Commerce confirmed these numbers and predicted that by 2006, the national IT workforce shortage would reach at least 1.3 million.[40]

An expert in IT personnel issues with TechForce, Inc. stated succinctly, "We're in a situation akin to running out of coal during the Industrial

Revolution. IT workers are the fuel for the nationwide IT revolution."[41] The Computing Research Association reported that revenue for employment advertisements for computer-related jobs more than doubled from 1997 to 1999. Statistics from 1996 show that 50 percent of new PhDs in computer science accepted positions in the industrial sector and only 26 percent took faculty appointments.[42]

Despite the dire economic slump of 2001, the ITAA released figures in May 2002 that were cautiously optimistic. The ITAA study found that the IT workforce has been bouncing back and that the IT workforce appears to be migrating south, with demand for IT workers in the Midwest and West having decreased, respectively, 68 percent and 71 percent since 2000. Managers surveyed stated that they would try filling 1.1 million IT jobs through 2003 but that nearly 600,000 jobs would go unfilled due to a lack of qualified workers.[43] This is less than the 1.3 million that Crabb predicted in 1999, but it remains a significant shortage.

IT will continue to be valued highly within the private sector. This is an unequivocal given. If faculty are not rewarded appropriately and compensated commensurately for their IT efforts and expertise, should faculty continue to labor in academe when statistics confirm that they could be making more, substantially much more, in the private sector? If faculty IT activities are undervalued or viewed unfavorably in promotion and tenure reviews, should faculty continue to focus their intellectual energies in this area?

> High-paying, fast-paced jobs in the computer industry are attracting both seasoned academics and newly minted Ph.D.'s who, in the past, would have opted for careers in higher education. Computer-science and computer-engineering departments are short on professors while undergraduate enrollments are booming.[44]

The theoretical underpinnings of higher education in the United States are being eroded by the realities of the marketplace. If this situation is to be resolved favorably for faculty, the academic sector must strive to resolve its institutional issues in evaluating and rewarding faculty for their use of teaching and publishing with IT. In the final analysis, it will be students who will derive the greatest rewards over time from institutional acceptance of faculty's intellectual efforts in using the avenues of electronic scholarship. The candid assessment, evaluation, and institutional recognition of the scholarly use of information technology within the ranks of academe continue to present and remain an unresolved problem.

A letter to the editor of the *Chronicle of Higher Education* is perhaps the best statement about the present realities of teaching and publishing with IT. Professor Tal of the University of Arizona, declared that:

Caught between administrative pressure to use new technologies and the certainty that older peers will not give credit for new-technology work in tenure or promotion review, [it is] easy for younger faculty members to resent comfortably tenured older peers for a kind of willful ignorance about technology and technological innovation in teaching and scholarship.[45]

Tal identified aptly the crux of the major issue that continues to confront the academic professorate in the twenty-first century. David William identified this issue just as aptly in a cartoon that portrayed a group of gossiping academics. One faculty member said to another, "Well, they say he's published, but only electronically."[46]

Notes

1. G. Philip Cartwright, "Information Technology: Considerations for Tenure and Promotion," *Change* (September/October 1994): 26–28.

2. Steffen Schmidt et al., Report of "Ad hoc Committee on Information Technology in Political Science" (September 1, 1999): 1–4. www.public.iastate.edu/~sws/apsa%20guidelines/itguidelines.htm.

3. Richard N. Katz and Julie A. Rudy, *Information Technology in Higher Education: Assessing Its Impact and Planning for the Future* (San Francisco: Jossey-Bass, New Directions for Institutional Research, No. 102, 1999).

4. Lynn C. Hattendorf Westney, "A Trivial Pursuit? Information Technology and the Tenure Track," *Campus-Wide Information Systems* 4 (2000): 113–19.

5. Seth R. Katz, "One Department's Guidelines for Evaluating Computer-Related Work," *Kairos: A Journal for Teachers of Writing in Webbed Environments* (Spring 1997). english.ttu.edu/kairos/2.1/coverWeb/katz/art2.html. See also in the section entitled "Tenure and Technology: New Values, New Guidelines": Cindy Nahrwold, "'Just' Professing: A Call for the Valuation of Electronic Scholarship" and Janice R. Walker, "Fanning the Flames: Tenure and Promotion and Other Role-Playing Games." english.ttu.edu/kairos/2.1/index_f.html.

6. Ibid.

7. Schmidt et al., "Ad hoc Committee."

8. Ibid.

9. Dorothy E. Leidner and Sirkka L. Jarvenpaa, "The Use of Information Technology to Enhance Management School Education: A Theoretical View," *MIS Quarterly* (September 1995): 265–91.

10. Lisa Guernsey, "Scholars Who Work with Technology Fear They Suffer in Tenure Reviews," *Chronicle of Higher Education*, June 6, 1997, A21–A22.

11. Karen G. Lawson and Nancy L. Pelzer, "Assessing Technology-Based Projects for Promotion and/or Tenure in ARL Academic Libraries," *College & Research Libraries* 60 (September 1999): 464–76.

12. Nancy E. Seminoff and Shelley B. Wepner, "Are Technology-Based Projects Valued as Scholarship for Tenure and Promotion?" *Journal of Computing in Teacher Education* (Spring 1995): 5–10.

13. Nancy E. Seminoff and Shelley B. Wepner, "What Should We Know about Technology-Based Projects for Tenure and Promotion?" *Journal of Research in Computing in Education* (1997): 67–82.

14. Walter Buchanan, "A Survey of Creative Endeavor Criteria for Promotion and Tenure of ET Faculty," *Journal of Engineering Technology* (Spring 1996): 30–36.

15. David Patterson, Lawrence Snyder, and Jeffrey Ullman, "Best Practices Memo: Evaluating Computer Scientists and Engineers for Promotion and Tenure," Computing Research Association (August 1999). www.cra.org/reports/tenure_review.html.

16. Linda L. Wolcott, "Tenure, Promotion, and Distance Teaching: A Study of Faculty Rewards and Incentives," (Arlington, VA: ERIC Document Reproduction Service, ED413861, 1997).

17. Kelly McCollum, "Colleges Urged to Use Technology to 'Promote Lifelong Learning,'" *Chronicle of Higher Education*, September 24, 1999, A39. See also: www.nasulgc.org/Kellogg/learn.pdf.

18. *Kairos: A Journal for Teachers of Writing in Webbed Environments* (Spring 1997). english.ttu.edu/kairos/2.1/index_f.html.

19. "Promotion and Tenure Guidelines for Work with Technology," CCCC, Committee on Computers in Composition and Communication, *College Composition and Communication* (September 1999): 139–42. See www.ncte.org/positions/promotion.shtml.

20. Deborah Lines Andersen and Dennis A. Trinkle, "'One or Two Is Not a Problem' or Technology in the Tenure, Promotion, and Review Process: A Survey of Current Practices in U.S. History Departments," *JAHC: Journal of the Association for History and Computing* (2001): 1–10.

21. Lawson and Pelzer, "Assessing Technology-Based Products," 464–76.

22. UIC (University of Illinois at Chicago) Peer Review Workshop, June 8, 1999, University of Illinois at Chicago, Chicago, Illinois.

23. Jeffrey R. Young, "Ever So Slowly, Colleges Start to Count Work with Technology in Tenure Decisions," *Chronicle of Higher Education*, February 22, 2002, A25–A28.

24. Rob Kling and Geoffrey McKim, "Scholarly Communication and the Continuum of Electronic Publishing," *Journal of the American Society for Information Science* (August 1999): 890–906.

25. H. Julene Butler, "Research into the Reward System of Scholarship: Where Does Scholarly Electronic Publishing Get You?" in *Filling the Pipeline and Paying the Piper: Proceedings of the Fourth ALA/AAUP Symposium*, ed. Ann Okerson, *Scholarly Publishing on the Electronic Networks* (Washington, D.C.: Office of Scientific and Academic Publishing, Association of Research Libraries, 1995), 67–77.

26. Blaise Cronin and Kara Overfelt, "E-Journals and Tenure," *Journal of the American Society for Information Science* (October 1995): 700–703.

27. Lizbeth Langston, "Scholarly Communication and Electronic Publication: Implications for Research, Advancement, and Promotion" (Arlington, VA: ERIC Document Reproduction Service ED403892, 1996). See www.library.ucsb.edu/untangle/.

28. Stephen P. Harter, "Scholarly Communication and Electronic Journals: An Impact Study," *Journal of the American Society for Information Science* 49, No. 6: 507–16.

29. Cheri Speier et al., "Faculty Perceptions of Electronic Journals as Scholarly Communication: A Question of Prestige and Legitimacy," *Journal of the American Society for Information Science* (May 1, 1999): 537–43.

30. Vincent Kiernan, "Rewards Remain Dim for Professors Who Pursue Digital Scholarship," *Chronicle of Higher Education,* April 28, 2000, A45–A46.

31. Aldrin E. Sweeney, "E-Scholarship and Electronic Publishing in the Twenty-First Century: Implications for the Academic Community," *Educational Media International* (March 2001): 25–38.

32. Langston, "Scholarly Communication."

33. Theresa Y. Neely, "The Impact of Electronic Publications on Promotion and Tenure Decisions," *Leading Ideas* (October 1999): 1–6. See www.arl.org/diversity/leading/issue10/tneely.html.

34. Lawson and Pelzer, "Assessing Technology-Based Product," 464–76.

35. Anita K. Lowry, "The Information Arcade at the University of Iowa," *Cause/Effect* (Fall 1994): 38–44. See www.educause.edu/ir/library/text/CEM9438.txt.

36. Barbara I. Dewey, "Beyond the Information Arcade™: Next Generation Collaborations for Learning and Teaching at the University of Iowa," Ed-Media/Ed-Telecom 98 World Conference on Educational Multimedia and Hypermedia & World Conference on Education Telecommunications. Proceedings 10th, Freiburg, Germany, June 20–25, 1998 (Charlottesville, VA: Association for the Advancement of Computing in Education, ERIC Document Reproduction Service, ED 428 659, 1998), 268–73.

37. UIC, Peer Review Workshop.

38. Lawson and Pelzer, "Assessing Technology-Based Product," 464–76.

39. UIC, Peer Review Workshop.

40. Don Crabb, "Is Information Technology Work Force Adequate?" *Chicago Sun-Times,* September 29, 1999, 73.

41. Ibid.

42. Peter Freeman, *The Supply of Information Technology Workers in the United States* (Washington, D.C.: Computing Research Association, 1999).

43. "Survey Sees Demand Returning for Information-Tech Workers," *AP Worldstream,* May 6, 2002.

44. Robin Wilson, "Computer Scientists Flee Academe for Industry's Greener Pastures," *Chronicle of Higher Education,* September 24, 1999, A16–A17.

45. Kali Tal, "Divisions Between Old and Young Professors Could be Dangerous to Academe," *Chronicle of Higher Education,* October 1, 1999, B3.

46. David William, "Well, They Say He's Published, but Only Electronically," *Chronicle of Higher Education,* November 26, 1999, B3.

Chapter 2

To Web or Not to Web?

The Evaluation of World Wide Web Publishing in the Academy

Kathleen Carlisle Fountain

Web Projects

As this collection of essays makes abundantly clear, universities continue to grapple with the value of their faculty's electronic publishing. Electronic journals are just beginning to be accepted and on-line courses continue to receive attention as more faculty employ courseware such as WebCT or Blackboard in their teaching. What is less often discussed, however, is the creation and maintenance of World Wide Web projects.

Unlike other electronic endeavors covered in this volume, a "World Wide Web project" refers to a stand-alone, creative work published solely on the World Wide Web. Materials provided on these Web sites often replicate the style of print publications. Virtual libraries, subject-specific guides, digitized texts, directories, biographies, and encyclopedias are common examples. However, the flexibility of World Wide Web publishing permits faculty to create nonlinear, experimental sites that bear no resemblance to traditional publications. Some of the most graphically sophisticated of these, like *Eating Disorders in a Disordered Culture*, produced by professors Kathryn Sylva and Robin Lasser, often have the look and feel of an interactive exhibit, with images and descriptions to create a virtual museum space.[1]

Faculty members typically create these sites at their own discretion, and they maintain creative control of design and content. In some cases, the site may be a one-person operation, with a single, technologically savvy professor mounting text and images on a university server, designing the layout, and updating links. In other situations, a professor might envision the final Web product and avail him- or herself of campus computing technology help to make the vision a reality. Still others create sites, then rely upon student assistants to keep them current. In nearly all cases, however, these projects are produced at the faculty member's option, without recommendation or preapproval.

In this way, a Web project differs dramatically from other on-line efforts like electronic journal articles or on-line courses. Electronic articles can still appear in peer-reviewed journals, and they are subject to editorial revisions. On-line courses may be mounted in response to campus pressure to use newly purchased course software, and thus are viewed favorably during review. Web projects are not generally subjected to this familiar editorial review. Any faculty member with server space can launch such a project, and it is almost never created at the insistence of campus personnel.

This type of professional communication is, as a result, fraught with problems when introduced into the performance review process. The study described below, conducted in 2000, found that many librarians and teaching faculty are satisfied with how well their work has been received, but the data also suggest that they are satisfied because they did not expect their campus to value the work at all. This chapter highlights the survey results and discusses the status of Web projects in performance reviews, the risks of Web publishing, and suggestions for improving the acceptance of credible, professional Web projects.

The Survey

In March 2000, 151 librarians (55 percent, n=83) and teaching faculty (45 percent, n=68) received surveys asking how their Web projects fared during performance reviews. The sample comprised individuals with sites accessible through a selective Internet gateway called *Librarians' Index to the Internet*.[2] Each selected project resided on a university (.edu) server and identified a single individual as the creator or editor. A total of 99 valid survey responses represented the state of Web projects in the performance review process.[3]

By selecting sites listed in this gateway, the survey sample targeted individuals whose projects received a favorable mention from a third party. The *Librarians' Index to the Internet* in this way indicated which projects served the needs of a wide audience and therefore might have given institutions cause to recognize the sites' importance. Sixteen survey questions sought to determine if the Web projects were well regarded and what institutional and individual factors contributed to acceptance of them as legitimate professional activities.

The Purposes of Web Projects

Librarians and teaching faculty chose to create World Wide Web projects that support each of the three traditional areas of professional achievement:

teaching/librarianship, scholarship, and professional service. In 2000, 42 percent reported that their Web work fit a professional service and development category, while 31 percent felt their sites supported teaching or librarianship, and 27 percent viewed their sites as scholarship. Only eight individuals viewed their work as unrelated to their profession.

In this sample, the academic faculty most often used their sites for professional service and development. This finding is not unexpected, because the professional lives of university faculty revolve around their expertise in a subject—whether for teaching or scholarship or professional service. Creating a Web project probably acquainted these faculty with useful sites related to their scholarship. It also may have enabled them to connect their students to on-line materials relevant to their courses. In the survey responses, the faculty expressed gratification from their colleagues' use of their sites, praise that served as signs of Web projects serving the profession.

Librarians more often selected "excellence in librarianship or teaching" as the primary criteria by which their work could be assessed. This finding closely paralleled two other studies conducted on technology produced by librarians. The early growth of the Internet as a research tool provided the impetus for librarians to organize and categorize Web pages into student-friendly and curriculum-appropriate groups of links. Karen G. Lawson and Nancy L. Pelzer surveyed administrators in research libraries across the U.S. and found that of the technology projects submitted by librarians during performance reviews, a librarian in every institution touted a subject-oriented Web page. Further, 88 percent of the libraries reviewed a librarian's "WWW-based tutorial/WWW major project."[4] These professionals frequently created technology projects, including those on the Web, to "improve library instruction" or because of a "library/university need."[5] Gail McMillian used Lawson and Pelzer's survey instrument to conduct a case study of Virginia Tech's library faculty, and she discovered these same patterns.[6] In short, most librarians in all three samples created Web sites to aid their work in their libraries.

Publishing Web Projects

As a nationwide trend, most individuals have relied on their own Internet accounts to load personal home pages. By 1998, 5.3 million America Online (AOL) members used the AOL template to create a home page.[7] This explosion of idiosyncratic and generally useless Web pages likely created the tarnished reputation of Web publishing. However, the adage that "anyone can put up a Web page" is as true on university campuses as it is through private Internet service providers. Typically one needs only university identification and an interest in Web design to receive server space permission. Despite this, a study found that campus professionals using "personal" Web space on university servers still commonly created home pages that served professional purposes, such as introducing a librarian to an intended audience of students and faculty.[8] Even though most individuals outside academia published with personal Web space, relatively few Web project authors in this study relied on the same personal directories. Of those who did, classroom faculty used this option more often than librarians.

As an alternative to a personal directory on a campus server, individual departments granted their faculty and librarians permission to load pages onto that department's official Web space. This appeared to be the most common form of Web publishing for those included in the survey, which may indicate a basic level of respect for the Web work. Of all 151 Web projects, 117 appeared to be loaded in an official directory. The Web projects of librarians often resided on library directories, which is to be expected since supporting the libraries' work is the primary purpose of the pages. In rare cases, such as Professor Jerry Goldman's *The Oyez Project*, a site may even have received enough support and prestige to earn its own server.[9]

The University of Iowa Libraries, in 1998, began offering an innovative Web hosting program called Bailiwick for members of the campus community who wished to "find a home for their scholarly research interests" on-line.[10] The libraries required faculty, staff, and graduate students to submit a proposal that described the Web project. If approved, they received access to server space and on-site technological assistance that helped make their project a reality. The library, in this way, provided an official electronic "home" for a project while simultaneously restricting the types of projects permitted. As will be discussed later, this model of Web publishing might serve the Web author well when he or she is undergoing performance review.

Evaluation of Electronic Work

The E-Journal Evaluation Advantage

The availability of electronic journals, or e-journals, has grown exponentially. In 1998, the *Science Citation Index* listed about 30 percent of its journals as on-line, and the *Library Journal* reports that figure has grown to 75 percent this year.[11] The 2002 edition of the *Ulrich's Periodical Directory* cited both print and electronic journals, including those periodicals available only in an on-line format.[12] Coinciding with this trend, libraries began providing easier access to electronic publications. Library databases, which once provided only citations, now offer full-text content with search results. Recent software developments offered libraries a solution for connecting citation-only databases to full-text articles in other on-line resources. Faculty and students continue to use more on-line journals in the course of their research as a result of these advances in technology. A case study conducted at Ohio State University found that "more than half of the faculty and graduate students at OSU report[ed] daily, weekly, or monthly use [of e-journals] by 2000."[13]

Not only have faculty discovered e-journals to read, they have submitted articles to these journals for publication. Many personnel committees have learned how to evaluate the quality of such journals. Blaise Cronin and Kara Overfelt found that a sample of Mathematics, Computer Science, English, and Sociology programs modified their promotion and tenure guidelines to adapt to faculty e-journal publishing. With these findings, the authors called the concern over acceptance a "non-issue" and credited it to the merit criteria of peer review, which is applicable in both print and electronic mediums.[14] Aldrin E. Sweeney's recent survey of the faculty and administrators in the Florida State University system supported these findings. Sixty-seven percent of those surveyed either "agreed" or "strongly agreed" that electronic publishing "should be counted in the tenure and promotion process." Some of his respondents did not commit to a blanket acceptance of all e-journals, but they wrote that journals subjected to peer review are meritorious.[15] Since Web projects, as discussed here, are often self-published, review committees lack this familiar peer review evaluation tool to effectively determine the worth of the projects.

Technology Evaluation

Only a few studies have tried to measure the evaluation of other nontraditional projects, but they indicate slightly increasing administrative approval. Nancy E. Seminoff and Shelley B. Wepner surveyed education faculty and deans around the country and discovered that the majority of the individuals who responded viewed the value of technology-based projects (e.g., software and videos) as equivalent to books and journal articles. On the other hand, when asked how their institutions perceived technology-based projects, most replied that "traditional scholarly work" received higher approval. Further, Seminoff and Wepner found that universities that valued teaching more than research tended to have a more favorable view of such work.[16]

The *Chronicle of Higher Education*, in addition to formal studies, provides the best anecdotal evidence in technology evaluation over the past nine years. In an article published in 1993, the *Chronicle* reported that some universities modified their tenure standards to accommodate software development and integrated classroom technology, and this provided the sense that higher education as a whole was beginning to accept technological work in the review process.[17] When Lisa Guernsey looked to faculty Web work in 1997, however, the professors discussed difficulties finding support in their institutions.[18] More recent articles echoed past recommendations to exercise caution when pursuing digital achievement but offered encouraging signs in anecdotes of faculty who earned tenure or promotion while contributing technology-based projects to their vita.[19] In each of these articles, the authors mentioned the personnel committee's difficulties in evaluating such things as constructing Web projects, editing mailing lists, and teaching on-line.

Web Project Evaluation

Trends

In 2000, the study of librarian and teaching faculty Web project authors found that universities generally appeared to value their on-line work. Although not all of the respondents felt as though their sites improved their vita, the majority provided indicators of institutional acceptance. Since the questions relied on the individual's perception of acceptance, the results substantiated the claims of research library administrators who expressed a willingness to count technology projects in the performance review process.[20]

Of those who submitted their projects during review, an overwhelming majority (82 percent) felt a general sense that their projects helped their final evaluations. Seventeen had not yet been through a review since they began working on their site, so they could not comment on the role it might play. Only one person, a tenure-track history professor, decided against submitting it because he felt his project was "not valued at my institution."

When asked to differentiate *how much* their project helped during review, librarians commonly perceived that their Web projects "somewhat helped" their vita and performance reviews. Academic faculty, however, did not report the same acceptance, and most remarked that their site was "not very helpful." One might expect these results, since organization of the Internet seems more closely linked with the professional activities of librarians. Statistically, the individual's profession proved not to directly determine how helpful one might find his or her project (see Figure 2).

Factors other than profession, as determined through a chi-square analysis, did measurably affect the probability that a Web project helped one's vita. Most notably, a review by peers at the academic department or library level notably improved the likelihood that the individual viewed the project as "very helpful." This review committee, although it did not guarantee acceptance, served to clarify the projects' value and decreased the authors' uncertainty during review. Thirty percent of the librarians and teaching

Figure 2 **Helpfulness of Web Project to Vita and Review**

100	Unknown		Unknown	
80	Not very helpful		Not very helpful	
60	Somewhat helpful			
40			Somewhat helpful	
20	Very helpful			
0			Very helpful	
	Librarians		Teaching Faculty	

Profession

faculty who lacked this level of review could not determine if their Web project helped or hurt their vita (see Table 2.1)

According to this study, assigned Web projects typically found more favor in performance reviews than those created voluntarily or only with encouragement. Admittedly, only four respondents, including two librarians and two teaching faculty, created their sites at the insistence of supervisors. Most of the respondents began work on their Web projects voluntarily, also with roughly equal numbers of librarians and teaching faculty doing so. Librarians, however, received significantly more encouragement to produce their sites than did teaching faculty.

The librarians and faculty who reported receiving some form of support during the development of their projects tended to be more satisfied with their institutions' recognition of their Web work. Universities most often offered support in the form of recognition, funding or staff assistance, software, hardware, and server space. Because the survey parameters required that the Web project resided on a university server, technically each respondent received the support of server space. Interestingly, only 5 percent of

Table 2.1

Helpfulness of Web Project to Vita and Review

	Total (N)	Very helpful % (N)	Somewhat helpful % (N)	Not very helpful % (N)	Unknown % (N)
Presence of Department- or Library-Level Peer Review*					
No	43	12 (5)	42 (18)	16 (7)	30 (13)
Yes	52	33 (17)	27 (14)	35 (18)	6 (3)
Total	95				
Demonstrated Value of Project by Including Reviews**					
No	35	17 (6)	31 (11)	29 (10)	23 (8)
Yes	37	43 (16)	38 (14)	14 (5)	5 (2)
Total	72				
Assignment of Project**					
Assigned as part of job	4	50 (2)	50 (2)	0	0
Voluntary, but encouraged	30	43 (13)	30 (9)	13 (4)	13 (4)
Completely voluntary	63	13 (8)	35 (22)	33 (21)	19 (12)
Total	97				

* $p = 001$.
** $p = 018$.
*** $p = 020$.

Note: Some percentages do not total 100; discrepancies caused by rounding.

those surveyed received any release time to create their Web project. Thomas J. DeLoughrey reported in 1993 a trend toward accommodating technology development through release time, but that trend was not commonly found among those working on sites defined here as Web projects.[21] Software likely earned more of this sort of university support, since it can be licensed or sold, unlike most faculty Web projects.

Present Evaluation Environment

Although the majority of those surveyed expressed a general satisfaction with the evaluation of their work and felt that their projects proved valuable to their vita, many librarians and teaching faculty worked in institutions where they endeavored to have their Web projects recognized, and evaluation criteria remained the chief impediment. Of the 99 surveys returned, only one person reported that the institution's guidelines on electronic projects were clear, and a few reported somewhat clear guidelines. Nearly all the rest, however, replied that guidelines were either not at all clear or did not exist. Guidelines proved to be the most important factor contributing to an individual's satisfaction with institutional recognition. Seemingly, each person who worked within established guidelines more clearly understood the way in which his work would be valued, and thus created sites deemed respectable within his institution. Clear guidelines also helped professionals avoid their own over-inflated expectations of potential rewards.

When they submitted their Web projects during the performance review process, librarians and teaching faculty demonstrated their projects' value with various forms of documentation. They commonly provided some combination of a description of the project, reviews, cited references, or number of Web site visits. Of these options, submitting reviews in support of the Web project proved to be the only reliable way to improve its perceived value. No distinction was drawn between end-user reviews or published printed reviews in the survey, but the implication is that committee opinions were swayed by the comments from outside the institution by those who use a particular Web project and regard it highly.

It appeared that, despite recommendations to develop criteria by which electronic work can be judged, librarians and faculty typically chose to create Web projects in a vacuum of review expectations. If professionally related, they often submitted their Web achievements with their files for periodic retention, tenure, or promotion reviews without anticipating significant rewards. They nevertheless hoped that the reviewer, whether a board or an individual, would recognize the site's value to the campus or the profession. Many received favorable reviews, while others heard that their work "remains problematic if examined under the light of traditional research and publication criteria."

Although Lawson and Pelzer found library administrators in research libraries open to accommodating technology-based projects (including Web sites) submitted in dossiers or portfolios, they identified a dearth of criteria of evaluation.[22] Little formal research exists on technology review in academic disciplines. Administrators in departments of education provided the only evidence of technology-based projects, specifically software and video evaluation.[23] Both studies offered evaluation criteria applicable to Web project review.

Risks in Web Publishing

Administrators and peer review committees may be open to new publishing formats, but anecdotal evidence has shown that faculty are somewhat wary of entangling themselves with technology projects.[24] As recently as 1997, faculty reported looking for new appointments at different institutions or abandoning their Web projects because of the lack of rewards.[25] Furthermore, Lizbeth Langston recognized that the established methods of publishing and teaching will continue to be rewarded more often and consistently.[26] Do faculty struggle for recognition more than librarians? Are those on the tenure track scared off by the reports published in the *Chronicle*? If recognition is so elusive, for what reason do academics undertake these Web projects?

When beginning this research, I anticipated that the profession of the respondents, whether librarian or teaching faculty, would significantly affect how much the Web project helped their vita. As previously mentioned, a librarian's job responsibility often includes the creation or maintenance of Web sites, specifically those that support the goals and mission of the library. This study, however, showed that while librarians tended to fare better than teaching faculty when submitting their Web projects during review, none of the statistical tests proved that their profession determined either how much their vita helped their review or how satisfied they were with their institutional recognition. In this way, librarians and teaching faculty faced similar risks when choosing to create and maintain Web projects.

Instead of predicting success, tenure status, it appears, played a larger role in determining who launched a Web project at all. Only 16 of the survey participants were on the tenure track instead of tenured. The majority had already received tenure, and several remarked that they had earned full promotion as well. A tenured social sciences professor, for instance, volunteered, "I would not have invested the time that I have to my Web site were I not already a full professor." Although the statistical analysis did not show a strong relationship between tenure-track status and lower perceived recognition by the institution, the dramatic minority of untenured Web project authors provides obvious evidence of Web publishing's risks. As Langston noted, traditional work earns higher rewards, and tenure-seeking faculty invested their time in safer activities.

During the summer of 2002, the tenure-seeking respondents received a supplemental list of questions asking them to discuss their experience within the context of their tenure status. Of those who replied, none considered their tenure status before undertaking their project. They, instead, showed a keen interest in adding to the field with their work regardless of how their universities might evaluate it. Donna Campbell, an English professor at Gonzaga University and author of the site *Literary Movements*, said, "I was never under any illusions that the Web work would count toward tenure or other kinds of professional development and didn't expect it to be counted."[27] Librarian Laura Cohen from the State University of New York at Albany, author of *Internet Tutorials*, expressed a similar sentiment. "I would have worked on this project anyway, because it was important to me and because it was a labor of love."[28] These replies help to illustrate why untenured faculty disregarded the caution of their peers and initiated Web projects anyway. They continued a trend seen in academic software development. Faculty spend time working with an innovative technology because it is interesting and compelling, regardless of risks.[29]

The reason Campbell and Cohen succeeded during review is not likely due to an enlightened review board, although that may also be the case. These faculty realized their risk, chose to work on Web projects, and continued to produce traditional work as well. In some cases, the Web project led to additional opportunities in these areas. Nicole Auer's *Bibliography on Evaluating Internet Resources* raised her professional status enough that, "my first and most significant article was invited because of my work on my Web project," even though the solicited article did not directly address the issues raised by the site.[30]

In this way, Web projects, in addition to potential recognition from an institution, offered intrinsic rewards. A tenure-track humanities professor echoed that sentiment. "Faculty and administrators, with a few exceptions, seem either unaware or perhaps mildly interested in these resources. Mostly they're indifferent. This doesn't disturb me because they are not the audience for whom I've created the site." When asked if he was glad he invested his time and effort into *CD HotList*, librarian Rick Anderson responded as any of the others might have. He said, "absolutely . . . what makes it worthwhile is the fact that it's helpful to people."[31]

Recommendations for Web Evaluation

The fact remains that faculty, whether librarians or academic faculty, who invest their professional time and energy into quality Web projects deserve to be evaluated in a substantive manner. Peer review is the most recognized measure of accomplishment, and it may be the easiest for a review committee to apply. Since Web projects do not fit the journal article model for publication, most personnel committees need knowledge of other criteria to enable them to pass substantive judgment on a colleague's Web project.

Web projects, for this reason, need augmented standards that adapt the ways in which accomplishments are judged. For example, if a committee determines that a faculty member's published book received sufficient national recognition based upon its use in classes nationwide, then this same committee could review a Web project and identify its importance with the same criteria. In this way, a Web site incorporated into syllabi to aid students' understanding of an academic subject cannot be considered a "hobby" unworthy of the professor's time.[32] Although this hypothetical personnel committee may not grant Web projects the same respect or relative value as a published monograph, nor does this author argue that they should, it can fairly and objectively conclude their worth by applying established standards.

Further, personnel committees should evaluate the project on its merits in teaching/librarianship, scholarship, or service as appropriate. The American Association for History and Computing's technology review guidelines specifically state that, "faculty members should receive proportionate credit in more than one relevant area for their intellectual work" if that work overlaps several areas.[33] The presumption in academia is that digital work replaces printed scholarly publication. As noted in this study, Web projects can serve a variety of purposes, and they should be reviewed with the standards most applicable.

As faculty across the country attempt to earn recognition for their electronic endeavors, professional organizations help define ways in which faculty deserve to be evaluated. Recommendations abound for the creation of university or department-level review guidelines so that faculty can anticipate expected standards of professional accomplishment. The responses received from librarians and teaching faculty proved a direct relationship between the clarity of guidelines and the respondents' satisfaction with institutional recognition, and they substantiate the suggestions in the literature.

The Modern Language Association of America (MLA) developed a set of recommendations for evaluation, which continues to serve as a model for guidelines approved in other professional organizations. MLA focused on the responsibilities of both administrators and faculty for an effective review, but it avoided defining merit criteria by which a digital project could be judged. The organization directed five tenets toward administrators: "delineate and communicate responsibilities" in the hiring process, "engage qualified reviewers" to judge digital work even if the expert is outside of the university, "review work in the medium in which it was produced," "seek interdisciplinary advice" on review decisions if the project is collaborative, and "stay informed about disability issues" so those who are disabled can contribute to the discipline through adaptive technology.[34]

Once the university establishes a framework for valuing electronic work, the personnel committee must assess each project's value individually. Seminoff and Wepner identified four factors as the most common evaluation tools for technology-based projects: contribution to the field or discipline, national recognition, well-researched data collection, and local recognition.[35] Similar factors are critical to the assessment of librarians' technology work, with the most important being uniqueness or creativity, scholarly contribution, local recognition, and national or international recognition.[36] Building on those findings, the following five standards provide for positive Web project evaluation and how they may be applied during the review process.

1. *Contribution to the Field or Discipline*: Similar to the test for uniqueness or creativity, a committee could ask its colleagues to discuss the originality of their work. The site should help students or professional scholars engaged in research. The Web project could be cited in a journal or a monograph highlighting noteworthy Web sites. Inclusion on the Multimedia Educational Resource for Learning and Online Teaching (MERLOT) site, a nationwide project that collects and reviews "digital learning materials," might allow committees to view evaluations already penned by Web-savvy colleagues.[37]

2. *Local Recognition*: If intended for a local audience, the Web project may generate local speaking engagements on the topic, campus or community awards, or local grant funding. The local newspaper might contact the Web project author for comments on a story as it applies to the topic of the site. In the case of the University of Iowa's Bailiwick project, the library exhibits recognition for selected sites by agreeing to host them on designated servers.

3. *National Recognition*: How have the faculty in the discipline responded to the Web project? If it is well regarded, faculty from around the country may adopt the Web project in class syllabi. The author of the site may receive awards from professional organizations or invitations to speak at national conferences. National recognition can also be evident though published reviews, links on other Web sites, or grant funding.

4. *Development of Project*: The reviewing body may wish to ask the Web project author for his or her design rationale. This could include scholarly, pedagogical, or aesthetic concerns. If the site includes a statistical component, a discussion on the collection of data, as mentioned by Seminoff and Wepner, might be necessary.

5. *Peer Review*: Although the committee cannot rely on editorial boards to scrutinize Web projects before publication, the projects may earn evaluative comments in other mediums that substitute for formal peer review. Awards from the discipline and the ability to secure grant funding for site development may prove to be two of the most important examples. References in books highlighting the most interesting and useful Web sites on a subject provide another technique for assessment. Finally, end-user e-mails serve as testimonials for the utility or limitations of these sites. Offering a committee several examples from this category should serve a candidate well during review.

The Importance of Documentation: Guidelines
for Supporting a Web Project

Librarians and faculty, as is evident from the Web project survey results, succeed in earning recognition for their Web projects based on how well they prove the projects' worth. Faculty on the tenure track are familiar with the process of compiling relevant achievements into a professional portfolio or dossier. This portfolio may contain examples of publications, student evaluations, letters of support from colleagues, and copies of syllabi. Faculty constructing a thorough explanatory narrative and a substantive file of evidence, whether touting traditional or electronic work, likely receive more positive evaluations from the personnel committees because the faculty members helped clarify the value of their work. Web work, in this scenario, should be treated no differently. As institutions settle on the method of evaluating digital work, the onus is on the faculty member to prove the professional value of the project.

This study of Web projects proves that providing reviews as evidence of a project's value makes the most significant difference in its acceptance. These reviews serve as indicators of peer approval or professional recognition as discussed in the previous section. Faculty with upcoming reviews should seek out sources outside the institution to evaluate their Web projects. For example, many selective Internet gateways, those recommending Web sites for specific audiences, accept recommendations for site additions. If the Web project author feels that the site is useful as curriculum support, he or she should list the project with the MERLOT project. MERLOT provides a panel of experts in each discipline to review those sites identified as the most valuable on-line resources.[38] A review in MERLOT is an explicit peer review of the work.

Experts may also be contacted to offer a letter of review for a personnel file. The guidelines issued by the American Association for History and Computing suggest that they will help locate such experts for committees if they find themselves overwhelmed by their charge to evaluate digital work.[39] The Web project author, however, can solicit letters of support from a colleague who is aware and supportive of the work. This proactive move will help demonstrate the value of the site to the inexpert reviewer.

Finally, if the Web project is integrated into a class syllabus, the syllabus helps demonstrate the applicability of the project in the academic lives of students. If the professor who created the site assigns it to students, the project may support his or her teaching portfolio. On the other hand, the adoption of the site in a colleague's class indicates either local or national recognition, depending on the professor's institution. Each of these syllabi further bolsters the supporting file and should be included with other documentation.

This study suggests that most librarians and faculty see their Web work as a worthwhile element of their professional development, and many reviewing bodies agree. Some institutions, however, remain inflexible toward the incorporation of digital accomplishments. Faculty struggling for recognition may wish to share applicable guidelines for digital evaluation, many of which are discussed in this volume, with their department chair, personnel committees, dean, or other supervisors. Exposing these individuals to suitable evaluation criteria may provide the impetus for creating institution-specific standards. This communication also presents the opportunity to discuss the value of a specific project with those who may eventually evaluate the work. As Cynthia L. Selfe is quoted as saying, "Know the tenure-and-promotion criteria at the institution you're working at. Have regular talks with your chair, and keep your chair informed about what you're doing and why."[40]

Long-lasting change will develop as those who presently create and maintain quality Web projects increasingly sit on personnel committees and evaluate their colleagues' work. Familiarity with the way Web work is disseminated and professionally accepted will help them knowledgeably consider the merits of subsequent work. In addition, as senior faculty, they may succeed in efforts to modify or clarify written evaluation standards and serve as mentors to technologically savvy junior faculty.

World Wide Web projects still await widespread acceptance throughout academia, but this study shows that reviewing bodies grant Web projects respect and credibility when their worth is well documented. This is not to say that this new mode of expression is a major factor in retention, tenure, and promotion decisions. Faculty, both in libraries and in academic departments, must still balance their electronic work with traditional projects to receive professional advancement. Fortunately, distinguished Web projects draw attention to the projects' authors and lead to additional opportunities. As one librarian remarked, "Once the national recognition came, the library soon followed." As faculty clamber for revised evaluation standards in their institutions, departments and libraries will develop tools for substantive evaluation of worthwhile Web projects.

Notes

1. Kathryn Sylva and Robin Lasser, *Eating Disorders in a Disordered Culture*, March 3, 2000, www.eating.ucdavis.edu.

2. The *Librarians' Index to the Internet*, www.lii.org, is a "subject directory" that compiles Web sites deemed useful for public libraries.

3. For a more complete methodology and statistical analysis, see: Kathleen Carlisle Fountain, "Perceptions of Acceptance: Evaluating World Wide Web Projects in Performance Reviews," *College & Research Libraries* 62, No. 3 (May 2001): 260–68.

4. Karen G. Lawson and Nancy L. Pelzer, "Assessing Technology-Based Projects for Promotion and/or Tenure in ARL Academic Libraries," *College & Research Libraries* 60 (September 1999): 468.

5. Ibid., 467.

6. Gail McMillian, "Viewing Results for Assessing Technology-Based Projects for Faculty Evaluations," 2000, lumiere.lib.vt.edu/surveys/results/.

7. Michelle Slatella, "Building Web Pages Is Child's Play," *New York Times*, May 7, 1998, G11.

8. Annette Haines, "Librarians' Personal Web Pages: An Analysis," *College & Research Libraries* 60, No. 6 (November 1999): 546.

9. Jerry Goldman,*The Oyez Project*, 2002, oyez.nwu.edu.

10. Paul A. Soderdahl and Carol Ann Hughes, "That's My Bailiwick: A Library-Sponsored Faculty Research Web Server," *Information Technology and Libraries* 19, No. 1 (March 2000): 29–34.

11. Lee Van Orsdel and Kathleen Born, "Doing the Digital Flip: Has the Advent of the E-Journal Finally Turned the Periodicals Industry Upside Down?" *Library Journal*, April 15, 2002, 51–52.

12. *Ulrich's Periodicals Directory* (New Providence, NJ: R.R. Bowker, 2002), x.

13. Sally A. Rogers, "Electronic Journal Usage at Ohio State University," *College & Research Libraries* 62, No. 1 (January 2001): 33.

14. Blaise Cronin and Kara Overfelt, "E-Journals and Tenure," *Journal of the American Society for Information Science* 46, No. 9 (October 1995): 702.

15. Aldrin E. Sweeney, "E-Scholarship and Electronic Publishing in the Twenty-First Century: Implications for the Academic Community," *Education Media International* 38, No. 1 (March 2001): 25–38.

16. Nancy E. Seminoff and Shelley B. Wepner, "Are Technology-Based Projects Valued as Scholarship for Tenure and Promotion?" *Journal of Computing in Teacher Education* 11, No. 3 (Spring 1995): 5–10.

17. Thomas J. DeLoughrey, "Professors Report Progress in Gaining Recognition for Their Use of Technology," *Chronicle of Higher Education*, March 3, 1993, A19, 21.

18. Lisa Guernsey, "Scholars Who Work with Technology Fear They Suffer in Tenure Reviews," *Chronicle of Higher Education*, June 6, 1997, A21–22.

19. Vincent Kiernan, "Rewards Remain Dim for Professors Who Pursue Digital Scholarship," *Chronicle of Higher Education*, April 28, 2000, 45. Jeffrey R. Young, "Ever So Slowly, Colleges Start to Count Work with Technology in Tenure Decisions," *Chronicle of Higher Education*, February 22, 2002, A25.

20. Lawson and Pelzer, "Assessing Technology-Based Products," 74.

21. DeLoughrey, "Professors Report Progress," A19.

22. Lawson and Pelzer, "Assessing Technology-Based Products," 471.

23. Seminoff and Wepner, "Are Technology-Based Projects Valued?" 8; Nancy E. Seminoff and Shelley B. Wepner, "What Should We Know About Technology-Based Projects for Tenure and Promotion?" *Journal of Research on Computing in Education* 30, No. 1 (Fall 1997): 67–82.

24. G. Phillip Cartwright, "Information Technology: Considerations for Tenure and Promotion," *Change* 26, No. 5 (September/October 1994): 26–28; DeLoughrey, "Professors Report Progress," A21.

25. Guernsey, "Scholars Who Work with Technology," A21.

26. Lizbeth Langston, "Scholarly Communication and Electronic Publication: Implications for Research, Advancement, and Promotion," in *Untangling the Web:*

Proceedings of the Conference Sponsored by the Librarians Association of the University of California, Santa Barbara, and Friends of the UCSB Library, April 26, 1996, see also ERIC Document Reproduction Service at www.library.ucsb.edu/untangle/langston.html ERIC, ED 403892.

27. The tenure-track faculty I interviewed by subsequent e-mail agreed to allow attribution to their quotations. All faculty and librarians surveyed in 2000 are cited confidentially. Donna Campbell, "Web Projects: Follow-up Questions," July 18, 2002, personal e-mail (July 18, 2002). *Literary Movements* is available at: www.gonzaga.edu/faculty/campbell/enl311/litfram.html.

28. Laura Cohen, "Web Projects: Follow-up Questions," July 19, 2002, personal e-mail (July 19, 2002). *Internet Tutorials* is available at: library.albany.edu/internet/.

29. Cartwright, "Information Technology."

30. Nicole Auer, "Web Projects: Follow-up Questions," July 19, 2002, personal e-mail (July 19, 2002). *Bibliography on Evaluating Internet Resources* is available at: www.lib.vt.edu/research/evaluate/evalbiblio.html.

31. Rick Anderson, "Web Projects: Follow-up Questions," July 18, 2002, personal e-mail (July 18, 2002). *CD HotList* available at: www2.library.unr.edu/anderson/cdhl/index.htm.

32. Young, "Ever So Slowly," A25.

33. The American Association for History and Computing, "Suggested Guidelines for Evaluating Digital Media Activities in Tenure, Review, and Promotion—An AAHC Document," *Perspectives* 39, No. 7 (October 2001): 33.

34. Modern Language Association, *Guidelines for Evaluating Work with Digital Media in the Modern Languages*, May 30, 2000, www.mla.org/reports/ccet/ccet_guidelines.htm.

35. Seminoff and Wepner, "What Should We Know About Technology-Based Projects for Tenure and Promotion?" 73.

36. Lawson and Pelzer, "Assessing Technology-Based Products," 470.

37. Thomas E. Malloy and Gerard L. Hanley, "MERLOT: A Faculty-Focused Web Site of Educational Resources," *Behavior Research Methods, Instruments, & Computers* 33, No. 2 (2001): 274. MERLOT is available at: www.merlot.org.

38. Malloy and Hanley, "MERLOT," 275.

39. The American Association for History and Computing, 33.

40. Young, "Ever So Slowly," A25.

Chapter 3

Valuing Digital Scholarship in the Tenure, Promotion, and Review Process

A Survey of Academic Historians

Deborah Lines Andersen and Dennis A. Trinkle

Scholarship and Technology

Formal historical research has traditionally been the backbone of the tenure, promotion, and review process in most academic history departments. While teaching and service are also weighed in cases of continuing appointment, peer-reviewed publication has usually been the critical focus of the tenure and promotion process.[1]

Information technology is starting to challenge this traditional academic culture. Cronin and Overfelt questioned how "the academic reward system is adjusting to changes in scholarly publication media and practices."[2] The focus of this research specifically looks to answer that question. Are history departments adjusting to changes in information media, creating policy that will reward digital scholarship in the areas of teaching, service, and research? Are there formal or informal policies at academic institutions that will reward this scholarship? What are the barriers that exist to this adjustment to change? And finally, are there broader policy implications that can be drawn from the case of history and applied to other disciplines attempting to use the products of technology in academe?

Defining Digital History

The Introduction of this book looks at "digital scholarship." "Digital history" is a subset of that area and requires some grounding in the literature. Traditional historical research has been based upon uncovering and interpreting evidence in the form of such primary source documents as letters, newspapers, diaries, journals, military or court records, and census data in order to create a historical argument.[3] Whereas "computer scientists often treat conference articles as significant forms of publication,"[4] traditional publication venues in history are of two sorts—the monograph and the peer-reviewed journal article. Historians also have traditionally worked alone. It is usual for papers and books to have single authorship.[5] As in other academic fields, the publisher of a monograph or the prestige of the journal is of critical importance when tenure and promotion committees evaluate the scholarship of a faculty member.[6] Unlike the sciences, history is traditionally underfunded in terms of research and travel dollars, and historians have tended to be technologically unsophisticated in their use of technologies for teaching as well as research, holding onto old computers until research projects are complete or maintaining file boxes of handwritten note cards while their computers sit unused.[7] These characteristics are changing, at least for a small percentage of historians.

Digital history has started to emerge in the past several years. One example of such history is in the creation of strictly electronic journals. Whereas some publishers have taken to making traditionally print-based journals also available in electronic format for subscribers,[8] individual historians and groups of historians have created e-journals that have no paper counterpart.[9] Without the constraints of the original paper medium, such journals are free to include sound and video bites, photographs, slides, and links to full-text document sources. They are not constrained by paper-based page counts. The medium has changed the presentation of the message.[10]

Another manifestation of digital history is in the form of CD-ROM or Web-based projects that create an interpretation of historical evidence by presenting the sources and creating links and text that guide the reader through the interpretative process.[11] Unlike the linear organization of a monograph—first page to last, these interpretations can be nonlinear. The reader has the ability to move forward, backward, and sideways through the text in a variety of ways depending upon the available links and his or her desire.

Also included in this mix of digital history are the teaching Web sites and projects that allow students to explore and interpret history through interactive games, class Web sites and discussion groups, geographic information systems, and computer-assisted design (CAD) programs.[12] Videotapes and audiotapes add to this mix.[13] These trends represent a sea change from the traditional classroom lectures. A cultural shift is beginning at least within some history departments across the United States. There may be just one or two faculty members who have decided to take the plunge and produce their work electronically. They have had to go beyond the realm of traditional historical research and teaching to learn from individuals in other fields such as computer science, geography, architecture, or music.[14] They have started to work collaboratively with these individuals.

The research presented here looked at the present state of digital product evaluation within U.S. history departments. As technologies change, there will be need for longitudinal research in how these digital history innovations have diffused across academic departments. Inevitably, technologies yet unheard of will, in the future, become new evaluation issues for academic departments.

Research Method

This research assessed the degree to which products of digital scholarship are used in the tenure, promotion, and review processes of history departments in the United States. To that end the 20–question survey contained both qualitative and quantitative questions, looking at formal and informal departmental and university-wide policies for granting promotion based upon the use of nontraditional media in teaching and research. Additionally, the survey asked about institutional support for technology-related activities and focused on differences that might surface between treatment of tenured versus untenured faculty members.

The sample for this survey was self-selected. In spring 2000, the survey was posted to the World Wide Web.[15] An invitation to participate in the survey was surface mailed directly to every history chair named in the Amercian Historical Association *Guide to Departments of History*. By the end of April, 66 chairs (a 10 percent response rate) had replied.[16] As a result of this sampling method, the findings of the survey are not generalizable to all history departments in the United States. The purpose of this survey was not to infer from the sample to the population, but instead to establish the degree of diversity among history departments in the United States. Often such survey techniques result in responses that are either very strongly opposed to or in favor of particular practices or ideas. The middle does not respond.[17] This was a benefit of the methodology for this research, since it surfaced stories based upon best and, arguably, worst practice in the field. The findings of this survey pointed to particular policies, or lack of policies, across the 66 departments. The findings suggested trends that are bound by traditional historical scholarship, and policy implications that could help new faculty members in their pursuit of promotion and tenure. Furthermore, the lessons gained from looking at technology-based scholarship in history, a field that has remained culturally very stable over time, may have implications for other academic disciplines.

The survey design consisted of forced-responses questions with a comments space after each. While the quantitative questions gave a sense of trends in the 66 history departments, the qualitative responses were rich in detail, in stories, in emotion, and in cautions for untenured faculty. The

1

I Policies

Question	Yes	No	Total
Does your institution have a formal, written policy for assessing technology-related activities in the tenure, promotion, and review process?	4	62	66
Does your institution count technology-related activities in the area of teaching?	2	2	4
Does your institution count technology-related activities in the area of service?	1	3	4
Does your institution count technology-related activities in the area of professional development/research?	1	3	4

findings in the next section concern both the quantitative questions and the qualitative remarks.

Survey Question Analysis

The first four questions (see Table 3.1) concerned *formal* institutional policies in relation to tenure, promotion, and review. Respondents were directed to skip the next three questions if they answered "no" to the first. Only 4 of the 66 departmental chairs stated that there were formal policies in place for dealing with technology-related activities, but none of the four stated that their institutions counted these activities in all areas of teaching, service, and professional development/research.

Examining the positive responses in Table 3.1, two chairpersons who answered "yes" to the first question *did not* answer "yes" to the subsequent three questions. Thus, although they indicated that their institution had a formal, written policy, it did not appear to cover teaching, service, or professional development and research! Of the other two chairpersons, one indicated formal policy in teaching and service, while the other indicated formal policy in teaching and research. Although this survey did not ask that respondents include a copy of the formal policies, future research could examine these policies.

The open-ended responses in this section of the survey mentioned both positive and negative aspects of technology-related activities. While one department chair stated that "anything to make access to materials easier and more understandable to students" would be counted in the area of teaching, another stated:

Part of the annual review of faculty and the regular reviews of tenure and promotion include assessment of all aspects of teaching. In recent years as more faculty have begun to use technology in their teaching, their performance evaluations include questions about the quality and effectiveness of the technology. Peer evaluation and class visitations are a second measure. In the tenure and promotion year, faculty are visited by their peers and by the department, and a written report is filed as part of the dossier. Third, in annual reviews, there are questions about the use and effectiveness of technology in the classroom. . . . Use of technology is thus a regular part of annual and special evaluations.

Similarly, department chairs cited positive examples of using technology in the service component of faculty members' jobs.

Those faculty who assist their peers in developing more effective uses of technology will list these activities as part of their service contribution to the department or institution, and it is a factor in merit review as well as tenure and promotion considerations.

On the other hand, comments about professional development and research tended to be more mixed. One chairperson stated, "What hasn't been directly addressed is the question of 'Is an on-line publication a publication?'" while another noted that, "The institution is not against the use of these materials in the review process, but is unfamiliar with a great many submissions in this area. Many professors in my department are not clear that this qualifies as research." On a more negative note, a third chairperson wrote,

I do not believe that most publications in electronic media earn much respect. These are seen as curiosities rather than as scholarship. The questionable level of "vetting" associated with computer publications is partly to blame. The basic unfamiliarity, with a hostility to technology among many of the members, especially the "humanistically" oriented, also plays a role.

The tension was strong between positive use and evaluation in the areas of teaching and service and negative repercussions from creating digital history products or publishing electronically.

The next two questions concerned university evaluation of nonprint scholarship (see Table 3.2). For both peer-reviewed journals, and database or digital creations, respondents were divided as to whether their institutions would value such activities. The two questions in Table 3.2 elicited the largest number of open-ended responses out of any in the survey. Twenty-five chairs

Table 3.2

University Evaluation of Nonprint Intellectual Products

Question	Yes	No	Total
Does your university value publications in electronic peer-reviewed journals in the tenure, promotion, and review process?	36	30	66
Would your university value the creation of a database or digital creation (Valley of the Shadow, for example) as an equivalent of a monograph?	22	44	66

commented on electronic peer-reviewed journals, and 17 commented on database or digital creation.

Of the 25 comments on e-journals, some were very positive, stating that "electronic, peer-reviewed journal articles are treated the same as traditional print articles," and that "these are treated as printed journals as long as they are peer-reviewed and tied to a recognized organization." There were several negative assessments as well. One chair noted, "I can only report my impression that such publication would be acceptable only if the author met minimum publication standards through print books and journals. . . . Work would have to be in addition to print publications." Another stated succinctly, "Frankly, if I am under review, I would not at this point publish electronically."

The comments on database and digital creation tended more toward the negative. Some chairpersons believed that digital creation might be considered as an edited volume, and probably not as the equivalent of a monograph. One chairperson stated, "at this point the monograph is the pinnacle of prestige." Another noted of his own research,

> I have created, with another colleague, an ongoing large Web site on African primary sources that is in the process of being turned into a database. Much of the information on the site comes from questionnaires that we have designed and distributed as well as research in a variety of sources. The work is being labeled "derivative" at this institution and not what a "real historian" does.

In general, individuals noted a lack of understanding of the nature of databases such as the African primary sources database ("Is a database more like an edited collection of source materials?"), a belief that they were not sufficiently peer reviewed, and a feeling that faculty have not thought of databases or digital creations as "a formal research submission."

Table 3.3

Informal Policies

Question	Yes	No	Total
Does your institution have an informal policy regarding the use of technology in teaching, professional development, or service?	37	29	66
Does your university have a consistently understood policy about how technology-related activities will be evaluated?	1*	65	66
Is there consensus among your faculty colleagues about how technology-related activities ought to be considered in the tenure, promotion, and review process?	5	61	66
Is there agreement between the faculty and the administration about the place of technology-related activities in the tenure, promotion, and review process?	6	60	66

*These bold figures indicated a strong shift from the responses to previous questions. Whereas 37 of 66 respondents said they had an informal policy, for the last three questions, no more than 6 said they had a consistent policy where there was consensus and agreement.

The four questions on informal institutional policies (see Table 3.3) started by asking if the institution had an informal policy in place. More than half of the respondents said "yes." Nonetheless, when asked in the next three questions if the policy was consistently understood, if there was consensus among faculty, or if there was agreement between faculty and administration, the numbers shifted strongly, with few (see the bold numbers in the table) indicating "yes."

As with the previous analysis of open-ended comments, those dealing with teaching and service tended to be more positive than those dealing with research. One chairperson stressed the role of the faculty member. "Individual faculty members who are active in technology-related activities need to take the initiative in framing it as scholarly work, teaching, or service. Documenting, for example, the peer-review strength of an on-line journal will have to be an individual faculty member's job." Another noted that:

> In an evaluation discussion of a faculty member, technology-related activities show commitment and engagement, but only in circumstances where the basic outline of competence is met. A faculty member would not be promoted or deemed meritorious for her/his technology-related activities if the student satisfaction ratings of the classroom experience were low. A divergent point of view on campus is that technology is robbing the faculty of resources (usually salary supplements) to improve the quality of their content delivery.

A third chairperson reflected on the tension between older and younger faculty members.

> There are two views offered informally by colleagues. The first one is held by older faculty and views technology as a toy/tool. They do admire people who use the many gadgets, but see it as a slightly wasteful but intelligent tool. Junior faculty are more intrigued by its uses but do not want to spend too much time out of their realm of research. However, their daily usage is much higher than the senior faculty.

Additionally, chairpersons felt the tensions between older and younger faculty, and between departments and administrations. One respondent stated:

> I believe that the administration is more sympathetic to technology-related activities than the faculty. As chair of the department, I received constant pressure from the administration to encourage faculty members to use technology in the classroom. My consistent reply was that older faculty members were not interested and that I could not in good conscience encourage younger faculty members to spend the time required by such activities because I know that various faculty committees judging tenure and promotion do not value those activities.

The general picture continued to be one in which teaching and service could benefit from use of technology-related activities but research and professional development were caught in traditional norms and modes of scholarship.

The next set of questions (see Table 3.4) was designed to surface differences in support for tenured versus untenured faculty in areas of technology-based research and course development. In the area of release time, the chairpersons were evenly split as to whether their departments would provide this kind of support. There was no statistically significant difference between the support given for tenured versus untenured faculty.

A shift in responses occurred in the last four questions (see the bold numbers in Table 3.4). Much more strongly, and again with no distinction according to tenure status, respondents said that their institutions did provide training and technical support. The open-ended responses were very helpful in understanding this difference. Whereas chairs saw release time as a scarce *departmental* resource, they explained that training support was at the university or institutional level, often from campus-wide teaching and computing centers. One chairperson gave an example of the use of technology support on his campus.

Table 3.4

Institutional Support for Technology-Related Activities

Question	Yes	No	Total
Does your institution provide release time or grants to *tenured* faculty for pursuing technology-related research activities?	33	33	66
Does your institution provide release time or grants to *untenured* faculty for pursuing technology-related research activities?	27	39	66
Does your institution provide release time or grants to *tenured* faculty for pursuing technology-based course development?	34	32	66
Does your institution provide release time or grants to *untenured* faculty for pursuing technology-based course development?	34	32	66
Does your institution provide training support to *tenured* faculty who wish to use technology in their teaching or research?	**55***	11	66
Does your institution provide training support to *untenured* faculty who wish to use technology in their teaching or research?	**53**	13	66
Does your institution proved technical support (instructional technologists, graphics experts, etc.) to *tenured* faculty who wish to use technology in their teaching or research?	**44**	22	66
Does your institution proved technical support (instructional technologists, graphics experts, etc.) to *untenured* faculty who wish to use technology in their teaching or research?	**46**	20	66

* As in Table 3.3, these bold figures depicted a change in chairpersons' responses. In these last four questions, chairpersons strongly indicated that their departments received technical and teaching support for tenured and untenured faculty.

The institution and college both have technology support personnel who work with faculty in the design, development, and use of technology. Our college support person has devised a simple click and drag folder system that allows faculty to place any print or digitized materials on the college server for classroom use. These activities are well used and effectively supported. The institution also has an office visits workshop program where tech staffers will come to the faculty member's office to work with him/her in addition to programs in the technical support area.

Table 3.5

Institutional Encouragement for Digital History

Question	Encourages	Discourages	No response
In general, does your institution encourage or discourage *tenured* scholars from digital research projects?	28	22	16
In general, does your institution encourage or discourage *tenure-track* scholars from digital research projects?	26	23	17
Does your institution encourage or discourage *tenured* scholars from digital teaching projects?	42	16	8
Does your institution encourage or discourage *tenure-track* scholars from digital teaching projects?	42	19	5

This was a strong statement about the kind of technology support provided to history faculty members at the college or institutional level.

The last set of questions asked history department chairs about institutional encouragement for digital history projects (see Table 3.5). This was the first set of questions that some respondents chose to leave blank. Again, the open-ended responses were helpful in sorting out this issue. Many stated that their institution or department neither encouraged nor discouraged digital history. One respondent commented, "There is no 'yes' or 'no' to this—it all gets done on an individual basis." Another remarked that, "The institution encourages digital teaching, but seems ambivalent about digital research at present." A strong theme in the open-ended comments was that the use of technology in teaching was encouraged at both departmental and institutional levels, while the use of technology in research could actually be detrimental to faculty coming up for tenure and review. One person related his own experience.

There is a double standard applied. Teaching with tech is accepted and generally promoted while research and publication in this area is "not" encouraged, rewarded or recognized. My own experience . . . in technology-related matters counted for nothing when tenure review came up. My effort to use technology and teaching together was only acknowledged, not rewarded.

Throughout this section there was no statistically significant difference between reported treatment of tenured and tenure-track faculty.

Findings and Policy Implications

The conclusions that arose from this study, and particularly from the open-ended responses, address not only how tenure and promotion cases in history departments use (or normally do not use) technology products, but also the apparent lack of formal means for dealing with digital history products within departments. Numerous chairpersons exhibited a "wait-and-see" approach, stating, "We haven't had a case yet," or "I do not think this has been tested or addressed." One individual went as far as to say that "one or two is not a problem" as long as the faculty member coming up for tenure also had appropriate peer-reviewed journal articles and/or monographs.

Combining the qualitative and quantitative analysis of the survey created a group of themes that appeared critical to departments of history, but that might also be generalized to other departments across university and college campuses. Department chairs identified culture, teaching and research, and faculty rank as important issues in defining and evaluating digital scholarship. These chairs also described current applications of digital history, formal and informal policy issues, and barriers to policy formation. Each of these themes helps inform scholarship in a digital environment.

Current Applications

In fields where technology is quickly changing the range and possibilities of scholarship, it is hard to pinpoint exactly what constitutes digital scholarship, or, for this chapter, digital history. Respondents in the qualitative section of the survey did give examples of what would be considered best practice in digital history.

Several respondents said that peer-reviewed articles should be indicators of high levels of scholarship, no matter what the medium of presentation. If this is to be a reality, then tenure and promotion committees at departmental and university levels would benefit from information about the peer-review policies of e-journals. At the same time, academic historians need to document their work, copying e-publications in case the on-line copy does not persist, and copying the peer-review statements of the e-journal to document the rigor of the process.

Other products of technology, such as databases or interactive Web teaching tools, might be weighted as edited volumes or as scholarly editions rather than being discounted altogether. There is a considerable time commitment that goes into creating an interactive computer simulation or a CAD program that allows students to reconstruct historic buildings. Documenting the time and effort of such products might help untenured faculty members showcase their work.

Furthermore, there is a continuum of possible technology-based products. Correctly, one department chair said that he would not give credit for someone using a computer. Should someone be given credit for using PowerPoint? For using electronic reserves for her students? For creating class Web pages that allow students to interact with one another and learn through out-of-class discussions? As new technologies come into play, history departments, and, in fact, all academic disciplines must remain alert to how new products of technology should fit into the tenure and promotion process.

Some of the best ways to create and change culture are through recognition and reward. Department chairs believed that universities and departments valued digital history. These products make schools more visible, giving advertising value and the potential for attracting new students and faculty. Administrations will be wise to create rewards for these methods of scholarship if they expect to reap the benefits of having them exist at their institutions. Faculty development grants, release time, paid conference attendance, and state-of-the art technology were all mentioned as ways to reward or encourage faculty.

The value of technology can also be seen in the technology centers across many university campuses. These centers serve as support organizations for faculty and graduate students, teaching them the finer points of using technology in their pedagogy. Perhaps there is a partnership to be formed between these organizations and history departments (and other departments where this is an issue) that would give greater credibility to digital media activities.

Finally, the future appears to require more, not less, collaboration. Academics in the sciences have, due to the nature of their fields and grant money, always been collaborators. They have worked out ways of identifying the part that individuals played in various projects when they came up for tenure and review. Historians draw upon such areas as art, music, and architecture, not to mention computer science, in the creation of digital history projects. Along the way, they will have to figure out how to assign authorship to various parts of projects, and they will need to develop a culture that respects and rewards work in teams. All of these products of digital scholarship are shaped by the culture of academic departments and by the universities that house them.

Culture

It is easy to argue that a university community is composed of a variety of subcultures. Scientists, humanists, historians, and artists all exist within the walls of universities, but they all conduct research in different ways depending upon the norms of their disciplines. The strength of universities comes from this cultural diversity. At the same time, it is a challenge to adopt tenure, promotion, and review policies that are consistent, while also taking this diversity into account. The challenge becomes even greater when a field that has traditionally published research in a particular manner (e.g., history with journal articles and monographs), moves to incorporate technologies more commonly seen in other disciplines. Added to this are the various levels of promotion and review at universities. Depending upon the size of the institution, an untenured historian might first be reviewed by her department members, then by her college, and finally by a university committee representative of the diversity of fields in academe. What is valued at what level of review may be seen differently at another.

Department chairs made a strong distinction between history departments and university administrations. Administrations provided technological support for the university in personnel, computers, and teaching institutes. They also pushed faculty to teach with technology. At the same time, history department chairs were nonetheless faced with junior faculty members who had spent too much time creating digital history in their research and teaching, and very possibly would not meet the traditional standards for tenure and promotion. One chairperson stated that they had not yet had a test case. This tension between departments and university administrations points to the culture and community of academic institutions.

Teaching versus Research

Throughout the survey comments a theme that should be underscored was the difference between technology for teaching and technology for research. Teaching with technology was considered good, if time-consuming, and not particularly valued for tenure and promotion. Using technology in the research and publication of history was not considered good by the majority of respondents and was considered to be an inferior product to the usual methods of disseminating research through peer-reviewed articles and monographs.

Senior versus Junior Faculty Members

Although in relation to the qualitative survey questions many respondents said that there was no difference in policy between tenured and untenured faculty members, there were, in fact, many differences mentioned. Senior faculty members do not have to worry about tenure, so the prospect of not being rewarded for digital history is not as large. Junior faculty members are probably the most technologically savvy but have the most to lose from using too much of their time on such pursuits. One respondent noted fear on the part of senior faculty—that technology products would become a teaching requirement for them since junior faculty were being rewarded for these endeavors. This was a reversal of the digital scholarship issue. It was not that junior faculty would not be tenured, but that senior faculty would be retroactively deemed less good and less skilled. If newer faculty are using Web pages, PowerPoint, multimedia, and real-time Internet connections to enliven their teaching, what do students think of more traditional faculty members who use more traditional lecture notes and discussion? Early adopters must find cultural bridges to their senior colleagues. At present, an identity gulf exists, and senior historians have difficulty imagining themselves pursuing the research or activities of their junior colleagues. This gulf triggers a variety of psychologically predictable defense and adaptive mechanisms, rather than fostering a broadened understanding of historical practice. This, again, is an issue of cultural tradition and community.

Barriers to Policy Formation

The idea of "wait and see" was problematic. Departments and universities should consider adopting policy before e-journal and computer-based scholarship becomes a larger issue in the tenure and review policy. On the other hand, if departments are bent on not creating policy, or on rewarding only traditional methods of scholarship and teaching, then those issues can be clearly delineated to candidates before they are offered positions. Newly minted history PhDs must be aware of this dichotomy between what administrations seem to want and what departments seem to reward.

Formal Policy for Tenure, Promotion, and Review in History Departments

The MLA and American Association for History and Computing policies mentioned in this book are strong starts to creating such policy. Part of cultural change is a shift brought on by younger faculty members replacing older ones as they retire. This change seems inevitable. It will require that newer faculty members negotiate their roles in advance of hiring and that departments create job descriptions including the part digital history will play in the intellectual life of the new faculty member. Additionally, those senior faculty members who believe technology has a role in their departments will have roles as mentors for new faculty. Finally, it seems that policy recommendations should be sensitive to cultural issues, while at the same time dealing with individuals who are about to be reviewed for tenure. There must be a safety net in place. This safety net should assure senior faculty that they do not need to participate in digital history. At the same time, it should be in place for creative, untenured faculty members who might make great advances in the field if they were not worried about the security of their jobs.

Formal policy is a two-edged sword. There is a strong possibility that history departments across the United States, if required to create formal policy, would vote in favor of the traditions of the field, today excluding products of digital scholarship from the tenure, promotion, and review process. The place of such institutions as the Modern Language Association and the American Association for History and Computing should be to create broad-based policies that departments and universities can adopt, rather than leaving policy formation to individuals and departments.

Tensions in Academe

The overarching findings of this research surfaced tensions that exist in the tenure, promotion, and review process—not just for historians, but also for all faculty members in academic institutions. There were those chairpersons from teaching institutions who said that research was not valued at their schools. For them, digital history in the form of teaching was a highly desirable and rewarded pursuit. Thus, this survey research surfaced the differences between institutions that required peer-reviewed publications and those that did not. More globally, the survey illuminated the central tension between teaching and research (and the amount of emphasis that should be placed on each) within institutions. This is especially evident with digital teaching products because they consume large amounts of time, while strictly peer-reviewed publications are necessary for tenure, review, and promotion.

Given the tension between teaching and research, it is not surprising that a very strong tension exists between the needs and actions of tenured versus untenured faculty members. Whereas tenured faculty members might have the time to create digital products without the worry of evaluation for tenure, untenured, younger faculty members are more likely to have the expertise to work in nontraditional media. Without formal guidelines for evaluating these technology-intensive products for teaching and research, it is possible that untenured faculty members will work in traditional publication media until they are assured tenure.

A less universal but nevertheless critical tension exists between single authorship and collaboration in technology-intensive scholarship. Whereas some faculty members, especially in the sciences, have usually worked in collaboration with their colleagues, humanists have worked alone. Academic departments that are not used to evaluating collaborative efforts will have to produce evaluation standards that take multiple authorship into account.

Finally, this research surfaced tensions that exist between departments and administrations as well as between departments and individual faculty members. In the first instance, university administrators seem to value strongly the products of digital scholarship. Creative teaching and Web sites are strong advertisements for drawing faculty, students, and donations to a university. At the same time, departments appear to value more strongly peer-reviewed publications that will assure tenure for faculty members and prestige for the department. In the second instance, departments need to make very clear to potential faculty members that there is a tension between digital scholarship for service and teaching, and digital scholarship for research and publication. Surfacing the department's assumptions about the new faculty member's role in these digital initiatives could greatly ease promotion cases, avoiding test situations where there is no policy, and providing mentoring before tenure review becomes an issue.

Some of these tensions have no remedy. They cannot be negotiated away or changed even through policy documents. Nonetheless, recognition of their existence is a critical first step in understanding the forces that are changing the face of academic tenure, review, and promotion. New information technologies are constantly surfacing. It seems clear that academics will continue to adopt these technologies, using them in their teaching and research. The challenge for departments and universities is to adopt policy that is broad enough so that it will incorporate new multimedia forms, and specific enough so that untenured faculty members can be rewarded for their endeavors. The challenge for national associations is to help create broad-based polices that will further scholarship and teaching, providing community-based support for those working in digital scholarship.

Notes

1. See M.E. Whitman, A.R. Hendrickson and A.M. Townsend, "Research Commentary. Academic Rewards for Teaching, Research, and Service: Data and Discourse," *Information Systems Research* 10 (1999): 99–109, for a discussion of the tenure, promotion, and review process among academic departments of information science; and Kathleen Carlisle Fountain, "Perceptions of Acceptance: Evaluating World Wide Web Projects in Performance Reviews," *College & Research Libraries* 62 (2001): 260–268, for a discussion of review in university library science and academic departments.

2. Blaise Cronin and Kara Overfelt, "E-Journals and Tenure." *Journal of the American Society for Information Science* 46, No. 9 (October 1995): 700.

3. See Deborah Lines Andersen, "Academic Historians, Electronic Information Access Technologies, and the World Wide Web: A Longitudinal Study of Factors Affecting Use and Barriers to That Use," *Journal of the Association for History and Computing* 1 (1998), available at mcel.pacificu.edu/JAHC/jahcindex.htm; also in Dennis A. Trinkle and Scott A. Merriman, *History.edu: Essays on Teaching with Technology* (Armonk, NY: M.E. Sharpe, 2001), 3–24; Donald O. Case, "The Collection and Use of Information by Some American Historians: A Study of Motives and Methods," *Library Quarterly* 61 (1991): 61–82; and R. Delgadillo and B.P. Lynch, "Future Historians: Their Quest for Information," *College & Research Libraries* 60 (1999): 245–60.

4. Rob Kling and Geoffrey McKim, "Scholarly Communication and the Continuum of Electronic Publishing," *Journal of the American Society for Information Science* 50 (1999): 890–906.

5. Jack B. King, "History Research into the 21st Century," *Reference Librarian* 47 (1994): 89–108.

6. Cheri Speier, Jonathan Palmer, Daniel Wren, and Susan Hahn, "Faculty Perceptions of Electronic Journals as Scholarly Communication: A Question of Prestige and Legitimacy," *Journal of the American Society for Information Science* 50 (1999): 537–43.

7. Andersen, "Academic Historians."

8. Speier et al., "Faculty Perceptions."

9. See the *Journal of the Association for History and Computing,* mcel.pacificu.edu/JAHC/jahcindex.htm, and the *Journal for MultiMedia History,* www.albany.edu/jmmh/.

10. Stephen P. Harter, "Scholarly Communication and Electronic Journals: An Impact Study," *Journal of the American Society for Information Science* 49 (1998): 507–16.

11. See the Valley of the Shadow, www.iath.virginia.edu/vshadow2.

12. See Laurel Thatcher Ulrich, *A Midwife's Tale: The Life of Martha Ballard Based on Her Diary 1785–1812* (New York: Random House, 1990), in book form as well as the interactive Web site at www.dohistory.org/. See also K.W. Carver, *Using Internet Primary Sources to Teach Critical Thinking Skills in History* (Westport, CT: Greenwood Press, 1999).

13. Karen G. Lawson and Nancy L. Pelzer, "Assessing Technology-Based Projects for Promotion and/or Tenure in ARL Academic Libraries," *College & Research Libraries* 60 (September 1999): 464–76.

14. Jamie Murphy, "Technology Training for Faculty," *Converge* 2 (1999): 30–31.

15. The authors distributed the survey via the H-Net history discussion lists and the American Association for History and Computing's closed e-mail list.

16. The research did not track the gender of respondents. All references are masculine, although this might not be the case.

17. Earl Babbie, *The Practice of Social Research,* 6th ed. (Belmont, CA: Wadsworth, 1992).

Chapter 4

Rewards for Scholarly Communication

Rob Kling and Lisa B. Spector

Introduction

Colleges and universities face questions common to all organizations, although their particular forms may be unusual. Who should be hired? Who should be retained? Who should be fired? Who should be rewarded if pay is based on merit rather than seniority? In North American colleges and universities, many of these decisions are made on the basis of scholarly merit, although the areas of evaluation often include teaching and professional service, as well as scholarship.[1]

There are over 3,000 colleges and universities in the United States that offer bachelor's and advanced degrees. They differ substantially in their missions, and consequently, in the criteria they employ for reviewing faculty for appointments, promotions, tenure, and other awards. In 2000, the Carnegie Foundation identified 151 universities as having strong doctoral research programs in at least 15 fields.[2] In contrast, the Carnegie Foundation identified about 600 master's colleges and universities and another 600 baccalaureate colleges based on the relative sizes of their degree programs. The primary missions of the colleges and universities in these broad categories differ in kind and in their relative emphasis upon research, various kinds of creative activities, teaching at various levels, professional service, and service to their local communities.

The majority of promotion and tenure reviews in the 600 baccalaureate colleges would necessarily differ in their criteria from the majority of promotion and tenure reviews in Carnegie's 151 "Doctoral/Research-Extensive Universities." Even within a specific university, different academic units may place different weights on research, service, and teaching for promotion.

Scholarly Publishing: A Wide Spectrum

It is common for academics to treat publishing as a binary concept: an article or book has either been published or not. This binary view of the publication status of a manuscript simplifies the work of reviewers who are making comparative judgments to decide who might merit promotions, grants, appointments, and honors. Reviewers compare the publication records of a group of candidates (and perhaps of their peers as well), often regarding documents simply as "published" or "unpublished."

We conceptualize publication as a multidimensional continuum, rather than as a discrete, binary category. Publishing conceptions are anchored in particular fields. It is often hard to evaluate precisely the relative quality and impact of several sets of paper publications. Adding e-scripts to the mix complicates evaluation.[3] But that is a feature of this new era of Internet-enabled, scholarly publishing.

Scholars' publication records are often heterogeneous; different publication venues or places dominate in different disciplines. Natural scientists publish primarily journal articles; humanities scholars are much more likely to publish books and book chapters.[4] However, within each field, many scholars publish in various places.

Electronic Publishing

"Purely electronic" publishing places have been the subject of considerable controversy in colleges and universities when claims about their legitimacy and status are made by authors, journal editors, members of search committees, and promotion committees. Authors usually have incentive to claim that their works have been published in high-quality places. The members of search committees and promotion committees are usually comparing a number of scholars, and may wonder how to readily sort the value of pure electronic publications into the mix of an author's traditional paper publications.

Scholarly publishing practices—especially those related to electronic publishing—have been the subject of many new kinds of projects, and of a rather cacophonous and sometimes confusing discourse that emerged in the 1990s. Enthusiasts for publication places that rely upon the Internet as a distribution medium emphasize potential advantages, such as enhanced speed of distribution, lower publication costs, new publication formats (such as hypertext), the accessibility of scholarship to larger groups of readers, and richer discourse about published works. These enthusiasts have created many new electronic publishing places, including authors posting their articles on their own Web sites, disciplinary repositories where authors can post their research articles (for example, arXiv.org), electronic versions of working paper series published by research institutes, peer-reviewed journals that are available exclusively via the Internet, and publishers distributing books via their Internet sites.[5] This list is suggestive and hardly exhaustive. In particular, the

list excludes publications that are available in both print and electronic form—
an important blend that has been the subject of some even more confusing
discussions.

A wide set of electronic publishing practices exists today,[6] and more
extensive scholarly electronic publishing is virtually certain over the next
decades. Nonetheless, these practices make many scholars and academic
administrators uneasy.[7] Some commonplace examples can illustrate today's
scholarly publishing practices, and pose questions about how they should
be viewed:

- arXiv.org, which was organized by physicist Paul Ginsparg around 1991,
  has been the most visible (or at least the most written about) exemplar
  of a disciplinary electronic manuscript (e-script) repository. It started
  as an e-script resource for high-energy physics but has been expanded
  to include all of physics, as well as mathematics and computer science. Authors must register to post their e-scripts in arXiv.org, but
  there is little editorial review of the posted e-scripts. By September
  2002, it included over 208,000 items. In August 2002, 58 e-scripts
  were posted in the section for High Energy Physics—Experiment.[8]
  By mid-September, some of these e-scripts were annotated as talks,
  conference articles that would appear in conference proceedings, peer-
  reviewed journal submissions (such as *Physical Review D*), and peer-
  reviewed journal acceptances (e.g., *Physical Review Letters*). Physicists
  like to refer to all of these e-scripts as "physics preprints." How should
  they be integrated into physicists' publication lists and be evaluated?
  Are they any more substantial as publications than are unrefereed e-
  scripts that physicists may post on their own World Wide Web pages?
- Many research institutes have shifted their paper-based working paper
  series and technical report series into electronic formats. Arguably, these
  e-scripts may be more widely available than their paper precursors.
  Should these e-scripts be evaluated as being as substantial as the paper
  precursors, or viewed as a new form of ephemera?
- *D-Lib Magazine*,[9] a peer-reviewed, pure-electronic (pure-e) magazine
  is widely read by scholars who are interested in digital libraries. How
  should its articles be evaluated?[10]
- *First Monday*[11] is a peer-reviewed, pure e-journal. Between 1996 and
  2002, there were many authors contributing and many readers.[12] How
  should articles published in *First Monday* be evaluated relative to other
  peer-reviewed journal articles?
- The *Journal of the Association of Information Systems (JAIS)*,[13] serves
  as the "flagship peer-reviewed research journal" of the Association for

Information Systems—the primary scholarly association for that field. *JAIS* is normally available only to members of the Association for Information Systems, while articles in the top paper journals, such as *MIS Quarterly, Information Systems Research,* and the *Journal of MIS,* are routinely available to scholars with access to good business research libraries. Should articles that are published in *JAIS* be viewed as ephemera or as substantial scholarly contributions? How should its articles be evaluated relative to those that are published in high quality established paper journals in the information systems field?

Later, we will explain the Kling/McKim framework, and then use it to analyze the effectiveness of publishing of these examples, in the Publishing on a Continuum section.

Some Nuances of Academic Reviews for Tenure, Promotion, and Rewards

One vexing issue in academic reviews is the way in which the nature of a publication place can serve as an "efficient surrogate" for the quality and impact of a publication. In this approach, the prestige of a conference, journal, or university press signals the scholarly quality of manuscripts published in that place.

In the effort to evaluate heterogeneous manuscripts, some reviewers may be tempted to simply delete all e-scripts and focus exclusively on paper publications. In short, "e-anything" must be ephemeral and lower in quality than paper publications. We believe that this attractive simplification is a mistake; the two "universes" of paper and electronic publications should not be delineated in such a cursory manner. A commonly held view is that any paper publication is more reliable than any electronic publication. There is a lot of misleading discourse that does not differentiate between places of a publication, within the electronic or the paper universes.

Carlson's article in the *Chronicle of Higher Education* reviews a study of scholars' use of on-line materials. The article is illustrative of this confusing discourse; "Almost 90% of researchers said they went on-line first . . ." and, "Most respondents tended not to trust on-line sources of information."[14] "On-line" can refer to a personal Web site, a technical report series, or an article in a peer-reviewed electronic journal that is also a paper journal such as *Science,* the *New York Times,* or e-mail. The *Chronicle* article does not differentiate between location (on-line) and specific place of publication (e.g., peer-reviewed journal or e-mail), by grouping all on-line places into one misleading category.

As we noted above, some kinds of e-script places, such as peer-reviewed, pure e-journals, attract such high quality e-scripts that they serve as flagship peer-reviewed research journals for their scholarly associations. In addition, the *Science Citation Index*, as well as other bibliographic databases, is also indexing the higher quality electronic-only journals, such as the *Journal of Artificial Intelligence Research (JAIR)* and the *Journal of Turbulence*.

Hybrid Publications: The Example of E-Journals

Most discussions of electronic journals (e-journals) conflate a number of different formats into one overarching, and sometimes misleading, category of "electronic journals." Much of the enthusiasm for e-journals in the early 1990s was based on specific assumptions: they would be electronic only, they could be peer-reviewed, and there would be no charges to their authors and readers. Concerns about the long-term archiving of e-journals and their academic legitimacy hinged on similar assumptions.[15] Today, the major scientific, technical, and medical (STM) publishers who offer electronic versions of their paper journals rely upon a subscription model in which they allow electronic access to individual subscribers or to members of organizations who purchase more expensive institutional (library) subscriptions.

For example, Okerson reviewed the history of journals and discussed a few e-journals of the early 1990s. She also provided a timeline from 1991 to 1999 and indicated the number of electronic journal titles that were listed in two directories. The number of titles grew from 27 in 1991, to 3,634 in 1997, and then to 8,000 titles in 1999. She briefly discussed the move by major STM publishers to provide World Wide Web-based access to their journals in the period 1996 to 2000.[16] Unfortunately, Okerson does not carefully distinguish between the relatively few journals that were published only in electronic editions in 1999 from the majority that were published in parallel paper and electronic editions. As we shall show in this chapter, these distinctions have substantial consequences.

The questions about the early "pure" e-journals took on a different character for journals with an established reputation and readership as paper-based journals that also provided parallel electronic editions. The distinction between an e-journal without any paper version and a paper journal with an electronic version matters when trying to answer questions about such issues as the legitimacy or the costs of e-journals. For example, we know of no evidence that prestigious paper journals, such as *Science*, have lost legitimacy after they established on-line versions in addition to their printed copies. The question of legitimacy seems to affect only the journals that are completely or primarily distributed in electronic form. Similarly, questions of costs will hinge on the number of printed copies a journal produces as well as the character of its electronic form. Finally, questions about a journal's accessibility and readership can depend on the extent to which it allows readers free access to electronic versions.

Following Kling and McKim,[17] we find it useful to distinguish at least four kinds of e-journals:

- *Pure e-journals:* journals whose text is originally distributed only in digital form. Examples include the *Electronic Journal of Communication*, the *Journal of Digital Information*, the *Internet Journal of Archaeology*, and the *Journal of Electronic Publishing*.
- *E-p-journals:* journals primarily distributed electronically, but they may have very limited distribution in paper form. Examples include the *Journal of Artificial Intelligence Research* and *Electronic Transactions on Artificial Intelligence*.
- *P-e-journals:* journals that are primarily distributed in paper form, but which are also distributed in electronic form. Examples include *Science, Physical Review*, and thousands of other scientific journals.
- *P+e-journals:* journals that are initiated with parallel paper and electronic editions that may be widely distributed. The *American Chemical Society's Organic Letters* is a p+e journal example.

There are many published discussions of the possible benefits of pure e-journals and their advantages over traditional "pure paper" journals (p-journals). However, those discussions often ignore three ideas. First, although beneficial changes may be possible from a technical perspective, the social structure of on-line publishing does not change as rapidly as the technical structure. Second, possible changes are often discussed without distinguishing to which type of e-journal they apply. Third, possible advantages are often analyzed separately, without taking into account how one advantage may trade off against another (for example, an e-journal's cost versus the variety of features offered). When looking at impact factors of an electronic journal for purposes of promotion, tenure, and review, it is important to distinguish whether or not a journal is well established, such as *Science*. We discuss impact further in the Framework and The Continuum of Publishing sections of this chapter.

Definitions

It is useful to clarify electronic publishing terminology. We define an electronic publication as a document distributed primarily through electronic media. The distribution medium is the defining factor, since an electronic publication may well be printed to be read and may be circulated post-publication in printed form. Conversely, most scholarly publications distributed in paper form have been electronic at some point in their creation, having been produced on personal computers and even typeset using software. According to this definition, a manuscript posted on a Web page (under a variety of restrictions or conditions), an article distributed via e-mail, or an article distributed via an e-mail-based distribution list, are all electronic publications.

In this chapter, we will use terminology that works across many disciplines to describe research documents.

Article

The common term "article" can implicitly refer to a publication place. The *Oxford English Dictionary* (OED) defines an article as "a literary composition forming materially part of a journal, magazine, encyclopedia, or other collection, but treating a specific topic distinctly and independently."[18] We will use the term "article" in a broader way to refer to any document that fits the OED's definition or that is in a form that could fit the OED's definition if it were published.

Manuscript, E-Script

"Manuscript" is the primary candidate for labeling articles that authors circulate prior to their acceptance for publication. The term "manuscript" is still widely used by journal editors to refer to articles that will be submitted or are under review. We will use the term "manuscript" to refer to articles that have not yet been accepted for publication in a specific place, as well as to articles that have been published in an institutionally sponsored place, such as a working paper series or an on-line server for research articles, such as arXiv.org. Electronic versions may be called e-scripts.

Preprint

We believe that the term "preprint" should be used in a strict sense to refer to articles that have been accepted for publication in a specific place. "Preprint" refers to a relationship between two documents, rather than a feature of a document in isolation. We will use the terms "preprint" and "e-print" conservatively—to refer to manuscripts in the form in which they are likely to appear in a conference proceedings, journal, or book (whether in printed form, electronic form, or both). "E-print," which some scientists use to refer to "e-scripts," plays off of its resonance with preprints, and we believe that e-prints should refer to electronic versions of preprints. We will examine the relative worth of preprints again in the Framework and the Continuum sections of this chapter.[19]

The Kling/McKim Framework for the Strength of Publishing

In 1999, Kling and McKim proposed a framework to assess the strength of publishing within scholarly communication. Prior to their work, there did not seem to be any research to evaluate when a publication is strongly or weakly published. Scholars are knowledgeable about the status distinctions within their fields and thus can identify a stronger journal within the field from a weaker one, and a peer-reviewed article in a journal from a talk that was accepted at a conference based solely on the abstract. However, there was no framework in place to analyze differences across fields and across all publications. The Kling/McKim framework explicitly defines three criteria: trustworthiness, publicity, and accessibility, to assess how effectively an article or book has been published within the scholarly community.[20]

Trustworthiness

The trustworthiness of a document is based on its quality indicators: "The document has been vetted through some social processes that assure readers that they can place a high level of trust in the content of the document based on community-specific norms. Trustworthiness is typically marked by peer review, publishing house/journal quality, and sponsorship."[21]

> Peer review is a particular form of vetting that is distinctive of the academic communities. However, scholars use other signs to assess the value of a document as well, often in combination—such as the reputation of a journal or publishing house as indicators of reliability. Peer-review practices vary across the disciplines. Some social science journals rely upon double-blind reviewing; many journals seek two to three reviews, while others (the *Astrophysical Journal*, for example) assign one reviewer to each article. Book publishers vary in the level of detail in a proposal that they require for review (from a short proposal through sample chapters to a full manuscript), and in the number of reviews. At the lower end of a scale of trustworthiness lie practices such as self-publishing, publishing in non-reviewed (or weakly reviewed) outlets (such as the working paper series of an academic department), or publishing in edited (but not refereed) journals. Even in non-reviewed or weakly reviewed places, the reputation of

the author (as perceived by the reader) may be a major factor in determining trustworthiness. This analysis of trustworthiness refers to institutionalized practices that are "beyond the person." Each scholar knows others whose works s/he trusts and would be eager to read in a prepublication form. But these judgments rest on a mix of highly personal knowledge, tastes, and interests.[22]

Even some collections of unrefereed e-scripts publish credible research. For example, about 90 percent of the e-scripts that are posted in the high-energy physics sections of arXiv.org are destined for future publication in conference proceedings and journals.[23] To write off e-scripts as entirely worthless until they appear in a paper place is a major judgmental error. On the other hand, we disagree with Arms,[24] who claims that the e-scripts posted on arXiv.org are equivalent in quality to peer-reviewed journal articles. The e-scripts published on arXiv.org are unrefereed research reports until they have been accepted for publication in a specific journal or conference. Many will be. However, we do not see why those that are not accepted for publication in a peer-reviewed place should warrant the stature of those that are.

As discussed in the introduction of this chapter, all electronic publishing is often grouped without distinguishing peer-reviewed from nonpeer-reviewed publications. This form of overgeneralization makes the evaluation of a publication's trustworthiness confusing. While the number of high-status scholars who currently publish in e-journals is smaller than those who publish in p-journals, drawing a conclusion from this would be specious, since the number of e-journals is much smaller than that of print journals, and few e-journals have been around more than a few years.[25] The guidelines that apply to evaluating paper publications for trustworthiness apply to electronic publications and vary in the same manner as paper.

Publicity

Publicity involves making the relevant audiences aware of a publication. The document is announced to scholars so that primary audiences and secondary audiences may learn of its existence. Publicity represents a continuum of activities from subscription, report lists, abstract databases, advertising and special issues, to citation. A book or an article is more effectively published to the extent that members of its primary and secondary audiences are made aware of its availability. In principle, e-publication (such as posting on a Web site or in a forum on the Web) would seem overwhelmingly more likely to effectively advertise a book or an article when compared with publishing in a paper journal, and to surpass the relatively limited efforts of many (paper) book publishers to advertise their wares. In practice, the differences are subtler, since relatively few established scholars regularly read (pure) e-journals or seek them out, and many book publishers are attempting to exploit the Internet as a publicity medium. Furthermore, many Web sites are "weak attractors" of reader interest. A major paper journal, with a well-established readership and reputation (e.g., *Science* and *Nature*) may be able to publicize the results of a study within a particular readership community far more effectively than a typical Web site.[26]

Accessibility

Central to the notion of being effectively published is a perception that an author's work can be readily located and obtained by interested scholars.

> Readers must be able to access the document independent of the author, and, in a stable manner, over time. Accessibility is typically assured by institutional stewardship as practiced by libraries, publishing houses, clearinghouses, and is supported by stable identifiers, such as ISBN and ISSN.[27]

The improvements of interlibrary loan services in the past decade have increased the effective accessibility of books and articles. Even so, "the obscure journal" that few scholars can locate or find still exists. The short-term accessibility of most documents posted on public access Web sites is relatively high in universities. People who have an adequate Web browser and good Internet connections can access the document independently of the author. Kling and McKim examined a variety of exceptions, such as journals or documents that are accessible only to members of an institution or organization.[28]

The long-term access of electronic documents is a broad and emerging topic, beyond the scope of this chapter. Briefly, we will mention some key points. Paper documents in libraries usually have a lifetime of 100 years or more. The paper version of a journal, *Nature*, for example, might be found in over 2,000 different libraries. One hundred years from now, many libraries will still hold back issues. Long-term access—10 years plus—is speculative for all electronic documents. Both e-journals and p-journals require maintenance, and it is often not clear who carries this stewardship for the e-journals. E-journals can lose their funding and become inaccessible.[29] There are many efforts under way to address this issue. For example, students are raising funds to pay for ongoing maintenance of the National Digital Library of Theses and Dissertations.

If a scholarly society sponsors an e-journal, it is likely to be well maintained and archived. There is no guarantee that sites such as arXiv.org will continue to receive funding, and the question of archiving those documents remains unanswered. Citation half-life counts vary greatly from field to field. In fields with long half-lives, digital preservation is critical, making institutional or society sponsorship critical. Some think that long-term preservation of digital collections is the most critical issue for library science today.[30]

A major strength of some of the better e-journals over tier-B and tier-C paper journals is that they offer much better publicity to their authors. Many of the tier-B and tier-C journals may circulate only a few hundred paper copies per issue. However, in many cases, the tier-B and tier-C journals may offer longer-term access. In 2001, Crawford examined the current status of 104 scholarly pure e-journals that were indexed in the 1995 edition of the ARL's *Directory of Electronic Journals, Newsletters, and Academic Discussion Lists*. Fifty-seven of these 104 pure e-journals had a URL for their gopher sites or World Wide Web sites. Only 17 of these 57 URLs worked in early 2001. After considerable search effort, he found the URLs of 49 of these 104 e-journals that were still publishing and were free to readers, as well as the URLs of 22 others that had ceased publication. Specialists in a field are likely to keep up with URL shifts. However, about 50 percent of these new pure e-journals survived for six years.[31] Over time, the sites of archives of deceased journals are taken down from the World Wide Web. In contrast, libraries that subscribe to journals (of any tier) usually retain their copies if the journal ceases publication.

The duration of access may differ in importance from one field to another. Generally, humanists value the ability to read publications in their fields that are decades or centuries old. Natural scientists rely more heavily on work published within the past ten years.[32]

Publishing as a Continuum: Paper and E-Scripts

Scholarly publishing is a complex continuum of communication places. A simple scale would range from the working draft of a manuscript that an author circulates at a seminar, to an article in a peer-reviewed place (such as a journal or book by a reputed publisher). However, many variations are possible, such as the reprinting of journal articles as chapters in books. This continuum of publishing occurs both in paper publications and in e-scripts.

In order to help gauge the strength of publication for an e-script, the first activity is to identify its character. The first question is whether the manuscript represents a dissertation, a working draft manuscript, a working paper or technical report in a series, a conference article, a book chapter, a magazine article, a peer-reviewed journal article, or a book.[33]

It is then possible to apply the Kling/McKim framework to the e-script, and to assess its strength of publication. This gives a framework to use to examine the e-script relative to paper-based manuscripts in the same class (e.g., preprints, talks, or books).

We will now use the examples from the introduction, analyzing their relative strengths and weaknesses, using the Kling/McKim framework to examine publicity, trustworthiness, and accessibility.

Repositories, Working Paper/Technical Report Series and Preprints

Repositories

arXiv.org contains over 208,000 e-scripts of talks, conference articles that will appear in conference proceedings, manuscripts submitted to peer-reviewed journals, and manuscripts accepted by peer-reviewed journals, in the fields of physics, mathematics, and computer science. How should the e-scripts be integrated into a physicist's publication list and evaluated? Are they any more substantial as publications than unrefereed e-scripts that a physicist may post on her own World Wide Web page?

Trustworthiness must be looked at on a document-by-document basis for evaluation. Only minimal review is required to post on arXiv.org. An e-script on arXiv.org that is later published in a peer-reviewed journal has a high level of trustworthiness, while a conference talk does not have the same quality indicators.

As we discussed in the definitions section, "preprint" is the terminology commonly used to describe all e-scripts posted to arXiv.org. This misnomer grants inflated trustworthiness to documents that do not have the "accepted for publication" or "published in . . ." markers. Considering a talk to be a preprint would add a false level of trustworthiness to those e-scripts. In fact, only some of the postings on arXiv.org are preprints, having been accepted for publication in a journal, and as such have the same level of trustworthiness as other articles published in the same journal.

arXiv.org is a highly visible e-script repository. Any e-scripts posted on arXiv.org gain some added publicity. A search on Google[34] will not yield results from arXiv.org because it is "robot blocked." Researchers who are aware of arXiv.org may easily search the site; arXiv.org is free to readers. The only prerequisite for short-term access to arXiv.org is Internet access.

Working Paper Series

Many working paper and technical report series are now available on-line. Should these e-scripts be evaluated as being as substantial as their paper precursors, or be viewed as a new form of ephemera?

The trustworthiness of working papers is the same, regardless of the publishing medium—electronic working papers retain the same quality indicators as the paper versions.[35] Within research universities, the working papers of a scholar early in her career may carry more weight than the working papers of a more experienced scholar when there are expectations of more strongly published work. Frequently, the marker, "in preparation" is added to a scholar's publication list. "In preparation" is not as highly weighted as a manuscript in a working paper series; placement in the series demonstrates that the work is at least in a full draft stage.

Journals

In this section we compare and analyze one pure-e magazine and two pure-e journals.

D-Lib Magazine (pure e-magazine). D-Lib Magazine is a pure e-magazine that is not peer-reviewed. How should its articles be evaluated?

D-Lib Magazine's trustworthiness depends on several factors, more complicated than those for peer-reviewed journals. *D-Lib Magazine* is widely read by scholars who are interested in digital libraries, and *D-Lib Magazine* is currently funded by the U.S. National Science Foundation as an adjunct to its research program on digital libraries. A pure e-magazine (or journal) in a field where there is not already another specialized magazine (or journal) may have enhanced trustworthiness. Scholars will publish their best work, knowing that their peers are reading it. The success of such an e-magazine (or journal), if free, with easy short-term access, and good publicity, may have a hypothetical edge over a new p-magazine (or journal) that an enterprising publisher may want to exploit.

D-Lib Magazine is widely read by scholars who are interested in digital libraries, and its table of contents is circulated on a listserv that is widely read in the field of information science (ASIS-L). Broad search engines can point to *D-Lib Magazine* articles, enhancing the publicity of its contents. Overall, *D-Lib Magazine* has a high level of publicity. Short-term access is easy with Internet availability, and articles are available in full text, on-line, for free.

The following two publications are pure e-journals. These journals are peer reviewed; therefore the quality indicators are equivalent to any peer-reviewed electronic, paper, or hybrid p-e-journal. Although similar in the level of trustworthiness, they differ in the levels of publicity, short-, and long-term access.

First Monday (pure e-journal). How should articles published in *First Monday* be evaluated relative to other peer-reviewed journal articles?

The wide topical breadth of *First Monday* means that there are many paper alternatives (such as *Information Society, New Media and Society,* and *Information Communication Society*). *First Monday* has a record of attracting many high-quality, and some lower-quality articles, making it comparable to its paper alternatives.

Although a pure e-journal, authorship is high. Between 1996 and 2002, almost 500 authors published about 400 articles in 75 issues. *First Monday* is indexed in INSPEC, LISA, and PAIS. Readership is also high: "In the year 2001, users from 536,046 distinct hosts around the world downloaded 3,117,547 contributions published in *First Monday*."[36] Apparently, publicity is also high. Short-term access to *First Monday* is easy, requiring only Internet access. Articles are available in full text, on-line, for free. Major search engines readily find *First Monday* articles.

The *Journal of the Association of Information Systems (JAIS)* (pure e-journal). Should articles that are published in *JAIS* be viewed as ephemera or as substantial scholarly contributions? How should its articles be evaluated relative to those published in high-quality established paper journals in the information systems field?

Access to *JAIS is* limited to Association for Information Systems members. Thus, *JAIS* has high visibility within the primary researcher circle of information systems and very limited publicity for secondary researchers.[37] This could reduce its impact over time. Limiting access to members only is a different—not a better or a worse—sort of access than p-journals have. P-journals can also have limited short-term access problems. They may or may not be available at certain institutions, depending on the research focus, perceived needs of their scholars, and funds available to the library or individual researchers.

The Tensions of E-Publishing in Perspective

The Rhetoric and Criteria of Research Reviews

We have examined the appointment, tenure, and promotion guidelines for about 20 of 151 "Doctoral/Research-Extensive Universities." The reviews typically evaluate teaching, research, and professional and university service. The criteria for expected research accomplishments differ by the rank of appointment or promotion. They also differ by the range of disciplines that the guidelines cover—from departmental or disciplinary to university wide. We have selected five short excerpts from much longer documents to illustrate the range of rhetoric and formal criteria used to judge faculty research during these career evaluations.

For example, the University of California's guidelines use the following wording to describe requirements for appointment or promotion as a tenured associate professor: "Superior intellectual attainment, as evidenced both in teaching and in research or other creative achievement, is an indispensable qualification for appointment or promotion to tenure positions."[38]

Professor-level appointments add this to the superior intellectual attainment: "A candidate for the rank of Professor is expected to have an accomplished record of research that is judged to be excellent by his or her peers within the larger discipline or field."

The criteria for one of its high-level professorial steps are: ". . . highly distinguished scholarship, highly meritorious service . . . excellent University teaching . . . [and] great distinction, recognized nationally or internationally, in scholarly or creative achievement or in teaching."

Advancement (or appointment) for a notably higher (and unusual) level of professorship: ". . . is reserved for scholars and teachers of the highest distinction, whose work has been internationally recognized and acclaimed and whose teaching performance is excellent."[39]

The criteria for tenure in the College of Literature, Science and the Arts at the University of Michigan are also broadly worded:

> Tenure in LS&A should be granted only to candidates who have demonstrated excellence in research and teaching and, in more modest ways, excellence in service. Excellent research should have a demonstrable impact on the area of study to which it is meant to contribute and should provide evidence for a strong presumption of future distinction. Excellent teaching should be demonstrated by evidence of a strong motivation to engage students in the learning process, by the rigor and scope of the courses taught and by course and instructor student and peer evaluations. The only overriding criteria for granting or not granting tenure is the quality, quantity, and impact of the candidate's research, teaching, and service.[40]

In contrast, the "Guidelines for Tenure and Promotion" for the University of Florida College of Health Professions note in the discussion of evaluating research for promotion to associate professor:

> The primary indicator of progress toward establishment of a national reputation shall be the publication of research findings in peer-reviewed journals of high quality (as indicated by, but not limited to, the judgments of experts in the field, the journals, rates of rejection, and empirically-based journal impact ratings). . . . The quality of research shall be judged as more important than quantity in evaluating the candidate's research contributions.[41]

The "Guidelines" list a broader set of research indicators, such as research funding, published book chapters, and editorial positions. However, the emphasis upon high quality, peer-reviewed journals is notable, and workable in the health sciences.

The Mathematics Department at the University of Arizona evaluates each of its tenured faculty annually "in each of the three primary areas of responsibility (teaching, research/scholarly activity, and service/outreach) according to a five-level scale. These annual evaluations are used to adjust workloads and to set salaries.

> The criteria for a rating of "Meets expectations" in research/scholarly activity are that the faculty member produce a yearly average of participation in at least one sponsored research grant or contract (as PI or Co-PI) or publication as author or co-author of one peer-reviewed document (books, book chapters, journal articles, conference papers, etc.) or activity as thesis or dissertation director for one graduate degree, or significant course or modular materials development dependent on deep understanding of a particular area, or any coherent combination of these four activities. (These criteria assume a 40% research load and should be adjusted to actual workload assignments.) As the frequency and nature of scholarly output varies with areas of concentration, even within mathematics, it is expected that the rating will be adjusted to reflect such variation, using departmental averages and comparison with peer institutions and general trends in mathematics departments.[42]

As in the health sciences, the mathematics department emphasizes peer-reviewed documents, but is more open to a variety of publishing places (e.g., conferences as well as journals). In contrast, the College of Humanities at the University of Arizona specifies different publication requirements for faculty in literature and area studies (books), scholars of language (journal articles), and for creative writers (books). The requirements for literature and area studies say, in part:

> Promotion to Associate Professor with tenure will normally mean the acceptance for publication by a reputable press of at least one single-authored interpretive monograph or a major work of scholarship (such as a scholarly edition, a biography, annotated bibliography, or calendar of plays with complete critical apparatus) that makes a significant contribution to the candidate's field. . . . Additional but not alternative evidence for promotion in this category of research will normally include the regular publication of scholarly or interpretive articles in refereed journals; it may also include the regular presenting of professional papers, winning grants and awards for scholarship, having one's work translated or reprinted, being cited by peers, and being selected for tours of duty at special institutes for advanced study.[43]

One may smile at some of these vague criteria. Is the excellence required for tenure at the University of Michigan a higher or lower standard than the "superior intellectual attainment" required at the University of California? The meanings of these vague criteria are sorted out in practice by comparisons of faculty under review with faculty in the same field at similar ranks and career stages at other major research universities. In practice, the level of accomplishment at the University of Michigan (Ann Arbor) and the major University of California campuses is comparable.

Most serious, pertaining to our concerns, is an understanding of how these general criteria influence the evaluation of electronic documents. For example, the Mathematics Department at the University of Arizona and the University of Florida College of Health Professions emphasize peer-reviewed documents as central indicators of quality. The University of Arizona's guidelines for promotion to Associate Professor with tenure in literary and area studies refer to the acceptance of a scholarly book "for publication by a reputable press." Some promotion guidelines are even more specific. For example, the Accounting Department at North Carolina State University specifies that the "number of refereed works normally expected for promotion are three or more to Associate Professor and eight or more to Full Professor."[44]

The quotation from the University of Michigan's guidelines identifies what we believe are the three major underlying criteria for scholarly evaluations: the "quality, quantity, and impact" of the works. Some universities' promotion and tenure guidelines explicitly stress that research and creative works should be evaluated and not merely enumerated.

The Grisly Work of Academic Reviewing

Substantive evaluation is time consuming, even for experts. Therefore, academic reviewers often seek "efficient indicators" of the quality and impact of publications. The publishing place—such as a peer-reviewed journal or a "reputable press"—often serve as quality indicators. Citation counts are sometimes used as indicators of impact, especially in the natural and social sciences. The impact of books can also be assessed through book reviews and the ways that other scholars discuss them (or ignore them) in related writing. All of these evaluation strategies are commonplace in academia and are well known to be imperfect.

Scholars in various fields attribute higher quality to some journals and book publishers than to others. An extreme example is that of business schools, where departments are often asked to stratify the journals in their fields into three tiers. In these settings, it is common to hear of faculty evaluated in terms of how many "tier A" or "tier B" journal articles they have published.

In the natural and social sciences, the Institute for Scientific Information calculates an "impact factor" for about 5,700 natural science journals and 1,700 social science journals, based on the fraction of articles in one year that are cited by other journal articles in subsequent years.

To what extent should the publishing medium—paper or electronic—be used as a quality indicator? During the 1990s, there were a number of surveys of faculty in various universities and various disciplines about their perceptions of the legitimacy of publications that appear in e-journals. Kling and Callahan note that these surveys rarely distinguish between different types of e-journals (i.e., pure e-journals vs. p-e-journals), and thus can be unreliable.[45] Today, the vast majority of e-journals are p-e-journals, and their status is anchored in their p-journal status. For example, *Science* has not lost status because it developed from a p-journal to a p-e-journal with *Science Online* as a parallel electronic edition.

The earliest surveys were conducted when "e-journal" meant "pure-e-journal"; but few faculty were familiar with them.[46] Academics will likely be more familiar with pure e-journals and their variety over time, and scholars' acceptance might improve with familiarity. Sweeney conducted a small survey of high-level academic administrators in the University of Florida system, and of faculty at one of the 109 Carnegie "research intensive" universities. The academic administrators were much less willing to include e-journal (probably pure e-journal) articles in tenure and promotion reviews. But about one-third of the faculty were critical of such inclusion.[47]

However, there are pure e-journals in many fields, and the question of their legitimacy is central here. For example, in mathematics, the peer-reviewed pure e-journals include: *Electronic Communications in Probability*, *Electronic Journal of Combinatorics*, *Electronic Journal of Differential Equations*, *Electronic Journal of Linear Algebra*, *Electronic Journal of Probability*, and the *Electronic Journal of Qualitative Theory of Differential Equations*. Should publications in these journals be automatically relegated to "tier E?" The University of Arizona Mathematics Department requires each tenured faculty member to publish one peer-reviewed article annually to receive a "a rating of 'Meets expectations' in research/scholarly activity." If its faculty chooses to publish in any of these journals, should their articles be counted as peer-reviewed or discounted? We will offer some guidance later in this section.

Other chapters in this book discuss the range of e-publishing projects and products that may be "on the table" for academic review. Most reviews are based on more than one document, i.e., there is usually a set of articles, and/or book chapters, and/or books to be evaluated. Some scientists' publication corpuses are composed almost completely of research articles in the primary journals in their fields. Similarly, some humanists' and social scientists' publication corpuses are composed primarily of monographs published by high-quality university presses. But we suspect that résumés with heterogeneous kinds of publications and places are more common across academia: some mix of conference papers, journal articles, book chapters, monographs, and textbooks.

The relative weight for these products varies by field (i.e., articles are usually more valued in the sciences while books are more valued in the humanities). These documents may vary by their character (e.g., an original research article versus a literature review or a text book versus a monograph). Documents are in different stages of their publication trajectories (i.e., under review, in press, or published in a specific place). Adding the characteristic "electronic" to some documents in this mix can further complicate the review of a scholarly corpus—whether the review is of an individual, a research institute (for national funding), or of a department (as in the case of the periodic Research Assessment Exercises in the United Kingdom).

In our experience, reviewers often try to simplify the cognitive complexity of their tasks by invoking simplified category schemes (e.g., unrefereed conference paper, peer-review journal article, or monograph from a major university press) to focus attention on some "high quality" portion of the corpus and to remove the rest from detailed consideration. We sympathize with reviewers who wish to simplify their reviews of complex academic corpuses by such focus (and we have done so ourselves in reviewing scholars for academic appointments and promotions). However, we caution against the attractive simplification rule: remove all e-scripts from detailed review.

As we indicated earlier, there are two primary perspectives that underlie academics' views of e-script publications.[48] The most common perspective emphasizes some information-processing features of electronic publishing and posits that electronic publishing can be relatively easy, inexpensive, and can lead authors to rapidly reach much larger audiences. An alternative "sociotechnical" perspective examines electronic publishing in a matrix of social practices, skill mixes, and support resources, which are often institutionalized in ways that turn electronic publishing into a complex venture whose virtues take considerable effort to realize. Many academics—both enthusiasts of electronic publishing and skeptics—accept the information-processing perspective.

The information-processing perspective underlies many enthusiasts' claims that scholarly electronic publishing can be much faster, much less expensive, and enable authors to more readily reach wide audiences than traditional print media. Skeptics often rely upon the information-processing perspective to characterize scholarly electronic publishing as "too easy" and ephemeral, leading to e-scripts that circulate "in a kind of ghostly netherworld of academic publishing."[49] Reviewers who take this point of view would remove all e-scripts from detailed review.

In our research, we have found that the sociotechnical perspective provides deeper insight into the virtues and limitations of scholarly electronic publishing. We will discuss key tensions of scholarly electronic publishing that are critical to evaluating e-scripts for tenure, promotion, and other rewards in the remainder of this section.

Pragmatics of E-Publishing

It is not "a snap!" for academics to publish their works on Web sites. It can require very complex pragmatics, including access to specialized computer programs and technical abilities (or technical support). The specific pragmatics differ for various kinds of publication places. Publishing on one's own Web site requires some basic skill with HTML. Publishing in an on-line working paper series may require little more than sending a manuscript as an e-mail attachment or on a disk to the person who manages the series' Web site. Publishing in a repository, such as arXiv.org, requires some basic abilities to fill in forms on-line and upload files. Publishing in an e-journal may seem as simple as publishing in a working paper series, but actually can be more complex because of a more involved editorial process (sometimes requiring rapid communication back and forth between authors and editors).

Responsibility for the formatting and layout of documents that are published differs in the world of e-publishing and in the print medium. In paper publishing, the publisher handles the layout. In pure e-publishing, authors are frequently asked to handle the layout. Many computing skills and programs are needed, as well as technical support. Some common word-processing programs may automatically translate a file to HTML, so it could seem that electronic publishing is easy. But communication between authors and e-journal editors can be complicated when the editors have shifted their markup language (such as TeX or HTML) to communicate copyediting changes to authors. Thus, authors must be familiar with these technologies for managing page layout. Of course, these markup languages are known by many academics and can be learned by people who are not information technology specialists. But the pragmatics of communication between authors and e-journal editors can require rapid turnaround within a few days prior to a journal issue being published.

In brief, one cannot assume that e-scripts take "almost no effort" to publish. When they require considerable effort to publish (i.e., "high friction"), they also require considerable effort to alter. Thus, the extent that e-scripts are easy to publish and alter at will depends to a great extent upon the pragmatics of the publication place and the author's skills (or abilities to enlist skilled assistants to do the work).

Post It and They Will Read It—The "Field of Dreams" Myth

Perhaps no topic is more misunderstood than the extent to which articles that are posted in on-line places will be widely read. As we indicated above in our discussion of publishing, places differ considerably in the extent to which they effectively publicize their documents (and the extent to which they are accessible for a long time after their initial publication).

Academic reviews in research universities emphasize the quality of a document (or a scholar's corpus) and the impacts of the scholar's document (and corpus). An extreme example is the scholar who posts an e-script on her personal Web site. This e-script may be accessed "worldwide"—if potential readers know about it and suspect that it is worth their attention. However, scholars' time (and thus attention) is limited. Consequently, we have not found many scholars searching for research in their fields via search engines. When they seek e-scripts, they are much more likely to visit specific places such as:

- disciplinary repositories (for example arXiv.org for particle physicists);
- select peer-reviewed "pure" e-journals (the *Journal of Artificial Intelligence Research*, for example); and
- select working paper series, such as that of the National Bureau of Economic Research, used by economists.

Thus, each of these is much stronger as a publication place than self-publishing on one's own Web site.

Scholarly Credit

Our main argument has been that e-scripts should not be automatically discounted in academic reviews, or treated as tier-E publications. Rather, they should be assessed, as are other publications in an academic's corpus under review. One key task is to sort publications into broad categories (e.g., books, journal articles, conference papers, working papers, and textbooks) and to note those that have been reviewed by peers. It is also important to note publication statuses, such as "in press." Some e-publishing enthusiasts have complicated this sorting by their elastic use of the term "preprint," or "e-print." As we noted earlier in the definitions section of this chapter, a document can be called a "preprint" once it has another publication place, such as a specific journal. Until that time, it is another unreviewed manuscript.

The next step is to evaluate the quality of the materials to be carefully reviewed. Publications may be evaluated using the Kling/McKim model explained in the framework section of this chapter. In some reviews, one has written evaluations from peers at other universities. Sometimes they are merely testimonials and provide little detailed insight. Others may clarify the stature of a publication place (for example, a journal or publisher) without evaluating the publications. Still other reviewers may evaluate specific works in substantial detail.

Conclusions

The medium of a publication—paper or electronic—does not influence its core scholarly content. The quality indicators, combined with the publicity and access of a document, determine the strength of publishing.

While the temptation (due to time limitations) for surrogacy is ever-present, the use of simplified evaluation criteria, such as ruling out on-line publishing, does not give a fair look at a scholar's work. E-publications should not automatically be deleted!

In fact, a broad continuum of publishing, both in paper and electronic form exists, and the Kling/McKim framework, though not definitive, is useful for tenure, promotion, and review evaluation purposes. Within this framework, we see that overall the strength of e-publishing differs from p-publishing in two major areas: publicity and accessibility. Through e-lists, publicity of e-publishing can be broad (in addition to the standard indexing and advertising done though societies). Short-term access (five to ten years) may be higher in e-publishing than p-publishing, although long-term access is, at least at this point in history, not as strong in the e-publishing world. These tradeoffs in strengths differ in importance from field to field. Historians may deem e-journals to lack permanence that is critical for their work. However, high-energy physicists may be more interested in high-level, short-term access and publicity.

This chapter is dedicated to the expansive thinking and research of Rob Kling who died on May 15, 2003. His vision in the field of social informatics spanned many disciplines. He also painstakingly analyzed and defined individual terms and concepts, thus clarifying existing murky discourses. For his intellectual curiosity, wide breadth of knowledge, perseverance, and clarity, we thank him.

Notes

Writing and research for this chapter have been funded by NSF Award #9872961 for the SCIT (Scholarly Communication and Information Technology) project (www.slis.indiana.edu/SCIT/). Disclaimer: "Any opinions, findings, and conclusions or recommendations expressed in this material are those of the author(s) and do not necessarily reflect the views of the National Science Foundation." This work was also funded by SLIS at Indiana University, Bloomington, Indiana. This chapter benefited from helpful comments by David Spector and Deborah Shaw.

1. In the United Kingdom, where academic salaries are negotiated nationally, there are similar questions about how to evaluate the relative strength of academic programs for national research funding via the "Research Assessment Exercise" (RAE). A discussion about the RAE and electronic publishing is explored further in an expanded version of this chapter: "Academic Rewards for Scholarly Research Communication via Electronic Publishing," available on the Center for Social Informatics Working Paper site: www.slis.indiana.edu/CSI/papers.html.

2. Carnegie Foundation, *Carnegie Classification of Institutions of Higher Education.* Table #1, 2002, www.carnegiefoundation.org/Classification/classification.htm.

3. For example, is a working paper posted on a personal Web site "published?" We discuss the nuances of weak to strong publishing in the Continuum of Publishing section.

4. Another field difference occurs in computer science. The Computing Research Association (CRA) is an ". . . association of more than 200 North American academic departments of computer science, computer engineering, and related fields; laboratories and centers in industry, government, and academia engaging in basic computing research; and affiliated professional societies" (from the CRA home page, available at: www.cra.org/). The CRA approved a memo stating that conference publishing is preferred to journal publishing for computer science experimentalists. See David Patterson, Lawrence Snyder, and Jeffrey Ullman, "Evaluating Computer Scientists and Engineers for Promotion and Tenure," Computing Research Association Best Practices Memo in *Computing Research News* (September 1999) www.cra.org/reports/tenure_review.pdf.

5. In this chapter we use the term "journal" to refer to a publication that primarily publishes research reports that are peer reviewed. We use the term "magazine" to refer to a collection of articles that is edited. The collection may be heterogeneous: research reports, interviews, book reviews, and news items, or it may be primarily of one kind. Further, the quality varies between magazines as well as within each magazine; the quality of journals varies between different journals and within each journal. Therefore, each magazine's and each journal's quality must be evaluated individually.

6. Rob Kling, Lisa Spector, and Geoff McKim, "Locally Controlled Scholarly Publishing via the Internet: The Guild Model," *Journal of Electronic Publishing* 8 (2002). www.press.umich.edu/jep/08–01/kling.html.

7. Aldrin E. Sweeney, "Tenure and Promotion: Should You Publish in Electronic Journals?" *Journal of Electronic Publishing* 6 (2000), www.press.umich.edu/jep/06–02/sweeney.html.

8. arXiv.org/list/hep-ex/0208.

9. www.dlib.org/.

10. "Pure e-" refers to a publication that is not published in print format.

11. www.firstmonday.dk.

12. We discuss this in further detail in the Publishing on a Continuum section of this chapter.

13. jais.aisnet.org/.

14. Scott Carlson, "Student and Faculty Members Turn to Online Library Materials Before Printed Ones, Study Finds," *Chronicle of Higher Education*, October 2, 2002, chronicle.com/free/2002/10/2002100301t.htm.

15. Rob Kling and Lisa Covi, "Electronic Journals and Legitimate Media in the Systems of Scholarly Communication," *Information Society* 11 (1995): 261–71.

16. Ann Okerson, "Are We There Yet? Online E-resources Ten Years After," *Library Trends* 48 (2000): 671–94.

17. Rob Kling and Geoffrey McKim, "Scholarly Communication and the Continuum of Electronic Publishing," *Journal of the American Society for Information Science* 50 (1999): 890–906.

18. *Oxford English Dictionary*, 2d ed. (Oxford, New York: Oxford University Press, 1989).

19. Further discussion about the cloudy discourse surrounding the terms "preprint," "manuscript," "e-print," and "e-script" is available in "Academic Rewards for Scholarly Research Communication via Electronic Publishing," available on the Center for Social Informatics Working Paper site: www.slis.indiana.edu/CSI/papers.html.

20. Kling and McKim, "Scholarly Communication."

21. Ibid.

22. Ibid. This concept of "career view"—trust based on a scholar's previous work—is examined in depth in Kling, Spector, and McKim, "Locally Controlled Scholarly Publishing via the Internet."

23. Heath O'Connell, "Physicists Thriving with Paperless Publishing," *High Energy Physics Libraries Webzine* (March 2002): 6. library.cern.ch/HEPLW/6/papers/3/.

24. William Y. Arms, "What Are the Alternatives to Peer Review? Quality Control in Scholarly Publishing on the Web." *Journal of Electronic Publishing* 8 (2002). www.press.umich.edu/jep/08–01/arms.html.

25. Kling and McKim, "Scholarly Communication."

26. Ibid. See Steve Lawrence, "Free Online Availability Substantially Increases a Paper's Impact," *Nature Webdebates* (May 2001), www.nature.com/nature/debates/e-access/Articles/lawrence.html, where citation analysis was used to study "119,924 conference articles in computer science and related disciplines." As we noted earlier, conference papers are the most prestigious form of publishing for computer science experimentalists. Their conclusion was "dramatic, showing a clear correlation between the number of times an article is cited and the probability that the article is on-line."

27. Ibid.

28. Kling and McKim, "Scholarly Communication."

29. So can p-journals, however, p-journals have an established archiving system in place in libraries. No system is infallible. About 40 years ago, an important preprint by Luisella Goldschmidt-Clermont, accepted for publication by the editor of *Physics Today*, was not published in that journal due to a change of editor and subsequent decisions. In recent years this preprint has become highly relevant in the high-energy physics communication discourse. When a search was done at CERN to find the

preprint in full, the only trace of it was a catalog card with an obscure reference number. A worldwide library search yielded no results; finally, the author was contacted, and fortunately she had a copy of her preprint. See Jens Vigen, "New Communication Channels: Electronic Clones, but Probably the First Steps Towards a New Paradigm," *High Energy Physics Libraries Webzine* 6 (March 2002), library.cern.ch/HEPLW/6/papers/2.

If Goldschmidt-Clermont had access to a computer during the 1940s and 1950s, her work would have been stored on a magnetic tape, which would no longer be retrievable. Electronic formats come and go, with some formats already being obscure, and others certain to become obscure in the future. While paper is not a guarantee of long-term archival success, the system is much more soundly in place than for e-publications. Also see Walter Crawford, "Free Electronic Refereed Journals: Getting Past the Arc of Enthusiasm," *Learned Publishing* 15 (2002): 117–123.

30. Dale Flecker, "Preserving Scholarly E-Journals," *D-Lib Magazine* 7 (2001), www.dlib.org/dlib/september01/flecker/09flecker.html.

31. Crawford, "Free Electronic Refereed Journals."

32. There are exceptions to these observations. For example, some contemporary astronomers often rely upon observational data that are decades or even centuries old.

33. As we noted in the introduction of this chapter, the trustworthiness of a document does not change because it is published electronically rather than in paper. A peer-reviewed article published electronically carries the same quality indicators as if it were published in paper. Also, of course, the quality of various p-journals and e-journals differs within each field.

34. www.google.com.

35. For an extensive discussion of Internet publishing of working papers, read Kling, Spector, and McKim, "Locally Controlled Scholarly Publishing via the Internet."

36. First Monday Basics, www.firstmonday.dk/idea.html.

37. Primary information systems researchers are likely to be members of the Association for Information Systems (AIS), which is the primary scholarly association for the field. Normally, access to *JAIS* requires AIS membership; however, "To promote readership of the Journal" *JAIS* was free and accessible to all readers, from July 1, 2002, to December 31, 2002, jais.aisnet.org/.

38. University of California, Office of the President, "Point 210–1 D. Academic Personnel Manual 210, d.," 5. 1992, www.ucop.edu/acadadv/acadpers/apm/apm-210.pdf.

39. Ibid.

40. University of Michigan, "College of Literature, Sciences and the Arts—Tenure Proceedings: Principles." (July 2001), www.lsa.umich.edu/dean/acad/promotions/principles.html.

41. University of Florida, College of Health Professions, "Guidelines for Tenure and Promotion," 2002, www.hp.ufl.edu/overview/ptguidelinesjuly2002.doc.

42. University of Arizona, Mathematics Division, "Annual Performance Review Processes, Criteria, and Measures" (January 1998), www.math.arizona.edu/overview/perf.html.

43. University of Arizona, "College of Humanities—Promotion and Tenure: Criteria." (2000), www.coh.arizona.edu/COH/facinfo/pandtcriteria2000/pandtcriteria 2000.htm.

44. North Carolina State University, Department of Accounting 1999, "Retention, Promotion, and Tenure Guidelines" (1999), www.ncsu.edu/provost/academic_affairs/rpt/guidelines/ACC.html.

45. Rob Kling and Ewa Callahan, "Electronic Journals, the Internet, and Scholarly Communication," *Annual Review of Information Science and Technology* 37, ed. Blaise Cronin.

46. Don Schauder, "Electronic Publishing of Professional Articles: Attitudes of Academics and Implications for the Scholarly Communication Industry," *Journal of the American Society for Information Science* 45 (March 1994): 73–100.

47. Sweeney, "Tenure and Promotion."

48. Rob Kling, Geoffrey McKim, and Adam King, "A Bit More to It: Scientific Multiple Media Communication Forums as Socio-Technical Interaction Networks," *Journal of the American Society for Information Science* 51, No. 1 (December 2000) 47–67.

49. Kling and Covi, "Electronic Journals."

Part II

Creation of Digital Scholarship

Cases from Academe

Deborah Lines Andersen

Creation and Transformation

In the Introduction, discussion hinged upon first defining digital scholarship and then looking at the forces that would cause digital scholarship to be valued, or not, within academic communities. The chapters in Part I looked at research that has explored how digital scholarship has been valued and assessed in the recent past. Central to the focus of this book, all these chapters address the issue of creation—how scholars create materials using technology and how the merit of these creations can be assessed for tenure, promotion, and review.

The next chapters present a change of focus. Rather than relying upon research *about* scholars, Chapters 5 through 9 have been written *by* digital scholars in the field. These chapters present stories about how digital scholarship occurs—how academics transform traditional mediums of publication and teaching into something greater through the application of information technologies. In each case the digital scholar speaks not only of the steps that transform academic work, but also about the evaluation of such products in the tenure, promotion, and review process.

Creating an E-Journal

In Chapter 5, Gerald Zahavi and Susan L. McCormick tell the story of the *Journal for MultiMedia History.* The strength of this chapter is first in its description of the creation of the journal, looking at the issue of producing a pure electronic journal in a field—history—that has clung very strongly to traditional patterns of research and research publication. This chapter gives insights into the creative talents and technical necessities that go into producing a journal in this form. It is a wonderful complement to Kling and Spector's earlier chapter on discriminating among and evaluating e-journals.

Second, Gerald Zahavi has chosen to share with readers his evaluation for full professor in the face of his own digital scholarship. Quoting external reviewers, Zahavi and McCormick provide a window into the review process, allowing us to read how others have viewed digital scholarship. The wording of the review letters, quoted verbatim here, serves as a model for others who must think about evaluating digital scholarship. Furthermore, Zahavi also allows us to read portions of his departmental review, quoting chairs and faculty members in his departmental review dossier. It is rare that anyone publicly writes about the promotion process in such personal terms. This chapter is a model for any faculty member, tenured or not, who is a digital scholar coming up for review.

Noteworthy in this chapter also is the notion of service, to the field of history and to the field of technology. Zahavi's reviewers spoke of his contribution to the university because of the creation of his journal—any university would be proud to have a journal originate from its faculty. In the case of the *Journal for Multimedia History*, a reviewer from academic computing also had high praise for the effort, stressing that, "*JMMH* is one of the first on-line journals at the University and it is the first site on campus to make use of streaming audio technology." Here is a case of both creation and transformation.

Creating Instructional Environments

The next three chapters in this section look at various aspects of teaching with technology. In particular, they emphasize the changes that can occur in teaching and learning with the addition of digital components.

Thomas P. Mackey explores digital pedagogy in the context of tenure, promotion, and review guidelines. Furthermore, Mackey tells the story of his Information Science 301 class—a class composed of upper-level undergraduate students. In particular, he explores the challenges faculty face in including technology in the courses, "making effective connections between theory and practice, managing the increased time demands of this work, expanding the role of teaching assistants, restructuring large classes, encouraging students to work in teams, and balancing content with technology instruction." Academics interested in creating such a course, or evaluators reviewing technology-rich coursework, will find this chapter to hold a wealth of information on technologies, classroom management, and pedagogical philosophy for moving from traditional to digital instruction environments.

Ian G. Anderson brings his experiences from Scotland to bear on our understanding of digital pedagogy in university history programs. He points out that, "In the UK the overwhelming majority of history courses that used computers were using database packages by the 1990s." Anderson's chapter provides valuable insights into how to think about learning outcomes, as well as lists of "benchmarking standards" for skills in history—standards that are broad enough to be applied to a variety of other disciplines. Furthermore, he gives examples of actual quantitative historical exercises, and checklists for such areas as "Learning Outcomes for Studying History with Computers," and "Learning Outcomes for Data Modelling and Representation." Anderson's chapter is extremely detailed, providing examples of pedagogy and evaluation for academics as well as tenure and promotion committee members.

Finally, moving to graduate education, Daphne Jorgensen's chapter looks at "adult learners who are pursuing advanced degrees through distance education via asynchronous learning networks (ALNs)." Whereas the previous two chapters dealt primarily with students in face-to-face classroom situations, this chapter explores the transformations that need to occur in a distance-education environment. Jorgensen takes us through the steps that she followed in order to teach a course in the use of media in teaching and learning for the State University of New York Learning Network (SLN). She shares her story, and the perspectives of her university colleagues "in shedding light on the work that goes into creating a rich on-line class community."

Creating Electronic Archival Exhibits

Jessica Lacher-Feldman works in the special collections library at the University of Alabama. She brings another perspective to this book—telling the story of creating an on-line sheet music exhibit for the university. She addresses the issue of how digital applications have required that archivists and librarians develop entirely new skill sets for their jobs, showing the reader how she used these skill sets to create a digital exhibition, *Over There! And Back Again: Patriotic American Sheet Music from the First World War*. Lacher-Feldman's chapter provides detailed explanations of timing, software, policy considerations, and selection choices when creating a digital exhibit, documenting the amount of time and expertise that are necessary to produce such a work. She also emphasizes the important role that such work can play in the life of the university, since, "it is . . . critical to consider the countless opportunities for innovative outreach, creating new and unprecedented access via the World Wide Web, and in developing partnerships within the university community that will draw positive attention to the repository, the academic institution, and the participants in the project."

Collaboration

The authors of these chapters were given free choice in how to pursue their topics. Nonetheless, and critically important for this book, they all talk about collaboration in one form or another in their respective chapters. Jessica Lacher-Feldman not only worked with a music professor to create the rich text for her on-line music exhibit, but she also emphasizes "developing partnerships" in order to "draw positive attention" to the various components of the university community.

Tom Mackey's chapter title includes the phrase "collaborative Web development." His use of the Web—having students teach each other through digital creation—requires that individuals work together to create Web pages that complement each other, forming collaborative Web sites that are strong learning tools. Similarly, Gerald Zahavi and Susan McCormick mention specifically "the collaboration of two scholars on a unique project that drew on their individual research and talents." The nature of e-journals requires partnerships. The authors provide one component, but the editors and technology consultants all have roles that one person simply could not fill in time or talents.

In a classroom setting, both Daphne Jorgensen and Ian Anderson found themselves working with others in order to produce digital environments for education. Jorgensen notes that three individuals drastically revised an ALN course, while Anderson discusses the development of modules, exercises, and Web-based materials in the context of his department at the University of Glasgow, specifically mentioning the role of the university archivist in creating teaching materials.

The topic of collaboration is critically important for this book. In the tenure, promotion, and review process, individual faculty members are evaluated based upon the contribution they have made in their service, research, and teaching. The digital scholar is almost certainly a collaborator. This means that review committees need to decide what type of contribution each individual has made in creative endeavors. In a paper-based world, coauthors are often asked to write letters explaining what each author contributed. Lacher-Feldman addresses the digital issue, noting that, "When work is being done collaboratively between two junior faculty members, it is critical to discuss how these end products will further both their positions within their departments and how they will be represented on each respective curriculum vita."

The process of creation and transformation in a digital environment requires a vast number of skill sets—probably more skill sets and time than any one person could own. The chapters that follow tell stories about how each of these individuals acted as a digital scholar—with the collaboration of others—to create products with technology that could not exist without it.

Chapter 5

Digital Scholarship, Peer Review, and Hiring, Promotion, and Tenure

A Case Study of the *Journal for MultiMedia History*

Gerald Zahavi and Susan L. McCormick

"The *Journal for MultiMedia History* is a free, peer-reviewed, on-line historical journal that presents hypermedia articles, documentaries, aural essays, and reviews. We showcase outstanding research in all fields of historical inquiry—research that incorporates audio, video and graphics, animations, and hypertext into presentations that would be impossible in a print journal."

So begins one of our promotional brochures publicizing the *Journal for MultiMedia History*. Founded in 1997 by Gerald Zahavi and Julian Zelizer, the *JMMH* has experimented with and promoted a digital mixed-media approach to augment composition and evidentiary presentation in history; it has challenged and expanded traditional approaches to historical publication. Before the arrival of the *JMMH*, the idea of presenting and disseminating historical, multimedia projects as discrete electronic journal "articles" had yet to be fully explored. No forum existed where scholars, students, and the public could read, view, and hear distinguished multimedia research in all fields of history, or peruse detailed reviews that also offered audio and video samples from reviewed works. Merging audio, video, graphics, and text offered historians an opportunity to make historical writing more rigorous *and* multileveled.

The *Journal* would demonstrate how hypertext and multimedia technologies could transform research, documentation, and publication of historical scholarship. As the first peer-reviewed electronic journal to present, evaluate, and disseminate multimedia historical scholarship, the *JMMH* also sought to help establish the standards of academic electronic multimedia publishing, matching those found in leading *print* historical journals such as the *American Historical Review* or the *Journal of Modern History*. We expected that administrators, tenure-review committees, and other deliberative groups looking to evaluate electronic academic historical publication for hiring, promotion, and tenure decisions would also find our reviews of Web sites, CD-ROMs, and other multimedia "products" helpful.

But from the beginning, we had skeptics. "A virtual journal in an academic world that has already rendered itself virtual? How appropriate!" That was how one colleague described our project. Although she missed the point, she did identify one of our major goals in initiating the journal. It was precisely *because* so much of what we were doing as professional historians seemed so separated and isolated from public life and discourse that we wanted to "get out on the Web." The *JMMH* emerged from discussions taking place within the department in the newly formed History and Media Committee. The work of historians, we were convinced, should not be restricted to the narrow margins of academic discourse; historical thinking and reasoning should be a larger part of American life and discourse. We felt that historians could help accomplish this by bringing history to the airwaves, to television, and to the Internet—and to people not typically exposed to academic history. The *Journal for MultiMedia History* would be one of several projects aimed at achieving this end.

We believed that digital, hypermedia publication would be exciting and accessible to an entire universe of nonacademic readers. Thus, it would accomplish one of our central aspirations: to expand the appeal and reach of our discipline through digital publication. As we wrote in our first issue, "We wanted to bring serious historical scholarship and pedagogy under the scrutiny of amateurs and professionals alike, to utilize the promise of digital technologies to expand history's boundaries, merge its forms, and promote and legitimate innovations in teaching and research that we saw emerging all around us."[1]

We knew we were entering untested waters and would need to convince others, *many* others, of the merits of our project. It was one thing to simply take a text journal and put it on the World Wide Web. Not to suggest that this is an unproblematic or unchallenging task, but it was another matter to create a publication that could exist *only* on the World Wide Web, that used streaming audio, video, and digital images as evidence—and as the foundations of historical arguments. As historian Christopher Tomlins recently pointed out, scholarly journals "exist to promote original scholarship, to accommodate it in its variety but also to influence its general direction and shape, to certify it as worthy of note and trust to whatever audience is reached, and to preserve it as such."[2] The *Journal for MultiMedia History* sought to accomplish all three of these goals in the realm of digital publishing.

Creating the Journal

The relative ease of access and availability of the World Wide Web for both publishers and consumers enhanced the potential of—and minimized some of the obstacles to—creating a new publication. The absence of significant print start-up costs, and the ability to identify and communicate with a potential audience of contributors and readers quickly and at little expense made creation of the *JMMH* feasible in ways that would not have been possible in a traditional print environment. Creating the *Journal* with mostly volunteer labor and minimal publishing costs allowed us to make it available free of charge, thus further reinforcing the "democratic" and "accessible" promise of the Web that many had described and lauded.

Our first challenge was to attract submissions, "to promote original research"—as Tomlins emphasized—in digital multimedia format. Without submissions, without scholars actually beginning to work in this mode, we would sink as a journal. After the initial decision by the History and Media Committee to proceed with this experiment, we put out a call for submissions, broadcasting it on H-Net discussion lists. We placed announcements on the History Department Web site and prepared and sent out brochures and flyers to history departments; we also distributed them at major historical association and conference meetings. In addition, the editors attended many sessions at various professional meetings around the country, seeking to identify scholarship that would best lend itself to this emerging medium. We sought out colleagues, and others working in related areas, looking for submissions or for recommendations and referrals to those doing relevant hypermedia work.

Unlike traditional text-based, print publications, we not only sought articles for the *Journal*, but we looked for researchers who had intriguing material but lacked multimedia know-how, or perhaps even interest. We challenged them with the opportunity and offered them the support that would allow them to think about their work in a new context and form. We were both eager and willing to undertake the added editorial labors that collaborative hypermedia composition and editing would entail. This was and still is a difficult task. We were not looking for text submissions; we wanted hypermedia articles that engaged visually and aurally rich topics, that fully used the potential of digital presentation and argument, and that experimented with new hypermedia syntaxes. Unfortunately, all too many of our submissions were text, and we generally rejected these.

From the earliest days, it was apparent to us that a strong peer-review system that operated on several levels was essential for the success of the *JMMH*. First and foremost, we recognized that scholars confronting their own hiring, tenure, or promotion concerns would both want and need to have their work appear in a peer-reviewed venue. For the *Journal* itself and for the development and legitimization of new forms of digital scholarship, close scrutiny and comment by peers in the field would be essential. Finally, reviews of the "products" of this new scholarship would help to establish standards and conventions that would serve as guides to assessing Web sites, CD-ROMs, or historical radio and video documentaries. The design and structure of the *Journal* itself, as well as the editorial process, reflected each of these concerns.

Producing the Journal

Editorial labor on a digital hypermedia journal is far more extensive and intensive than in a traditional print journal. Not only are there the usual concerns about the content of a submission, style and grammar, and typographical proofreading, but there are also judgments to be made on whether substantive content truly represents—or could represent—the best use of a multimedia format. Practically, this means that submissions are subject to at least one additional layer of review. All submissions undergo an initial review of form and content by the editorial staff; some are rejected as clearly not appropriate for the journal because of their weak content, lack of appropriate multimedia elements, or both. On occasion, the editors are drawn to original work that has the *potential* for a worthwhile article if only the authors undertook the challenge of framing, or reframing the research and writing in hypermedia form. In this scenario, a discussion with the author(s) ensues, and we encourage him, her, or them (multiple authors are common in these cases) to reshape their compositions.

Sometimes the multimedia elements are present, but the underlying content is weak. In such situations, we encourage revision and resubmission before sending the work to outside reviewers. In rare cases, a submission clearly will demonstrate both substantive scholarship and mastery of the complexities and possibilities of digital scholarship. In this event, the work is sent to two outside reviewers, experts in the subject area of the submission. A final decision to publish—or to publish with revisions—is made after receiving the readers' reports. At this point, the editorial team works collaboratively with the authors to refine and revise the article. Part of this process also includes considerable design and layout work, to make sure that the finished piece reflects the author's unique aesthetic vision while also ensuring that it conforms to the overall "look" and style of the *JMMH*.

Thus, editorial work at the *JMMH* is often a *very* collaborative process between the author(s) and the editors. Production of most pieces—reviews *and* articles—involves working closely with each author, preparing the visual and aural elements of reviews and articles, and often writing or revising the HTML and JavaScript code that creates the "look" of the finished pieces.

"I Can Almost See the Lights of Home," published in 1999 in the *Journal*, suggests the importance of the collaborative process between editors and authors. Termed an "aural essay" by joint authors Alessandro Portelli and Charles Hardy III, this extended and innovative work explored place, form, time, and the act of historical interpretation; it was an attempt by two oral historians—one from Pennsylvania, in the United States, and the other from Rome, Italy—to create a new *aural* history genre that counterpoised the voices of subject and scholar in dialogue, the dialogue that takes place in the real time of an oral interview *and* the one that occurs as interpretations are created and scholarship is generated. Dialogic elements pervaded the work—in the conversations between Portelli and Harlan County, Kentucky, residents—the subjects of the essay—and in the verbal exchanges between Portelli and Hardy as scholars discussing the oral interviews that Portelli collected. "I Can Almost See the Lights of Home" was also an instructional manual on authoring in sound and a manifesto of sorts. It challenged *oral* historians to truly explore the full dimension of the sources they create and use in scholarship—to engage the "orality" of oral sources. It challenged *all* historians to consider alternative modes of presenting interpretations, modes that render the very act of interpretation more visible while preserving and respecting the integrity of primary sources.

"Lights" was an example of the collaboration of two scholars on a unique project that drew on their individual research and talents; it also highlighted the expanded editorial input of *JMMH* editors in the development and production of the feature article. Although it began as a purely audio project, after several discussions with Hardy and Portelli, the two decided to submit it to the *Journal* and reconfigure it for the World Wide Web. After outside reviewers gave their thumbs-up to the submission, *JMMH* editors worked closely with the two authors to construct the on-line version. The initial aural essay, "I Can Almost See the Lights of Home" (which received the Oral History Association's 1999 Non-Print Media Award for outstanding use of oral history), provided the genesis and the linchpin for the *JMMH* article. Portelli and Hardy were asked to write additional essays that would further elaborate on and develop their contributions to the project and reflect on some of the larger issues suggested in "Lights." They willingly agreed. Both referenced the original "essay in sound," but also provided a complex, multilinear exploration of the subject matter. The success of "Lights" as a hypermedia work is attested to by one reader, Roy Rosenzweig, a prominent practitioner of and a pioneer in hypermedia historical scholarship. He termed the work "a spectacular piece of work—a brilliant melding of form and content and probably the best use of the Web for scholarship that I have seen."[3]

In a few cases, submissions to the *JMMH* arrive in fairly polished hypermedia form. Tom Dublin, for example, along with Melissa Doak, submitted an excellent piece titled "Miner's Son, Miners' Photographer: The Life and Work of George Harvan," an in-depth profile of Pennsylvania documentary photographer George Harvan and his work. They did so only after more than a year of ongoing discussions with the editor. When completed, "Miner's Son" included 280 photographs, hours of oral interviews, flash-slide exhibits, and an analytical essay with hyperlinks to various visual and aural resources. After hundreds of hours of collective and collaborative labor—mostly by Dublin and Doak, but also by many technical consultants at the University of Binghamton and at the *JMMH*—the final work emerged as a powerful demonstration of how to use the full potential of electronic publishing in scholarship, focusing on visual and audio subject matter.[4]

In fact, with such works as "I Can Almost See the Lights of Home" and "Miner's Son, Miners' Photographer," the *JMMH* had a profound influence on promoting original works—exploring, in particular, new presentation modes for oral history. As a recent review article in the *Journal of American History* acknowledged, "The effect of the sound files paired with contemplative writing is more evocative of place and thought than are most standard journal articles."[5] That is precisely what we hoped multimedia publishing would help accomplish.

Still, stimulating multimedia digital publication and successfully soliciting and attracting quality submissions have been our greatest challenges. It has slowed our progress considerably. The young scholar wants a quick jump start to a career, and a new and untested medium and publications venue is hardly attractive. The anticipated labor and widespread technophobia of older scholars and those far removed from technology have also held back submissions.

Teaching, Research, and Reviews

For those interested in exploring the pedagogical and research implications of new digital technologies, the *JMMH* created a "Teaching and Research" section that explores ways in which pedagogy and research are being rapidly transformed by the World Wide Web and by multimedia. Other essays provide guidance in using the Web to conduct research by evaluating subject-specific Web sites. Corinne Blake's "Teaching Islamic Civilization with Information Technology" (vol. 1, *JMMH*) is an extensively hyperlinked article that offers a comprehensive review of Web-based resources for students and scholars of Islam and Islamic Civilization. The author pulled together a broad array of materials and presented them in a highly useful, innovative, and analytical fashion. Demonstrating one of the unique problems and possibilities of on-line publication, Professor Blake is now reviewing and revising her essay to incorporate new scholarship and to remove links to sites that no longer exist. The *JMMH* staff is still debating how to present the revised version while preserving the original work.

In a similar fashion, Robert Griffith's "Un-Tangling the Web of Cold War Studies; or, How One Historian Stopped Worrying and Learned to Love the Internet" (vol. 3, *JMMH*) gives students and scholars a road map to on-line resources pertaining to the Cold War. Other articles offer advice and guidance on integrating Web development into pedagogy. Adrienne Hood and Jackie Spafford's "Student-Constructed Web Sites for Research Projects: Is It Worth It?" (vol. 1, *JMMH*) makes judicious use of hypertext to demonstrate the promise and perils of integrating Web page construction projects into course assignments. In "Creating Instructional CD-ROMs" (vol. 3, *JMMH*), Ian Anderson summarizes the work of the History Courseware Consortium at the University of Glasgow, Scotland, in developing CD-ROM and on-line multimedia resources for undergraduate instruction. Noting that the use of computers in historical research has followed divergent paths in the United Kingdom and in the United States, Anderson suggests that the development of Web-based teaching materials may offer common ground for historians on both sides of the Atlantic.

Our attempt to meld concerns about content and form extends to other sections of the *Journal* as well. For example, when seeking reviewers for Web sites, CD-ROMs, and the like, we select experts in the field and not in hypermedia. In our guidelines to reviewers, we specifically ask them to evaluate the content *and* the way the content is presented—whether a particular medium is used well—and to offer comments on the ability of a "non-media-savvy" person to take full advantage of the "product." Of course, as access to and use of the Internet have exploded in the past few years, even some of the more technophobic souls are comfortable exploring on-line and digital materials. Nonetheless, we have always believed that those who are knowledgeable about a particular subject are the best equipped to evaluate the substantive content of a work and to secondarily assess the effective use of the medium—the ease, aesthetics, elegance, and appropriateness of use and presentation. We are first and foremost a *historical* journal and strongly believe that it is always the content that must drive the technology, thus ensuring works of substantive scholarship.

The Historical Profession and Digital Hypermedia Publishing

Throughout the sections and "pages" of the *JMMH*, we aspired to achieve what Tomlins described as another of the primary functions of a scholarly journal: the certification of research and publications "as worthy of note and trust to whatever audience is reached." As we wrote in our founding statement, we wanted to "utilize the promise of digital technologies to expand history's boundaries, merge its forms, and *promote and legitimate* [emphasis added] innovations in teaching and research that we saw emerging all around us." Unlike other creative multimedia work on the World Wide Web, the *JMMH* was to be peer-reviewed.[6] In fact, the *JMMH* was the *first* peer-reviewed, on-line journal of historical multimedia scholarship.

Multimedia historical scholarship was and still is in its infancy; the *genre* has yet to "take off." Many scholars are still wary of, and lack skill in, the techniques of digital multimedia publication. Historians concerned about professional visibility and establishing academic reputations, including graduate students preparing for a competitive job market, are hesitant to wade into the rising waters of a seemingly foreboding digital ocean. By creating a peer-reviewed journal, we began to address these apprehensions.

Throughout academe and within the historical profession, considerable attention has been directed to the ways in which digital scholarship should be evaluated and rewarded. The American Historical Association (AHA) recently ran a series of essays on the topic in its monthly newsletter, *Perspectives*. As one contributor noted, "It is becoming increasingly important to explore the potential of electronic publication in disseminating academic work. While many are discussing the theoretical issues involved in publishing in this new medium, there are already several experiments underway that are producing examples of peer-reviewed electronic publications in the field of history."[7] The *JMMH* was cited as one.

The key issue in the relationship between digital publishing and hiring, promotion, and tenure reviews—the essence of the academic reward system—is quality control, or peer review. A second participant in the *Perspectives* forum made the following essential point: "Once the complex process of developing and designing these scholarly works is complete, the next major challenge is to make certain that they are accepted within the academic world as significant scholarly contributions that are equivalent to their print counterparts." The term "equivalent to their print counterpart" in this case implies a *quality* equivalency. The American Historical Association has, in fact, moved forward on several fronts to ensure quality assessments of digital scholarship. It has created a new prize, the Gutenberg-e Prize, and an associated digital publishing program, which recognizes quality historical works and dissertations with multimedia/digital promise, helping transform them into Web sites. As described on the AHA Web site: "The program is not intended simply to reward excellence in scholarship with yet another prestigious prize but rather to use prestige—the bluest of ribbons awarded by the grandest of juries with the full authority of the AHA behind it—to set a high standard for electronic publishing. By legitimizing electronic publishing, the AHA hopes to change attitudes of academics toward e-books. By making the most of the new media, the program may also contribute to a new conception of the book itself as a vehicle of knowledge."[8]

In addition, the AHA has recently approved a set of guidelines for evaluating electronic publications, "recommending that they be reviewed alongside other publications in their field. . . . The guidelines also recommend that reviewers consider the ways in which historical scholarship is enhanced or otherwise affected by the use of digital technology in the publication." The ultimate arbiters, however, as historian Kate Wittenberg has noted, are engaged university faculty members. "Certain elements must be in place to create an environment conducive to innovation," she writes, "including an interested and responsive faculty (at both a senior and junior level) and leaders within the various parts of the university who can play a critical role in encouraging the creation and acceptance of new models for scholarly communication."[9]

Increasingly, historians are attempting to come to grips with standards that can be used to judge digital scholarship. Historian Robert Townsend has attempted to establish a foundation for evaluation criteria. Acknowledging the growing recognition of the legitimacy of digital publishing, he has emphasized the need to establish clear and distinct quality standards. "Insofar as tenure and promotion remain tied to the production of articles and monographs," he recently wrote, "it seems vitally important to assess how on-line publication can extend history scholarship in new directions, while maintaining its integrity as good scholarship. To facilitate a new understanding, we need to do a better job of differentiating the types of scholarship on the Web—and the function and value of each—to both sketch out what is possible and lay a groundwork for incorporating this form of scholarship into the academic reward system." He then offered a detailed analysis of on-line scholarship (including a sample from the *JMMH*) and suggested a typology for organizing and evaluating such scholarship:

> As a starting point, I propose three distinct categories of electronic scholarship—*textual* (materials that are simply reproductions of print articles), *supplemental* (articles and monographs that use hyperlinks to other primary and secondary sources on the Web for illustrative purposes), and *foundational* (texts that are built "from the ground up" and fully integrate

other electronic resources into their arguments). . . . The categories proposed here would measure on-line history scholarship by how closely the
argument and evidence are brought together. This places particular importance on two factors: the level of interpretive guidance an author provides
to readers in guiding them through the linked materials, and the depth of
the related material created by the author.[10]

Such thoughtful considerations to matters of standards are critical if digital scholarship is ever to be accepted by the historical profession as a whole.
More scholars, senior and junior, need to join Townsend in formulating evaluative standards.

Tenure, Promotion, and Digital Publishing: A Case Study

But doing serious history on-line takes more effort and work than history
that goes from the word processor to the printed page, so the possibilities
of the on-line medium will remain stifled until we develop the institutional
support and incentives to do it properly.[11]

The increasing legitimacy of digital publishing can be gauged not only in the
numerous high-quality historical projects available on-line, in the growing
recognition by historical associations of the significance of digital publishing, and in the concern of scholars for establishing standards and rewards,
but also in the tenure and promotions review of multimedia scholars and
publishers. Examining the experience of *JMMH* editor Gerald Zahavi, who
recently underwent one such review, offers us additional evidence of the
evolving understanding and acceptance of digital publishing by scholars and
academic institutions.

In 2001–2002, Gerald Zahavi came up for promotion to full professor at
the University at Albany. Since so much of his work in the previous half
decade involved digital media, it was a major focus of outside reviewers as
well as of the departmental, college, and university review committees evaluating his record.

Perhaps most valuable to understanding the sea change in professional
estimates of the importance of multimedia scholarship are the contents of
confidential letters from outside scholars solicited by the department chair
(writers, unless they choose otherwise, are normally not identified to the
candidate). These external evaluators, without exception, emphasized
Zahavi's digital publications and editorial work in their assessment of his
case. One outside evaluator wrote: "To cut to the chase, *Talking History* [a
radio program and on-line aural history archive] or the *JMMH* alone would

be impressive professional service to the field. That Gerry has been able to produce both—and team them together with related on-line resources—is an amazing accomplishment, and product of a prodigious amount of work. This is work on the cutting edge of digital scholarship."[12] Clearly, digital publication and editing was being taken seriously in the promotion process.

Surprisingly, outside readers of the promotion file sometimes demonstrated a detailed knowledge of the *JMMH*: "Equally impressive is how the journal has improved both conceptually and stylistically from one issue to the next. The graphics and design are cleaner and more engaging, he has introduced video, and Volume Three demonstrates a growing understanding of the syntax of digital scholarship. The *JMMH* is unique. It is the only peer-reviewed clearinghouse on multimedia historical scholarship, and as such it is *invaluable* for historians interested in scholarship appearing in digital media." This writer recognized the contributions that peer review made to the profession, really highlighting the case that Tomlins made in his essay in *Perspectives*. Furthermore, as this reviewer's additional comments acknowledged, the peer-review process was the only way the *Journal* could establish a reputation that could compete with established and respected text journals that drew many, many, more submissions from young scholars.

One of the most informative letters noted the importance of examining both traditional *and* digital publishing in evaluating candidates. It acknowledged that digital work could sap intellectual energies that might go into traditional print publications, but was nonetheless worthy of equal recognition: ". . . the world has changed with the advent of the Internet and the WWW, and the academy has altered accordingly, albeit at a glacially slower pace. Professor Zahavi has chosen to demonstrate the scholarship required by the academy in both traditional and digital form. As a result, he has published fewer pieces in prominent print journals and devoted energy that might have gone into finishing the second monograph to pioneering online publication. My hat is off to him. Zahavi has managed to distinguish himself in two arenas." This same writer, demonstrating familiarity with other existing on-line projects, went on to emphasize the importance of the *JMMH* as a model for future hypermedia publishing, "There are three online journals devoted to history and new or multi-media that qualify as 'native' history new media publications: *The Journal for MultiMedia History*, *Common-Place*, and *The Journal of the Association for History and Computing*. . . . Only *The Journal for MultiMedia History* attempts to use new media and Web technology to 'do' history and furnish access to a wide audience as well as exhibit an understanding of the on-line design criteria."[13]

Another reviewer noted, "For the past many years there has been much discussion directed at the issue of how historians can approach and cultivate new audiences for our work, and the importance in a democracy of doing so. At Albany, we are being instructed everyday in how to do this." The contributions of the *JMMH* in this respect were critical:

> A glance at any of the issues reveals an extraordinary creative and complex sense of the American past and the ways that our understanding of that past can be communicated to wider audiences. In every issue major American historians have been enlisted to bring to that audience the latest in historical scholarly commentary, or to review electronic media of historical note. The journal consistently, in my mind, avoids easy popularization while making the textured complexity of the past understandable to a wider audience of not only academic scholars but also students, teachers, the educated layperson and professionals in historical or other institutions such as: historical societies, museums, community agencies and local history projects.[14]

Still another emphasized the importance of the work on the *JMMH:* "Zahavi has pioneered in historians' use of new electronic media . . . [and] has exhibited remarkable leadership in this very new and rapidly evolving field. That leadership is particularly evident in his editing of the online publication, *The Journal for MultiMedia History*. The journal is at the cutting edge of the use of the new media in historical research in both providing an outlet for some of the most creative work being done by social historians today and at the same time stimulating historians to experiment and take full advantage of the potential that the new media offer."[15] This comment captured precisely those points made by Christopher Tomlins concerning the second core aim of any scholarly journal, namely, to "promote original scholarship, to accommodate it in its variety but also to influence its general direction and shape."[16]

The department chair appointed a committee (the Ad Hoc Promotion Evaluation Committee) to review Zahavi's record, including outside letters, and to report its recommendation on promotion to the department. The report produced by the committee not only provided a detailed review of Zahavi's text publications but also of his multimedia and digital projects—including a digital version of a text article about General Electric's Association Island (used as a management summer camp for a half century). For many faculty in the department, the review of a colleague deeply engaged in multimedia digital publishing was an eye-opener: "The strength of the work lies in the written text (or at least it does to this dinosaur), but the media components certainly do add dimensions to the written text," wrote one member of the committee. "You are no longer simply a reader; you listen and you look (you also point and click). If one picture makes you want to see more pictures, you click and your wish is granted. If you don't believe that someone could really have said what Gerry claims he said, you click on the name and you hear him say it. You don't merely read about the Great Elm, you see it, and, if you desire to get more of the mood of the time, you click again and listen to a song that the campers would have sung. The piece also includes two corporate films, one from 1925 and one from 1954. You actually see how the camp has changed from a place where men engaged in play, parades, hard-drinking, and joviality to a formal, business-focused, regimented world, far from the traditional notion of a summer camp."

Besides being a contribution to scholarship, Zahavi's multimedia work was also viewed as a component of his "service" contributions to the university. The head of the Academic Computing Center at the University at Albany highlighted Zahavi's work on the *JMMH*: "Dr. Zahavi founded and remains the editor of the on-line *Journal for MultiMedia History*. Established in 1997, the early days of the World Wide Web, it is active and tremendously popular. *JMMH* is one of the first on-line journals at the University and it is the first site on campus to make use of streaming audio technology." A former assistant director of the university's Center for Excellence in Teaching and Learning likewise acknowledged and praised Zahavi's expertise in the area of multimedia and Web development in the field of history. Student evaluations, too, noted Zahavi's expertise in "new educational technologies and methods" designed to "break historical research away from 'dry, academic treatises' and make it come alive for his students." One student acknowledged that Zahavi had a profound impact on the way s/he handled teaching: "I have included multimedia pieces in my syllabi. . . ." Another stated that he came to graduate study at the University at Albany's history department in part because he learned about *Talking History* and the *JMMH* as an undergraduate.

The final report to the department concluded, in part, "Professor Zahavi has also given a full measure of service within and for his home department. He has brought national visibility to history at Albany through the *Journal for MultiMedia History*, the path breaking peer-reviewed electronic journal of which he is co-founder and editor." After the presentation of the Ad Hoc Committee's report, on February 14, 2002, the department began its deliberations. Department minutes reveal the various views expressed at that meeting concerning the general and specific merits of digital multimedia publishing. Thus, it is a valuable document, one that provides direct and detailed evidence of how digital scholarship is being considered in promotion decisions. The minutes record the reactions of individual members of the department. (They are not identified by name.) One faculty member emphasized the importance of looking at substance and not form:

It is not the mode, but the dissemination of knowledge that is critical. . . . Zahavi's work has been focused and broad, *and* he has done it using different modes of scholarly production. Every time a new mode is used, there is a significant learning curve. The use of different modes is more important than one might initially think. For example, when looking at the "Association Island" work and seeing the high-level corporate administrators actually relaxing around the campfire, it becomes impossible to think about the "man in the gray flannel suit" in quite the same way again. In addition to the fact the use of different modes of presentation adds context and dimensions to material that otherwise would not exist, it is clear that part of the motivation for using different modes of presentation is Professor Zahavi's commitment to engage a larger and larger audience. He has clearly done this, and by doing so, has gained an international reputation.

It was also clear that the deliberations provided a *learning* opportunity for many faculty members. Some, admitting their own ignorance of electronic multimedia publishing, were hesitant to judge digital projects; they relied on outside evaluators. According to the minutes, one acknowledged, "the evaluation of scholarship now is different from the ones used when he and others in the department 'grew up.' In terms of the changes in technology, he sees himself as part of 'the dinosaur's club.' He thought it behooved those colleagues who are not able to do what Zahavi can do to rely on the evaluation of those who can. The outside letters are powerful and unanimous in their endorsement of this promotion."

A *substantial* portion of the discussion over promotion focused on the "nature" of digital publishing and hypermedia. Although the unfinished status of some of the digital projects undertaken by Zahavi was a source of some controversy, it was also an opportunity to make an important point: "the on-line editorial project ['Remembering Attica,' an archive of aural and visual works edited by Zahavi pertaining to the Attica insurrection of 1971] will always be 'in progress.' That is precisely its advantage over the written editorial project—it can always be added to as more material becomes available," retorted a colleague. The discussion of digital scholarship continued— part instruction, part evaluation. One could hardly imagine anything like the following in a debate over the merits of monographs:

The world of books and the world of computers require different rational processes. People who read books are dealing with linear syntax and grammar. Computer language differs from linear texts. Hypertexts have tags that lead from a written text to another document that might add a sound layer or a video layer. The logic of multimedia text is associative or layered, rather than linear. Professor Zahavi's use of multimedia creates an entirely new experience of the past. First he empowers the reader. The reader can make choices while engaging with the article: to read the text, to see a video, to listen to a song or a speech. Zahavi invites the reader to make associations and add layers to layers. Secondly, he reproduces a piece of the past in the round: the words, the sounds, the sights. Professor Zahavi is fundamentally a traditionalist, but one who blends traditional goals with innovative production.

Faculty members were encouraged to see scholarship in terms beyond text publications. "We define ourselves too narrowly if we are going on printed text alone. . . . [T]he 'Attica Revisited' piece could easily be turned into a monograph, but it simply works better in the electronic form. We are talking about different forms, not about substance or value. . . . This orange just happens to be as good as this apple."

Following the department's deliberation—the department voted 15 for promotion, 0 against, with 2 abstentions—the case went to the College of Arts and Sciences' Tenure and Promotions Review committee and to the dean. Predictably, here too the issue of how to weigh electronic publishing was debated. The dean suggested the importance of the *JMMH*—and electronic publishing—when he drew upon an argument made by one of the outside evaluators: "while the quality of his publications is very high, the quantity is lower than sometimes expected, but it is made up for with his electronic journal."

This case study is illustrative of more than one academic's experience with promotion and digital scholarship. It demonstrates that as scholars and members of review committees come to understand the nature, the complexity, and the possibilities of multimedia formats, even the "dinosaurs" among them are able to consider scholarly production in a new light. External evaluators, unknown to one another, were able to thoughtfully and independently assess digital publications. At every decision level *within* the institution, evaluators were open and willing to be educated about new modes of scholarship. The outcome might well be different in other institutions; however, a review of the records pertaining to this promotion case *does* suggest a growing familiarity with, and greater appreciation of, the rigorous demands of substantive multimedia scholarship by many historians—and a greater willingness on the part of committees to view this work favorably in hiring, tenure, and promotion reviews.

The Future

It would be inaccurate to suggest that multimedia scholarship—and *publishing*—are not without obstacles. In fact, we have encountered several serious impediments in publishing the *JMMH*. Multimedia historical scholarship is perhaps just past infancy, approaching the toddler stage; the *genre* has yet to "take off." Some scholars are still wary of, and lack skill in, the techniques of digital multimedia publication. Historians concerned about professional visibility and establishing academic reputations, including graduate students preparing themselves for a competitive job market, are still hesitant to wade into the rising waters of a seemingly foreboding digital ocean. We understand these concerns and will continue to address them. Slowly but surely, the digital merging of aural, visual, and textual historical analysis is coming of age. For those seeking to include digital scholarship in their teaching or research portfolios, there are grounds for cautious optimism. The path-breaking articles and reviews in the *Journal* reflect the excitement we felt when we first imagined the *JMMH*; they only begin to suggest the enormous possibilities open to historians ready and able to experiment with digital multimedia scholarship. We hope that they will inspire more scholars and students to courageously explore research that blends the conceptual and theoretical with imaginative multimedia presentations.

Notes

1. *Journal for MultiMedia History*, 1 (1998).

2. Christopher Tomlins, "Don't Mourn, Organize! A Rumination on Printed Scholarly Journals at the Edge of the Internet," American Historical Association, *Perspectives* (February 1998).

3. Roy Rosenzweig to Charles Hardy, April 4, 2001 (e-mail).

4. *Journal for MultiMedia History* 3 (2000).

5. Mary A. Larson, "Potential, Potential, Potential: The Marriage of Oral History and the World Wide Web," *Journal of American History* 88 (September 2001): 600–601.

6. Philip J. Ethington, "Los Angeles and the Problem of Urban Historical Knowledge," *American Historical Review* 105 (December 2000) cwis.usc.edu/dept/LAS/history/historylab/LAPUHK/index.html. The *AHR*, the premier journal in our discipline, has begun experimenting with multimedia on-line scholarship; in the December 2000 issue it offered its first "exclusive e-AHR multimedia article."

7. Kate Wittenberg, "Digital Technology and Historical Scholarship: A Publishing Experiment," *Perspectives* (May 2002), www.theaha.org/perspectives/issues/2002/0205/0205pub4.cfm.

8. www.theaha.org/prizes/gutenberg/Index.cfm [AHA Gutenberg-e Prizes from the American Historical Association for dissertations and monograph manuscripts in history].

9. Wittenberg, "Digital Technology."

10. Robert B. Townsend, "All of Tomorrow's Yesterdays: History Scholarship on the Web," *Perspectives* (May 2002), www.theaha.org/perspectives/issues/2002/0205/0205pub3.cfm.

11. Ibid.

12. Evaluation letter. Since writers are rarely identified to the candidate (unless they choose to be identified), they are, for the most part, not identified here. The remaining comments are not attributed.

13. This same writer added: "'I Can Almost See the Lights of Home—A Field Trip to Harlan County, Kentucky' (*Journal for MultiMedia History*, 1999), for example, could not be written or understood as history without new media technology. As the piece demonstrates, sound adds immeasurably to the historical narrative. In this sense, some but not all of the articles in the *Journal for MultiMedia History* serve as useful models for combining history and new media. It is to Professor Zahavi's credit that he experiments with, new media so that students and faculty have worthy examples for study."

14. Charles Hardy, evaluation letter.

15. Tom Dublin, evaluation letter.

16. Tomlins, "Don't Mourn, Organize!"

Chapter 6

Transforming the Learning Process

A Case Study on Collaborative Web Development in an Upper-Level Information Science Course

Thomas P. Mackey

Technology in the Classroom

Much of the discourse about digital technology and tenure review focuses on the work of faculty as producers of digital projects, software, and presentations. What is often missed in this conversation is the perspective of faculty who challenge students to produce their own technology projects. Teaching students to gain critical thinking skills in the digital production of information is a different process than developing instructional materials for students to view. To do so requires us to rethink the scope of what we teach and how we integrate software, labs, technical instruction, and student participation into the core themes and objectives of our courses. There should be generalized and scalable guidelines for institutions to evaluate this work as part of tenure review to advance and encourage creative uses of technology in the classroom. We also need to differentiate between the use of digital media for faculty-centered publication or presentation and the development of student-centered pedagogy through technology. Faculty who use technology for publication, presentation, or transformation of student learning should have a clear sense of how these approaches may or may not be considered in a tenure decision.

Students as Producers of Digital Information

Jeffrey R. Young argued that, "a growing number of institutions are working to include digital creations in the tenure folders that form the core of a candidate's professional portfolio."[1] This may include a Web site, multimedia project, or on-line course developed by faculty. The questions addressed by Young are important and challenge the institutional definitions of publication and the extent to which teaching is valued, especially at research universities. At the same time, this focus on faculty as producers of digital information is itself a traditional construct that further supports the fact that what really matters is faculty publication. This approach to technology and tenure review fails to recognize what is potentially transforming about new media when students create digital information, and ultimately why we should value and measure the importance of this work.

There is much more to consider than whether or not a digital project produced by faculty can be reviewed in the same way as a traditional print publication. Digital technologies challenge some of our basic assumptions about teaching and learning. Transforming a classroom into a digital environment requires faculty and students to make connections among discipline-specific and interdisciplinary course content, technology skills, and information literacy. Students should have the opportunity to develop digital information in a meaningful way to produce knowledge and to gain critical insights about this process. The goals of this work should be to prepare our students to be critical readers of digital technologies and to be active developers rather than passive viewers of new media. This is not accomplished through the development of faculty-centered Web sites, multimedia, and PowerPoint presentations for students to read as an alternative to print or lecture. We must teach our students and ourselves to share in the responsibility of development and to open a dialogue about the production of digital media as an active learning objective. Teaching students how to develop their own presentations, Web sites, and multimedia projects must be supported and encouraged by the tenure review process.

Although teachers familiar with technology may have a clear understanding of why they are using it, and institutions may value innovation in the classroom, we do not have generalized and scalable standards for how to measure or even fully define this kind of work. Michael Day argued that, "in the best of worlds, we would be free to innovate with technology to our hearts' content, confident that our innovations would be recognized at evaluation, tenure, and promotion time as long as they were backed up by sound pedagogical theory."[2] Without consistent guidelines, or even a common understanding about the importance of teaching with technology as a potentially transforming learning process, this ideal world for innovation is simply not realistic. Junior faculty especially must be careful about how innovative they are in the classroom because institutional support for this work varies by campus.

The problem with this cautious approach is that it prevents innovation in the first place. Faculty may be less inspired to take a risk and to try new approaches to teaching with technology if they do not have the support of their institutions. This further perpetuates the traditional definitions of tenure and promotion that place a higher value on publication in print over teaching and service. Dianne Lynch presented a convincing argument that faculty are not exactly transforming their teaching through innovative technology, primarily because they are not using it. Lynch said that, "when it comes to applying digital technology in the classroom, the biggest obstacle for higher education has nothing to do with resources or wiring."[3] According to Lynch the biggest problem is faculty members because many are simply avoiding new technologies. She pointed out, for example that "while 80 percent of public four-year colleges make course-management tools available to their faculties, professors actually use them in only 20 percent of their courses."[4] Lynch did not identify the tenure review process as an impediment to the use of technology in the classroom. She suggested that the problem has more to do with faculty who already have tenure and do not necessarily have an incentive to revise their courses with technology. Given the reluctance of so many faculty members to use course management systems or to develop Web syllabi, it seems clear that institutional support is needed to encourage the use of technology in the classroom. Although tenured faculty may not have an incentive to radically reinvent their pedagogy, this complacency should not be perpetuated in junior faculty who may want to experiment but are afraid to because they are concerned that the work will not be valued at the time of their own tenure decision. Tenure review should be an opportunity to encourage and support new approaches to teaching and should reflect a digital environment that continues to change in distinct ways.

Without clear guidelines that recognize and support teaching with digital media, there are fewer incentives for exploring technology in the classroom and fewer opportunities for innovation in research. A lack of institutional support creates a false disconnect within the research-teaching-service triad. Technology considerations intersect teaching, research, and service and should be envisioned as an integrated process. Faculty must feel free to try new approaches to pedagogy in the classroom and to consider the research and publication potential of such work. This may lead to an expanded role for teaching assistants and students in the research process. If we remove barriers between teaching, research, and service through explorations in technology, we may be able to further engage our students in scholarly research and writing. For example, students may be invited to participate as respondents in an on-line survey or as members of a focus group, or as researchers who locate scholarly materials in the library and on-line for an actual research project. These documents could be reviewed, organized, and shared through student-developed Web sites. By involving our students in a real academic process that reflects and possibly informs our own research interests, we may be more successful at teaching the core concepts of our disciplines than we are when simply lecturing in a classroom. Technology assists in this process because it provides a way to share documents and to create links between resources.

An approach to tenure review that diminishes, confuses, or completely ignores the potential for technology as a transformative medium works against some of the primary challenges posed by new media. One of the challenges often examined in the discourse has to do with how we conceptualize research and publication in digital environments. This concern addresses how to review a Web site or multimedia project produced by faculty in relation to the traditional standards of a peer-reviewed journal article. Most junior faculty would not take the chance that their institution would measure these different forms of publication in the same way. Young argued that while some progress has been made in this area and some colleges have developed new guidelines to consider technology projects, "review committees may not take technology work seriously, so [junior faculty should] stick to traditional academic activities, like publishing journal articles."[5] The incentive for tradition seems clear, but the problem for faculty interested in teaching with technology goes beyond their own definition of publication or whether or not their teaching is valued. Another challenge posed by digital technology is that it requires students to produce their own work in order to think, explore, and write in new ways. Digital technologies must be applied and experienced from a development and production standpoint. This approach radically alters what happens in the classroom because when students are digital writers of information, rather than digital readers, they are engaged in a process of critical thinking and the development of their own ideas. This shift in how we envision writing and teaching, and in turn the digital classroom, has been a concern of hypertext and Web theory for some time. The visual, dynamic, and textual characteristics of hypertext and the Web challenge our definitions of composition and pedagogy in these environments.

Hypertext and Web Theory

Before the Web, George P. Landow argued that hypertext "has the potential to make the teacher more a coach than a lecturer, and more an older, more experienced partner in collaboration than an authenticated leader."[6] For Landow, hypertext offered the potential to enhance collaboration, interdisciplinarity, and critical thinking. This approach "reconfigures the instructor"[7] because traditional notions of "power and authority"[8] are shared between teacher and student in a collaborative hypertext environment. Jay David Bolter described the computer as a "writing space"[9] that "offers a new surface for recording and presenting text together with new techniques for organizing our writing."[10] This was a fundamental rethinking of the computer from simply a machine for convenience or tabulation to a conceptual space to think and create. Richard A. Lanham argued that, "the digital revolution offers the most extraordinary opportunities to teach the arts in new ways"[11] because the technology expands traditional roles and creates "a dynamic oscillation: you simply cannot be a critic without in turn being a creator."[12] Michael Joyce authored the first hypertext fiction "afternoon, a story" using storyspace software.[13] He argued that hypertext transforms the way we understand texts because it "enables interaction between viewers of its material and those who created or gathered that material."[14] Joyce recognized the collaborative potential of this technology "in university and industry research settings, especially the World Wide Web (WWW)."[15] Several years into the Web revolution, we continue to see the use of the Web in a range of educational contexts, from on-line syllabi to course management systems, but many faculty are still reluctant to engage with this medium for student-centered writing and collaboration.

Tim Berners-Lee is recognized as "the inventor of the World Wide Web."[16] He developed the Hypertext Transfer Protocol (HTTP), the Universal Resource Identifier (URI), and a program actually called "WorldWideWeb" that allowed users to browse and edit Hypertext Markup Language (HTML) documents through a point and click interface.[17] Berners-Lee discussed the Web as a medium for the production of new ideas and not simply a tool for accessing and retrieving information. He insisted that the development of Web browsers should include an editor function, because as he said, "without a hypertext editor, people would not have the tools to really use the Web as an intimate collaborative medium."[18] Berners-Lee emphasized the production of new knowledge through the Web as a collaborative opportunity that supports the need for pedagogy that challenges students to actively develop information in a shared digital environment. Charles Jonscher argued that, "the Net has removed the asymmetry, the yawning divide, between producer and consumer, and this is indeed a completely unprecedented feature in any mass medium."[19] He also asserted that on the Web "each of us can be a publisher and a broadcaster as well as a reader and a viewer"[20] because traditional roles are expanded and reversed. Our understanding of publication is not only challenged as a format question but is also reenvisioned through sweeping redefinitions of authorship and audience.

Digital Pedagogy

Approaches to pedagogy must consider the changing roles of teacher and student in a digital environment and the degree to which our students participate in this process as originators of digital information. According to Lynch, most faculty are not engaging in new technologies at all. She refers to a Campus Computing Project survey that found "in more than one-third of their courses, college instructors still don't even use e-mail to communicate with their students, much less integrate innovative on-line applications into their curriculums."[21] If faculty members are not using e-mail, or course management software to deliver content, it seems unlikely that they will take the next step to teach their students how to explore and produce knowledge in a digital environment. Lynch suggests many reasons to explain the reluctance of faculty to engage with new technologies, such as the time commitment needed to develop on-line materials, concerns about publishing course content for the Web without copyright protection, and even the fear that faculty will be perceived by students as being less skillful with technology than they are.[22] These are all valid concerns and should be addressed as part of the problem standing in the way of technological innovation in the classroom.

Lynch does not address, however, one of the key reasons that faculty may avoid technology. Faculty must have a tangible reason for integrating technology into their teaching. Although the process may seem mysterious at times, tenure review is a concrete professional reality that defines the goals and objectives of faculty for an extended period of time. The early adopters of technology may have a clear understanding as to why they are using it, but this does not mean they are fully supported in doing so through the tenure review process, nor does it mean that others will follow. If fundamental change is going to take place in the classroom and if the promises of new technologies are going to be fully realized, we cannot simply rely on the early adopters to chart the course of action for everyone else. This problem requires an across-the-board, institutional response based on scalable guidelines to evaluate innovation with new technologies in the classroom and not simply a redefinition of what we mean when we use the term "publication."

The Information Environment: A Case Study

Many of the issues concerning teaching with technology and tenure review can be further illustrated in a case study of an information science course I have been teaching at the University at Albany since fall 2000. ISP301: The Information Environment is a three-credit, upper-level core requirement of the undergraduate program in the School of Information Science and Policy. This course explores a number of key concepts in the field of information science, such as information architecture, Web design and usability, the history of information science and technology, the digital divide, information ethics, and copyright. My approach to this course is to teach information science topics in concert with information literacy and information technology. My students are immersed in a digital environment through projects and assignments that require them to explore information theory and apply research methods. Although the challenges in balancing theoretical course content, information literacy, and technology competencies are ongoing, I believe that this course design is effective in foregrounding the integrated and potentially collaborative nature of these issues.

This case study demonstrates some of the challenges faced by faculty when integrating technology in their courses, challenges such as: making effective connections between theory and practice, managing the increased time demands of this work, expanding the role of teaching assistants, restructuring large classes, encouraging students to work in teams, and balancing content with technology instruction. The work of this course is intended to engage students in a collaborative digital environment in support of course themes and the development of critical thinking. This is not to suggest that this is an ideal framework for doing so or that this particular class is the only model that exemplifies this approach. This case study illustrates a process that places students at the center of technology development as an intentional strategy to apply hypertext and Web theory. ISP301 provides a picture of what a course with an integrated technology component looks like. This is not simply a question about whether technology projects should be given consideration as a publication in a tenure review discussion. In this case, the entire course is a technology project; and while this work is not a publication, it does intersect my research and service interests. For me, the process of integrating technology and information literacy into ISP301 is essential to the course content and reflects my philosophy of teaching, that students must be active participants in this practice.

Information Theory

As a core requirement of the Information Science and Policy undergraduate program, ISP301: The Information Environment introduces students to some of the key theoretical ideas in the field. For example, ISP301 explores the development of print and book culture, the expansion of libraries and museums, the emergence of computing, hypertext, electronic books, digital libraries, the Internet, and the Web. These topics intersect the transformation of information and communications over time and provide a contemporary context for Web development, interface usability, information architecture, collaboration in digital environments, content management, Web accessibility, and the challenges posed to copyright and intellectual property by digital technology. These topics are ideal for student-centered assignments that interconnect information literacy and information technology because students produce their own documents for the Web. Students synthesize a wide range of library and on-line resources and produce original content through the development of their own research, writing, and code.

Information Literacy

Students at the University at Albany complete a one-credit information literacy requirement as part of our general education program. Librarians teach many of the one-credit courses that fulfill this requirement. ISP301 is an upper-level, three-credit course that infuses information literacy concepts as fully integrated learning objectives in combination with a technology component. ISP301 requires students to work with library resources, both on-line and on campus, to conduct academic research. Students learn how to access Web-based resources such as the University Libraries Web-based catalog Advance, EBSCO, ArticleFirst, and on-line scholarly journals such as the *Journal of the American Society for Information Science and Technology*. Each semester, this part of the course is developed in collaboration with librarians from our research library. I work closely with library faculty to develop assignments and to discuss ways to integrate information literacy concepts in the course. Library faculty also visit ISP301 at least twice a semester to facilitate lectures focused on such topics as library research methods, specialized databases, how to navigate the library Web site, how to differentiate between scholarly, trade, and popular sources of information, and how to evaluate Web sites. Students also complete three library tutorials about research methods, evaluation of Internet resources, and prevention of plagiarism. These Web-based resources have been developed by our librarians and support the key information literacy concepts addressed in class. This collaboration between faculty and librarians is useful from a teaching standpoint, but it also models for students the interdisciplinary nature of the field and the collaborative opportunities that are possible within this framework.

The information literacy component provides a rigorous approach to academic research methods and is an effective way to bridge information theory and information technology through practice. As students gain an understanding of key information science concepts, such as information architecture, Web usability, copyright, and the digital divide, it is important for them to pursue these topics through their own research and production of original Web pages. This approach reinforces topics explored in class while providing an opportunity for students to apply research methods within an information science context. Students gain critical thinking skills through the evaluation of Web sites, scholarly journal articles accessed through on-line journals, and popular sources, such as Web sites, on-line newspapers, and magazines. They are challenged to differentiate among these different sources of information and to write a scholarly journal critique that compares a peer-reviewed scholarly journal article with at least two popular sources of information. Students work in Web teams to apply these skills toward the development of two research-oriented Web sites.

Information Technology

The information technology component of this course is focused primarily on collaborative Web development. Students learn how to produce original Web pages through the production of their own HTML, XML, and XHTML code. They also learn how to create digital images for their Web pages and how to transfer files to a UNIX environment. Rather than experience technology as a separate requirement, students in ISP301 approach information literacy through the production of their own Web documents in collaboration with others. Students evaluate a wide range of resources such as scholarly journals, newspapers, magazines, and academic Web sites, while gaining skills in Web development. This requires the ongoing integration of information theory, literacy, and technology throughout the course in lectures, readings, Web-based instructional materials, and assignments.

Lectures explore information science themes and make explicit connections through PowerPoint to Web-based resources such as information sites, media files, archival footage, and Web-based radio interviews.[23] Students are also required to read scholarly resources available through our Electronic Reserves system, which is facilitated by our library. The ISP301 Web site features an on-line syllabus, as well as a detailed timetable for every class session, due dates, readings, and hypertext links to Web-based resources.[24] This Web portal links to instructional materials for computer lab and has external links to Web-based tutorials that further support the technical procedures that we cover in class.

Expanded Role for Teaching Assistants

Teaching assistants play an important role in the course, including technology development and support. The time considerations of teaching with technology are very real, and over the past two years I have continued to expand the role of teaching assistants to help manage and support the course. With over one hundred students in ISP301 every semester, support from teaching assistants is essential, especially given the focus on such time-intensive requirements as Web development, research, writing, and collaboration. Teaching assistants attend lectures and participate in Web team discussions. They also troubleshoot student questions during my computer lab, or they teach their own sessions. They also hold office hours and respond to student questions about the course. The office hours offered by teaching assistants often resemble a "Help desk," with many questions from students about the technology. Teaching assistants also evaluate individual and Web team projects.

Teaching assistants develop Web pages that link to all of the student Web team projects. For each Web project, students create one individual Web page and participate in the development of one Web team page. This creates a visible on-line structure for students to see how their Web pages interconnect with the work of peers and instructors. For example, my ISP301 home page links to pages developed by the teaching assistant, which then link to student Web team pages and then to individual student pages. The information architecture for the ISP301 Web site illustrates collaboration at all levels. Students produce research-oriented Web sites that everyone in the class has access to through the Web team page, teaching assistant page, and the main ISP301 page. As such, the Web portal for ISP301 is not a static syllabus that simply provides a digital replica of the paper version, but rather it is a dynamic site with ongoing participation from students, teaching assistants, and instructor. This site expands as students engage with course concepts and apply research and technology skills in collaboration with peers. We build the site together over the duration of the semester. Student learning and exploration of ideas are visible on this site and reflect the ongoing development of research, writing, and code.

This approach challenges the traditional ways in which information is presented and produced in a large lecture class. In order to balance course content with research and technology, it is necessary to integrate these concepts in the lecture center and computer lab. Faculty may be reluctant to divide the time spent on traditional course content with research and technical instruction, but it is absolutely required for students to engage with theory through digital media. Spending time to teach students how to make a Web site may be seen as nonacademic work that should be covered in vocational workshops, but in order to fully integrate the technology into assignments it must be addressed as an essential component in the course. The most effective way to accomplish this is through instruction. This may be a difficult realization at first but it may lead to new ways to deliver established course content. For example, it is useful for students to examine course topics through the production of their own Web pages. Even with such extensive technology requirements, I still manage to cover a great deal of information in ISP301. At the same time, the development of technology skills allows students to make a contribution to the production of information through their own Web sites.

This approach requires a restructuring of the traditional large class into smaller sections. In my course, I developed a Web team format to facilitate student participation in lectures and to reinforce the conceptual focus on collaboration. This restructuring allows me the opportunity to work with student teams during lecture and to extend the collaborative work students complete beyond class time. Although I do present formal lectures, I also try to provide opportunities for Web teams to process and respond to this material in almost every class session. This allows for interactivity within the lecture setting and also reinforces teamwork focused on problem solving and conceptual ideas and not just on learning how to construct a Web page. The traditional lecture format is usually centered on the delivery of core concepts based on required readings, research, and disciplinary themes, topics, and definitions, but this approach must be modified to include technology instruction and interactivity. Trying to balance active learning through Web development and deliver theoretical course content is difficult in a lecture setting, but this is an opportunity to take advantage of the collaborative potential of this new medium. My approach is to teach students how to use these tools without reducing the course to a series of "how-to" workshops in Web design. This is accomplished through the ongoing intersection of theory and practice in both lecture and lab. What is most important is that students explore the tools of digital production and understand this as a process of writing and critical thinking within an information science context.

WebCT

WebCT is a course management system for faculty to post Web-based materials in a secure environment and to facilitate interactivity among students online.[25] WebCT enables faculty to make external links to Web sites, to create on-line quizzes and surveys, to post lecture notes and PowerPoint presentations, to generate student groups, to facilitate discussions through an on-line bulletin board and chat room, and to post student grades in an on-line grade book. At the University at Albany, WebCT is supported by the Center for Excellence in Teaching & Learning (CETL)[26] and Academic Computing.[27] CETL administers all WebCT course accounts and provides faculty with help desk support, documentation, instructional and best practices workshops, and one-on-one consultations centered on the pedagogical considerations of using this software. Academic Computing manages the technical infrastructure, including the server and software, and course backups, and also provides help-desk support for students.

For instructors concerned about the time commitment needed to develop on-line course materials, WebCT is an ideal interface because it provides a fairly easy-to-use point-and-click environment to develop Web-based materials and assignments. WebCT is used extensively in ISP301, and I have found it to be a flexible and robust system for posting lecture materials, grades, and links, and for facilitating communication among students. Response to this software from students has been positive, because they find easy-to-access course materials, as well as an on-line grade book that allows them to immediately see their grades, once posted. WebCT also allows me to involve teaching assistants in course development, communication, and evaluation. In WebCT, teaching assistants have the responsibility of co-instructor. They evaluate essays and bulletin board responses posted by students, and post grades for in-class assignments and homework. Teaching assistants help to maintain the grade book and respond to student questions posted on the bulletin board or sent via the private e-mail function. At times, teaching assistants enforce course policy about on-line etiquette, especially related to the messages posted on the WebCT bulletin board. Teaching assistants have their own unique identity in WebCT and their ability to instruct students is shared with me in this digital space.

PowerPoint lectures are posted in WebCT so that students can study these materials for exams or for their own curiosity. WebCT is also used to post links to resources that are not available on the ISP301 Web site, such as links to free software downloads that students may find useful for this course. For example, if students do not have PowerPoint on their computer they can download a free and legal version of the PowerPoint player from the Microsoft Home page. WebCT is a space for the exchange of ideas among students on the bulletin board. Students are required to respond to structured essay questions about core themes discussed in lecture, such as Web accessibility issues, the digital divide, and topics that emerge from readings. Given the size of the class, students are not required to respond to more than one or two other students in the bulletin board, but my goal for this assignment is for students to have a relatively spontaneous writing experience in the public space of WebCT. For me, this individualized approach to writing in a public space, which requires a reconceptualization of audience since they are not simply writing for the evaluator of their work, is more important than trying to force a conversation among 150 students. At the same time, all of the bulletin board assignments do require students to respond to at least one other student posting. Student responses in this course generally indicate that they do have a sense of what their peers contribute to this digital forum.

WebCT Survey Tool

WebCT provides a survey tool that I use to ask students specific questions about the way they perceive their own information literacy and information technology skills. At the start of the course, I survey students about their familiarity with specific technologies as well as information literacy concepts. It is invaluable to have a sense of where students are, or where they think they may be, before the course begins. Rather than assume that students have no skills in these areas, it is essential to find out what they know and adjust the course design accordingly. I share the results of the survey with the students to reinforce course objectives and to include them in the process. Students also complete an exit survey based on the same questions to assess learning outcomes. This instrument allows me to measure student skills perception and to modify the current course plan for the following semester. The exit survey is useful because it allows students to review their learning outcomes. Many of the terms that may have been unknown to students at the start of the class may be more familiar at the end of the course.

Although a similar survey could be facilitated on paper, the entrance survey reinforces the fact that ISP301 is a virtually paperless environment and that most of the work in this course takes place on-line, even though we meet face to face. Admittedly I do provide handouts on occasion for key assignments as well as for homework and in-class participation assignments. Most of the work produced by students in this course, however, is either developed for the Web or submitted via WebCT. In my view, this focus on Web development and WebCT reinforces the potential creative and collaborative possibilities of the digital environment. Students think about the production and distribution of their documents as individuals or in collaboration with peers. In some cases, these are documents for a public audience, such as a Web page or bulletin board response, but in others this information is developed and transmitted from the student to the instructor. Digital documentation provides opportunities to apply technologies in support of skills development, but more importantly to think through the production and transmission of information as a cognitive exploration.

E-Mail and Class Listserv

Several years ago it was necessary to teach students how to use e-mail. This is no longer the case, although there is still a need for teaching the responsible use of e-mail (including e-mail etiquette) and the collaborative possibilities of electronic communications. Students arrive to class with a familiarity with popular e-mail interfaces, but they are less familiar with using their e-mail accounts to apply to a group listserv or to collaborate with student teams on academic projects. The ISP301 class listserv is a convenient way for me to send announcements about grading, lectures, and further context about readings and course materials to the entire class. It is important to have such an immediate form of communication for addressing course-related issues beyond the scheduled class time.

Students are encouraged to use e-mail to communicate with their Web teams and to share files as their Web design work progresses. WebCT provides students with a private e-mail function and bulletin board exclusively for their Web teams. They also have access to a space in WebCT for file sharing. Students can upload a wide range of files to Web team directories in WebCT, including HTML and XHTML documents, digital images, and Cascading Style Sheets (CSS).[28] This allows for communication and file sharing within student Web teams for project planning, problem solving, and codevelopment. Student teams meet face to face based on their own planning needs, and they often make arrangements for their actual meetings in WebCT virtual space.

Web Team Assignments

All of the assignments in ISP301 require students to use technology in some way to locate information sources, to communicate with other students about course content and projects, and to write and/or to produce their own Web-based information documents. Students engage in a digital environment focused on the critical evaluation of information sources and the creative production of information projects. Although the specific requirements change each semester, students generally create two Web projects, with one individual page and one collaborative page for each project.

In fall 2002, students created their own Web portals to useful information sites. Students made links to five search engines and five news sites. They also linked to sites based on specific information science themes either discussed in class or discovered through their own research. Each Web team united the individual student pages through a common Web team page. The purpose of this assignment was for students to conduct on-line research to find credible and reliable Web sources of information and to organize these sites thematically. Students were encouraged to expand their search for information science topics using the BUBL Information Service.[29] This Web site provides links to professional and academic Web resources with a particular focus on library and information science, and information technology.

As students applied research methods and the critical evaluation of Web-based resources, they also learned HTML, Cascading Style Sheets, UNIX, and how to arrange information in tables, a common HTML element that allows developers to create manageable structures to organize data and format the look of the page. The Web team pages linked the individual pages thematically and created another layer of organization that allowed the class to make sense of hundreds of individual information Web portals that linked to research-oriented Web sites. This first project required students to develop effective search strategies, evaluate Web resources, explore information science topics, and participate in a large-scale collaborative Web site.

For their second project, students developed evaluation Web pages that looked critically at Web sites within specific genres, such as search engines, university sites, news sites, or library sites. Students were required to locate six sites and evaluate these sites based on the usability criteria we examined in class, such as page design, information architecture, content, and accessibility. These criteria are informed in part by some of the characteristics defined by usability expert Jakob Nielsen in his book *Designing Web Usability: The Practice of Simplicity*[30] and his Web site useit.com.[31] Students were also required to develop Web pages based on the 12 guidelines for accessibility[32] defined by the World Wide Web Consortium (W3C), with an understanding of the Web Accessibility Initiative (WAI).[33] This required students to carefully develop their HTML code and then validate their pages using the W3C's MarkUp Validation Service.[34]

The Web team assignments focused primarily on the critical evaluation of popular, professional, and academic Web sites. The information literacy objectives for this course, however, extend beyond the Web to include scholarly journal articles. In previous semesters I required students to write comprehensive research Web pages that included several sources of information. This assignment was effective because it required students to synthesize a wide range of information sources and to publish this work on the Web, but I had two concerns about this original project that led to a revision of the assignment in fall 2002. First, my sense from reading student essays in prior semesters was that the scholarly journal articles referred to in their essays were not always closely examined. I wanted to encourage a closer reading of scholarly articles through a revised assignment. I also had concerns about requiring students in such a large class to basically post their formal research papers as Web pages. With over one hundred students in this course every semester, I did not want to encourage the development of a resource for potential plagiarism. This view was shared with a few students who expressed concern about posting their writing and research sources on the Web.

Given these considerations, I designed an assignment that required students to write a scholarly journal critique focused specifically on one scholarly journal article in relation to two popular sources of information, such as newspapers and magazines. This assignment encouraged students to summarize the article, evaluate the research methods used by the author, examine the bibliography or "works cited" page, analyze the author's conclusions, and then compare the scholarly journal article with two popular sources.

Students wrote essays using their word processing program of choice, and then they submitted these files to the secure environment of WebCT. This assignment required students to apply their research and critical thinking skills in the evaluation of three sources, with a particular focus on a scholarly journal article. They were also required to gain an understanding of how to transfer files in the WebCT environment.

In many ways this assignment proved to be more difficult than the collaborative Web projects. Although the specific focus on one scholarly journal article did result in many essays that examined the journal articles directly, most of the essays summarized the articles without a close or critical reading. The emphasis on fewer resources did not generally result in more complex readings and may have contributed to more superficial responses. In addition, the file transfer process in WebCT seemed to be more confusing to some students than transferring files to UNIX, although this may have been the case because we spent more time doing so in UNIX than in WebCT. In addition, without a collaborative requirement this assignment seemed to reinforce a traditional format where individual essays were disconnected in a closed, secure space for the instructor that prevented student-centered peer review. This assignment interconnected the core information themes in this course, i.e., theory, literacy, and technology, but the audience for this work was limited to the instructor and teaching assistants. Some of the confusion about how to upload files in WebCT and how to critically evaluate a scholarly journal article must be addressed in future revisions of this assignment. Although students did engage in an important evaluative process through their research and writing, this assignment did not always contribute to a deeper understanding of the content examined. In a few cases, the file transfer process in WebCT may have prevented a focus on content and communication in digital environments through confusing interface usability.

Web Design as Literacy

As soon as I learned the basics of HTML, I realized that the process of making Web pages allowed me to think in new ways about the textual, visual, and conceptual associations in my writing and to participate in an emerging new medium, the World Wide Web. My experiential insights at the time were supported and encouraged by an examination of hypertext and postmodern theory in the fields of English Studies and Art History. Teaching with the Web provided an opportunity to put theory into practice for my own interdisciplinary explorations, pedagogical interests, and professional development.

The participatory aspect of this process still generates excitement and curiosity in the classroom. Learning HTML, digital imaging, JavaScript, or any other creative digital media is not so much about acquiring a portfolio of disconnected technology skills, but rather, about learning a new literacy that places one in conversation with others. Students in an information science program are particularly interested in learning about technology, but in my prior experience teaching Human Diversity, Composition, and in Project Renaissance—an interdisciplinary program for first-year students at the University at Albany—I have found that students with a wide range of interests are eager to explore ideas through the development of Web sites.

Although technologies are always changing and access continues to be an issue, we need to learn and teach these tools and to think about the context for each application. In ISP301, it is important for me to foreground the specific technologies students will learn and to provide a meaningful context for why we are using them. It is also important to try to demystify the technologies somewhat and to help students gain confidence in learning this new language. The primary goal of the course is focused on how students understand information from a variety of media sources and how they produce new information in collaboration with others. This requires the codevelopment of information theory, literacy, and technology.

Digital Intersections

By framing this case study within a discussion of technology and tenure review, my primary goal is to expand the conversation beyond questions of faculty publication and presentation in print or digital forms to include an analysis of the intersections among teaching, research, and service through student-centered collaborative Web development. I do not see my own technology development and teaching in ISP301 as publication, but I do see it as an opportunity for research and publication in print and/or digital forms. The sense I have from my own institution is that teaching with technology is valued, but I would not expect my work in this area to count toward or as publication in a tenure review decision. At the same time, without clearly defined and scalable guidelines across institutions of higher learning it is difficult to tell how this approach to teaching is generally understood or evaluated in any context.

I am not arguing that this work should be given special consideration because it takes a great deal of time to develop a course with technology, even though it does. Faculty members who are committed to other theoretical perspectives have the potential to spend as much time thinking through and developing courses as those who use technology. What I am arguing for, however, is a discourse that considers the value of teaching with technology as a way to engage students in critical thinking, collaborative writing, and the original production of digital information. We also need guidelines to help define the importance of this work in the classroom and to encourage faculty to use digital media in their teaching across the curriculum to advance educational goals.

Practical considerations in the profession require faculty to successfully prepare for tenure review with a clear understanding of the guidelines that will be used in the evaluation of their work. This is a professional development opportunity that should reflect a wide range of faculty activities and effectively encourage technological innovation in teaching, research, and service.

Notes

1. Jeffrey R. Young, "Ever So Slowly, Colleges Start to Count Work with Technology in Tenure Decisions," *Chronicle of Higher Education*, February 2002, chronicle.com/.

2. Michael Day, "Teachers at the Crossroads: Evaluating Teaching in Electronic Environments," *Computers and Composition* (2000): 31.

3. Dianne Lynch, "Professors Should Embrace Technology in Courses. . . ," *Chronicle of Higher Education*, January 18, 2002.

4. Ibid.

5. Young, "Ever So Slowly," 1.

6. George P. Landow, *Hypertext: The Convergence of Contemporary Critical Theory and Technology* (Baltimore, MD: Johns Hopkins University Press, 1992), 123.

7. Ibid.

8. Ibid.

9. Jay David Bolter, *Writing Space: The Computer, Hypertext, and the History of Writing* (Hillsdale, NJ: Lawrence Erlbaum Associates, 1991), 10.

10. Ibid.

11. Richard A. Lanham, *The Electronic Word: Democracy, Technology, and the Arts* (Chicago: University of Chicago Press, 1993), 107.

12. Ibid.

13. See www.eastgate.com/catalog/Afternoon.html.

14. Michael Joyce, *Of Two Minds: Hypertext, Pedagogy, and Poetics* (Ann Arbor: University of Michigan Press, 1995), 20.

15. Ibid.

16. See www.w3.org/Consortium/#background.

17. Tim Berners-Lee, *Weaving the Web: The Original Design and Ultimate Destiny of the World Wide Web* (New York: HarperCollins, 2000), 28–29.

18. Ibid., 57.

19. Charles Jonscher, *The Evolution of Wired Life: From the Alphabet to the Soul-Catcher Chip—How Information Technologies Change Our World* (New York: John Wiley & Sons, 1999), 175–176.

20. Ibid., 176.

21. Lynch, "Professors Should Embrace Technology in Courses," 1. For more information about the Campus Computing Project, see www.campuscomputing.net/.

22. Ibid., 2–3.

23. See www.npr.org.

24. See www.albany.edu/~mackey/isp301.

25. See www.Webct.com.

26. See www.albany.edu/cetl.

27. See www.albany.edu/computing/.

28. Cascading Style Sheets (CSS) allow Web developers to separate styles such as fonts, background colors, table borders, and so on from the actual content of an HTML, XML, or XHTML document. This can be done using external style sheets, embedded styles, or inline styles. CSS is a recommendation from the World Wide Web Consortium (W3C) and provides Web developers with control over the presentation of Web documents by linking to a separate file with a .css extension or from within the document in the head or within separate elements. For more information about CSS, see www.w3.org/Style/CSS/.

29. See bubl.ac.uk/.

30. Jakob Nielsen, *Designing Web Usability: The Practice of Simplicity* (Indianapolis, IN: New Riders, 2000), 15.

31. See www.useit.com.

32. W3C defined 12 guidelines for Web developers to make their pages accessible to individuals with disabilities. Requiring students to make their pages Web-compliant based on these guidelines is an effective way to extend the scope of Web design beyond the how-to of making Web pages to more complex policy issues and considerations related to human experience with technology. At the same time, this requirement emphasizes the importance of developing clean code and understanding the syntax of the code in relation to presentation and audience. For more information about the W3C guidelines for Web accessibility, see www.w3.org/TR/UAAG10/.

33. As part of its mission to improve Web accessibility, W3C established the Web Accessibility Initiative (WAI), which provides guidelines and resources for Web developers interested in making sites accessible for individuals with disabilities. For more information about the WAI, see www.w3.org/WAI/.

34. Students check their code for syntax errors and conformance to the Web accessibility guidelines via the W3C MarkUp Validation Service that allows students to validate their files. For more information about the W3C MarkUp Validation Service, see validator.w3.org/.

Chapter 7

Technology in the Classroom

A United Kingdom Experience

Ian G. Anderson

Computers in History Teaching

Today almost all historians use a computer in some aspect of their work. Even if it is simply word processing or e-mail, many do so in their teaching, and some make intensive use of computers in research. These historians are likely to fall into one of three categories: those who make no use of computers in their research or teaching, those who use computers in their research but not in teaching, and those who have caught the Internet bug and are seeking to make more use of this technology. For tenure-track historians, there may well appear to be more pressing priorities than using computers in their teaching. This chapter might persuade those who make no use of computers in their teaching that their promotion prospects will improve if they do. For those who have already taken the first steps down this route, this chapter provides a pedagogic framework in which to effectively integrate computers into history teaching. Moreover, this chapter goes a long way toward ensuring that historians can prove that using computers in their teaching is effective through evaluation. It is hoped that this strategy will help scholars make the most of computers in the classroom, whatever the extent to which they are deployed.

This chapter draws extensively on developments in practice in U.K. higher education as well as on the author's experience of designing history courseware and teaching history courses that make use of computers. Particularly important sources have been surveys of developments in history teaching, national benchmark criteria for teaching quality review, and recent research on implementation strategies for integrating Information and Communication Technology (ICT) into history teaching. Although based on U.K. experience, it is hoped that the ideas presented here are sufficiently generic to transcend national or institutional boundaries.

Why Use Computers in History Teaching?

Historians today face a very different educational environment than did their predecessors. As students are increasingly seen as consumers of educational services, universities become more mass—rather than elite—education systems (at least state-supported universities), and as the relevance of university education to a rapidly changing employment market is increasingly scrutinized, the purpose, range, and quality of teaching becomes more significant. Certainly the political agenda has increasingly sought to justify university education on utilitarian grounds—the educational equivalent of asking what it costs, not what it is worth.

To many, these are not desirable circumstances, but it is in this context that introducing computers to history teaching can be seen as an easy way in which to make history more relevant to employers' needs, more attractive to students, and "proof" of the usefulness of history teaching to those outside of academia. However, as Spaeth and Cameron point out, these are not arguments that advocates of historical computing are most likely to use or that other historians are likely to find most persuasive.[1] Using computers in history teaching does provide useful transferable skills, but only to some students, in some circumstances, and using certain applications. Many students have sufficient computing skills from their pre-university experience, and those who do not are often better served by basic computing skills courses. Nor do most computer programs in use in history, such as Web browsers, require a great deal of expertise to operate. Furthermore, computer skills are just one transferable tool that history students can acquire in pursuing their degree. Second languages, group work, writing, and oral presentation are just some of the other skills that students can develop. Rather, the strongest justification for using computers in history teaching is that it helps students become better at understanding historical subjects and the historical process, makes historical study more interesting (perhaps even fun), and makes history teaching more rewarding.

Using computers does not mean throwing the historical baby out with the bathwater. Using computers in the classroom complements, not replaces, traditional teaching methods, helps reinforce, not diminish, historical understanding, and enhances, not reduces, other transferable skills. The student using computers to study Western civilization is no less likely to have to attend lectures, seminars, or tutorials to demonstrate a thorough understanding of the subject or to write term papers. Computers are not a panacea to the challenges facing the discipline nor are they a technological Trojan horse.[2] This chapter seeks to persuade the reader that the computer can help to enhance the learning and teaching of history.

For historians involved in the stressful tenure process, using computers in their teaching may seem a luxury they can ill afford. Introducing new technology and experimenting with new pedagogies may seem something that only the security of a tenured professorship would allow. Tenure-track historians may well see their main priorities as research and publication, with teaching new courses, or introducing new technology into them, as a secondary concern.

While research and publication are important and necessary factors in securing tenure, they are not in themselves sufficient. A portfolio of evidence needs to be provided and should include distinct courses that are able to attract students (and not just away from other history courses) and that are positively evaluated. Therefore, tenure-track professors who neglect the range and quality of the teaching they provide do so at their peril.

In one important respect, the environment of U.S. historians will be different from their U.K. counterparts. Until the advent of the World Wide Web, there was less of a tradition of using computers in history teaching in the U.S. compared to the U.K. Historical computing in U.S. institutions was almost exclusively associated with high-level quantitative analysis, using statistical programs such as SPSS. In the U.K., the overwhelming majority of history courses that used computers were using database packages by the 1990s, and little emphasis was placed on quantitative techniques beyond simple descriptive statistics.[3] Parallel to this development, and aided by it, was the progression of historical computing courses from the postgraduate to the undergraduate curriculum. As database packages became easier to use, students were able to analyze primary sources more thoroughly, without having to learn advanced computing or statistical techniques that were most appropriate for postgraduate research training. In contrast, U.S. institutions persisted with statistical programs and made less use of databases. As Spaeth and Cameron point out, there were valid cultural and organizational reasons for this, history being considered as a social science rather than a humanities subject and the more flexible U.S. degree structure being the most significant. The advent of the World Wide Web has opened the eyes of many historians to the potential benefits of computer technology. However, it is easy to forget that not all faculty have been swept up in the computing revolution.

In what Mawdsley and Munck have termed the first computer revolution, the advent of powerful mainframe computers heralded a new age of historical research to the minority of vocal converts.[4] Whether called cliometrics, scientific history, quantification, "new" history, econometrics, or social science history, the use of computers in history has not easily shaken off its association with quantification and the impression that it is only a number-crunching machine.[5] Although many U.S. institutions skipped the database phase of U.K. universities, U.S. historians were quicker and more enthusiastic adopters of the Web. This has done much to the number-crunching notion, but historians seeking to diversify the computer applications they use beyond the Web may still encounter similar arguments—that using a computer diverts students from the periods, events, people, or places they are supposed to be studying. Worse still is the argument that it distances history students from the process of constructing historical understanding itself.[6]

Developments in computer applications have largely mitigated these factors. Even powerful database management systems such as Access are easy enough to use for students to start making meaningful analyses without prolonged technical training. Spreadsheet programs are able to perform sophisticated statistical analysis, and even SPSS is more user friendly today. Moreover, as subsequent sections of this chapter seek to demonstrate, using such applications brings students closer to the subjects they are studying and makes them more aware of the processes and methods historians use. This is achieved through aligning the use of computers with particular learning outcomes and ensuring that these are assessed and evaluated appropriately. While historians have always been aware of the learning outcomes that the study of history sought to achieve, it is only in recent years that these have been stated explicitly and reconsidered in the context of higher education.

History Today

A 1987 study of the undergraduate curriculum in U.K. Higher Education concluded that, "history remains one of the subjects least susceptible to external manipulation."[7] Fifteen years later, history is no less susceptible than any other subject to the rapidly changing circumstances in which it operates. Funding per student has fallen as student numbers and staff-student ratios have increased; library funding has fallen, dramatically in real terms; the demands, prior experience, and expectations of students have become increasingly influential; new regimes of research and teaching quality review have been introduced; modularization of undergraduate degrees has become almost universal; and great advances in information technology have been made. The details of these changes may be unique to the U.K., and many have been controversial, but most are familiar trends in higher education institutions in the developed world.

Of these changes, the increased use of information technology in the history classroom is one of the most significant. Of course, historians have been using computers in their teaching almost as long as in their research. At the University of Glasgow, a dedicated computer lab for history teaching was established in 1985.[8] Undergraduate options in computing for historians continue to this day, as do specialized postgraduate courses. Glasgow also housed a number of national initiatives promoting the use of information technology in history.[9] Glasgow's experience is by no means unique, and there is a wealth of experience on effective educational practice on which to draw on both sides of the Atlantic. The dissemination of this experience through organizations such as the Association for History and Computing (AHA) has aided the organic growth of computers in history teaching from the 1980s.

Supply-side factors have also driven some of the increased use of computers in history. Hardware and software advances and the widespread availability of electronic and digital resources for historians, particularly since the advent of the World Wide Web, have also been major factors. On the demand side, students have identified some level of computing use as an essential transferable skill. In departmental teaching quality reviews, the use of ICT is one of the evaluative criteria encouraging faculty to adopt computer technologies. However, a more significant factor in the increased use of computers in history teaching in the U.K. has been changing attitudes about the purpose of history teaching.

There have always been faculty who have critically reflected on the nature of history teaching and the skills with which it aims to equip students. It has also been a discipline open to change, but this has been predominantly at the instigation of individual historians, developing their research and teaching interests within the confines of their own courses. However, the predominant attitude reported in 1987 (certainly among the larger, more established departments) was that the goals of history teaching were self-evident, that explicit skills did not need to be taught, particularly employment-related ones such as ICT, and that the cultural value of history was a self-sufficient objective.[10] By 2002 one of the most pronounced changes occurred in the way in which the purpose of history teaching is perceived. There is greater emphasis on transferable and study skills and more diversity in teaching methods. Independent, active, student-centered, and resource-based learning all feature more heavily in today's predominantly constructivist learning environment. Even within the more "traditional" departments, the linking of teaching aims and learning outcomes with content, teaching methods, and assessment is far more explicit.

The catalyst for many of these changes in the U.K. was the introduction of independent, national, subject-based teaching quality assessment (TQA). This was perhaps the most controversial development of the 1990s and has only just been abandoned in favor of institution-led review. Nevertheless, this development forced historians, whether they liked it or not, to think more closely about what history teaching was supposed to achieve, to state this explicitly, and to document and evaluate their teaching aims, learning outcomes, methods, and forms of assessment.

Simultaneous to the development of national teaching quality review was a relentless drive to increase participation in higher education under both the Conservative and Labour governments. Under Conservative government, the emphasis was on increasing the numbers participating in higher education. Under Labour government, the desire for increased participation has continued, but the emphasis has shifted to broadening participation to include those traditionally underrepresented in the student population. This includes students from less advantaged backgrounds, ethnic minorities, and mature students.

As a result of these pressures, questions that had concerned a few historians became the concern of many. What is the purpose of studying history? What skills and understanding do historians expect of students? What are the transferable skills historical study develops? What learning skills do students acquire? How can history teaching cater to an increasingly diverse student body? Within these broad questions was consideration of the role of computers in teaching history. What is the use of computers in history? How important is it? What learning outcomes can the use of computers facilitate? Are these learning outcomes restricted to transferable IT skills? Can the use of computers assist the development of other learning outcomes in history? What role can computers play in providing effective, inclusive, and flexible learning environments?

Theory into Practice

The increased attention paid to questions about the purpose of history teaching has led to an affirmation of the traditional benefits of historical study and a more coherent expression of the transferable and study skills students acquire. Consideration of these skills is an important starting point to introducing computers to the history classroom or making the most effective use of existing provision. It is the first stage in an iterative and critically reflective process by which aims, outcomes, course content, teaching methods, and assessment can be aligned. This process makes no apologies for being essentially constructivist in theory. It sees historical knowledge and understanding not as external and independent of the learner (as objectivists/positivists would contend) but something students actively construct for themselves.[11] This approach does not seek to impose a particular version of constructivism but to align theories of practice with the practice of teaching history with computers.

The first stage of this process is consideration of the intended learning outcomes. Such a back-to-basics approach may seem excessive, but unless the intended learning outcomes are fully espoused it is far harder to align these correctly and hence to furnish credible evidence to support claims for the effective use of computers. Therefore, this stage is fundamental for those seeking to use computers appropriately and effectively in their teaching.

In the 1993–94 higher education quality assessment review of history the *Overview Report* commented that:

> Learning outcomes for history programmes typically include analytical skills, critical evaluation, problem solving, independent thinking, synthesis of complex information, and written communication, as well as specialist knowledge. Other transferable skills, such as oral communication, presentation, and the ability to work in teams are also identified as learning outcomes.[12]

However, in the mid-1990s, historians had yet to fully embrace the aims of history education expressed in terms of learning and transferable skills. The *Overview Report* goes on to say that, "There was considerable variation in the extent to which a commitment to the development of these (skills) was evident in curriculum design, classes observed, and assessment methods."[13]

In terms of constructivist theory, the *Overview Report* found a misalignment of outcomes, content, and assessment. Ensuring that outcomes, content, and assessment are aligned, reviewed, and evaluated is not just good educational practice but is vital for the promotion, tenure, and review process because it enables faculty to provide *substantive evidence* of good practice in the use of computers. Of particular importance is establishing a clear link between learning outcomes and assessment, as it is the appropriate assessment of learning outcomes that provides particularly compelling evidence. Without it, faculty are unable to prove that students have achieved the learning outcome or that computers have assisted in this process. The assessment itself does not need to be extensive or count toward students' final grades, but students generally perform better when a learning outcome is assessed. This applies to all learning outcomes but is particularly important with learning and teaching innovation where the expected benefits need to be demonstrated in practice.

The following scenario provides a simple example of how this process can operate. By 2000, the national Quality Assurance Agency had developed a comprehensive set of generic skills. The so-called benchmarking standard identified the following skills to be acquired through the study of history:

- Self-discipline;
- Self-direction;
- Independence of mind, and initiative;
- Ability to work with others, and have respect for others' reasoned views;
- Ability to gather, organize and deploy evidence, data and information; and familiarity with appropriate means of identifying, finding, retrieving, sorting and exchanging information;
- Analytical ability, and the capacity to consider and solve problems, including complex problems;

- Structure, coherence, clarity and fluency of oral expression;
- Structure, coherence, clarity and fluency of written expression;
- Intellectual integrity and maturity;
- Empathy and imaginative insight.[14]

This "benchmarking-standard" is used here to represent a fairly typical and generic skill set. Although the benchmarking standard does not make any specific recommendation as to how these skills should be taught, there is at least one clear case where the use of computers would be highly appropriate. It is difficult to imagine in today's networked environment students being able to "identify, find, retrieve, sort or exchange information" without resorting to electronic library catalogues, on-line finding aids, search engines, e-mail, distribution lists, or on-line discussion groups and bulletin boards. The QAA's benchmarking-standard goes on to mention the "use of information technology for bibliographic and archive searches" as one of the means by which students could have their analytical and communication skills assessed.[15] In this scenario there is a clear case where one can align an intended learning outcome and assessment.

Therefore, if a course includes an information-retrieval learning outcome, there is an immediate starting point for using computers. This could be accomplished in a number of ways. One might ask students to locate specified texts or sources via the library catalogue, searching other institutions' OPACs, on-line archival finding aids, or Web sites. Students could be asked to locate materials that would require the use of more than one information retrieval method. They could note which method or methods they used, how long it took, and how effective they thought it was. These answers could be written down, e-mailed to the tutor, or shared on an electronic bulletin board. Assessment could be carried out by the tutor or by students' peers. Criteria for this assessment could include: Did students find the resources requested? Did they use an appropriate retrieval method? Were they able to evaluate its effectiveness? and Were they able to share this information? Such an exercise would be particularly appropriate for students in their first year of study. It would promote familiarization with important information sources and overcome the problem of students managing to avoid any contact with the library for as long as possible.

Even a simple exercise like this can be developed further. One of the skills identified in the "benchmarking-standard" is analytical ability. Analytical ability can be demonstrated in many ways, through tutorial discussions, term papers, presentations, examinations, and project work. A method that makes use of computers is to ask students not only to locate material but also to consider its authenticity and credibility. With increased use of the

World Wide Web by students, an exercise that analyzes the material they find can be particularly valuable. There persists among students an inherent faith in on-line material that they would not grant to print.

As an example of how effective this can be, the reader can try this exercise.[16] Go to a Web search engine—Google is particularly good, as it allows one to search specifically for images—and see how many unique images of the Magna Carta can be found. At the last count, there were at least 17. This, of course, raises the question, "Which image is of the real Magna Carta?" One can easily dismiss the $19.99 versions available with an optional, and no doubt tasteful, mahogany-effect frame. Likewise, one can dismiss the multitudinous versions supposedly embellished with the coats of arms of the Barons present at the signing in Runnymede. This still leaves a number of fairly promising candidates, Ross Perot's eponymous version among them. There are images of the Magna Carta in the British Library, the Bodleian Library at Oxford, Salisbury Cathedral, the Library of Congress, and the National Library of Norway. These are all reputable institutions—which of these holds the "real" Magna Carta? Of course, the point of this exercise is to demonstrate that there is no single version of the Magna Carta. It has been revised several times since it was first written in 1225, and even the first version was duplicated in order for it to be proclaimed simultaneously in different locations.

If one changes this exercise to a standard Web search instead of just for images, one will also find numerous transcriptions and translations. This raises further questions for students. What version of the Magna Carta is being transcribed or translated? By whom? Why? When? What are the credentials of the individual and/or institution responsible? Can one actually find any of this information? Such questions may be most appropriate to medieval history or methods courses, but this exercise can be adapted to any course where one wants to pique students' critical faculties, particularly in regard to on-line sources. Of course, there are ways in which this can be done using noncomputing methods, but this exercise makes good use of the range and variability of information hitherto inaccessible without the use of the World Wide Web.

A variation of this exercise is used at Glasgow University for a class of masters students. This is a typical one-year masters course, with a dissertation component leading to an MPhil in History qualification. The purpose of the session is twofold. The first, nonassessed component is designed to introduce students to a range of on-line information sources and to challenge students to think about the authenticity and credibility of the sources they find. The second component is an optional assessed exercise to be completed in the students' own time. They are asked to locate sources on a historical topic of their choice and to evaluate the retrieval strategies they used and the provenance of the sources they located. This is to be presented in a brief report of not more than 500 words. The class takes place in a single, supervised, two-hour lab session where students are provided with a hand-out listing the sites to visit, the sources to locate, and some of the questions they should ask of them. The sites include data and text archives, Web sites, and discussion groups. Prior to commencing the lab work, students are briefed with a twenty-minute overview of modernist and post-modernist approaches to source reliability in order to provide a theoretical context. This comple-ments similar sessions provided by the university library and archives.

The examples provided above make use of nothing more complicated than a Web browser. They can all be integrated into courses quickly and easily, can relate to both transferable skills and historical learning outcomes, and can be expanded to provide resource-based, independent learning. At-tainment of the learning outcomes could be assessed specifically or as a com-ponent of a traditional assessment such as a paper or project.

However, the examples above make limited use of the potential of com-puters. More intensive use of computers can be made to bring students closer to the subjects they are studying, support a wider range of learning outcomes, and deepen IT skills.

Expanding Horizons

Expanding the use of computers in the history classroom does require greater planning, resources, and technical knowledge; but the rewards can be great, and the same model of establishing outcomes, assessment, content, and teach-ing method can be used. This section presents examples of computer use in support of both historical learning outcomes and more advanced ICT skills. This approach is reflected in the QAA's benchmark statement, where the assessment section includes the recommendation that departments consider students having their critical and communication skills assessed by the "use of information technology to answer questions about historical data, includ-ing statistical and/or graphical analysis of historical data sets and to present findings in a variety of appropriate forms (bar graphs, pie charts, etc.)."[17] The key feature here is that it is the students' critical and communication skills that are being assessed. Transferable ICT skills are a desirable benefit, but it is the critical historical skills that are primary.

This "computer as a tool" approach is by far the most typical intense use of computers in history and can be applied to different levels of study. At Glasgow University, second-year economic and social history students take two, hour-long sessions in which to work in the computer lab instead of traditional tutorials.

Table 7.1

Extract from Census Worksheet

HOUSEHOLDS AND SERVANTS [QS 1–5 1 MARK EACH; Q 6, 2 MARKS; Q 7, 4 MARKS; QS 8–9, 2 MARKS EACH. TOTAL = 13 MARKS]

	GORBALS	SANDYFORD
(1) How many individuals were listed as 'heads' of households?		
(2) How many individuals were listed as servants of these heads?		
(3) How many servants were female?		
(4) How many female servants were under 25?		
(5) How many servants were Scottish born, but came from areas outside Glasgow and its adjacent counties?		
(6) What % of female servants were single?		
(7) Did the servants in **Gorbals** work in the households they lived in? Comment.		
(8) The servants in **Sandyford** were not all doing the same type of work. What were the three most common types of work they did?		
(9) Were Irish people likely to get a job as domestic servants in Sandyford? Comment.		

The table above asks about household composition in both districts.

Suggestion: For finding servants in **Gorbals**, you will have to use RELN; but in **Sandyford**, you will find it easier to use RELCOD. Find out before you begin how the Sandyford servants in RELCOD are coded. (You will have to use SCH, RELN, and RELCOD to do this.)

These second-year students study a survey course on British economic and social history and use the lab sessions to study a subset of census enumerators' returns for two contrasting districts of Glasgow—the Gorbals and Sandyford areas. The enumerators' returns are held in two, unrelated, flat files in a Microsoft Access 2000 database. Each file contains just over 400 records, sufficient for students' results to have some meaning, but not an intimidating or unmanageable set of data.

Students are provided with detailed handouts that take them from opening the databases through a variety of queries designed to illustrate both the strengths and weaknesses of the source of computerized historical data and of the type of historical enquiry possible. Students are then provided with a comprehensive worksheet that asks them to answer a series of questions on household and family structures, employment, and social status. Students are required to provide these answers as well as the queries they used to arrive at them. A set of questions from the worksheet is provided in Table 7.1.[18]

At the end of the worksheet, students write a 1,000–word report. They are asked to consider the results from the worksheet and their implications, to compare the two districts, and to comment on the differences and on any limitations of the census database as a historical source. Marks are mainly given for students demonstrating that they are able to reach historical conclusions from the data on the nature of households in the two areas, and for students' assessment of the strengths and weaknesses of using the database. Both this report and the students' completed worksheets are assessed coursework.

The assessment tests both students' ability to use database software and their capacity to follow lines of historical enquiry, marshal evidence, present it coherently, and evaluate the strengths and weaknesses of the methods they used. Second-year students go on to undertake simple statistical analysis using Microsoft Excel in their second term, building on the ICT skills developed in term the first and furthering the range of methods available to them for historical enquiry. These database exercises have proved immensely valuable and durable. Commitment to the use of ICT was praised in the 1996 teaching quality review of history at Glasgow, particularly by economic and social history.[19]

Honors-level students at Glasgow (third and fourth years in the Scottish system) have further opportunity to specialize through two honors modules on studying history with computers.[20] Comparing and contrasting these two modules demonstrate similar teaching methods, sources, and assessment formats but different learning outcomes. The modules are "Studying History with Computers" and "Data Modelling and Representation for Historians." Both modules run for ten weeks, comprising 20 hours of lectures and 20 hours of labs. In both modules, students explore a variety of data derived from census enumerators' returns, the Doomsday book, probate records, court records, and poll books. In both modules, students also have the same form of assessment. Their coursework is continually assessed through a combination of project preparation work (25 percent), group presentation (15 percent), and database project and report (60 percent).

In spite of these similarities, the two modules have subtle but distinct differences in what they hope students will achieve. The "Studying History with Computers" module emphasizes how computers can be used to explore historical problems and debates as well as examining historical analysis and methods. The learning outcomes for this course are stated below.

Learning Outcomes for Studying History with Computers

Students who successfully complete the module should be able to:

1. Understand the main forms of computer-aided analysis used by historians, particularly their use of database management and statistical software, and be able to evaluate interpretations based upon such evidence.

2. Be familiar with the census and with other sources which historians have analyzed with the help of the computer, and understand the limitations and irregularities of such sources and methods of analyzing them.

3. Be able to retrieve information from simple and complex historical databases in order to address historical questions.

4. Be able to use spreadsheets and other software, as appropriate, to present data and to conduct more rigorous quantitative analysis.

5. Be able to use computer-based data to address historical issues and interpretations.

6. Write a clear and well-supported extended essay based upon computer-based and other evidence, using graphs and tables where appropriate, and

7. Be able to work productively as a member of a small team.[21]

In these learning outcomes, computer skills are well to the fore, but the ultimate aim is to further historical analysis and interpretation. In the "Data Modelling and Representation for Historians" option, the aim is not on the analysis and interpretation of historical questions or debates. Instead, the primary learning outcomes are for students to understand the nature of historical sources, in particular their structure and relationships, the type and nature of the data they contain, modernist and post-modernist methodologies, how to model sources, understand the principles of database design and implementation, and how to represent data in a variety of graphical and tabular formats. Students are still expected to develop the historian's skills in source analysis and interpretation but through the study of them as data types. Therefore, understanding data types, database structures, and methods for data modeling come to the fore. The learning outcomes for "Data Modelling and Representation" are provided below.

Learning Outcomes for Data Modeling and Representation

After completing the module, students should be able to:

1. Identify existing and potential applications of databases in research.

2. Identify strengths and weaknesses in original data sources, and be able to employ strategies for dealing with the data irregularities.

3. Identify the advantages and shortcomings of different database systems.

4. Be able to design and create databases using data modeling techniques.

5. Apply the skills they have acquired to the planning, design, and analysis of a historical database.

6. Determine the time and cost involved in database creation and data entry.
7. Retrieve information from simple and complex historical databases in order to address historical questions.
8. Document a database according to recognized standards.
9. Recognize the principles of good data representation.
10. Represent quantitative data in an appropriate tabular or graphical format, and
11. Manage and carry out an independent project, including writing a clear and well-supported extended report.

Placing greater emphasis on the techniques of modeling and representation, rather than analysis and interpretation, is not typical, and may be unique. Nevertheless, it remains a valid approach to using computers in history because, like "Historical Study with Computers," it still sees the computer as a tool to assist historical inquiry and not as an end in itself.

The examples above have all used databases and spreadsheets as the computer application in the classroom. Indeed, in many eyes, historical computing is synonymous with databases and quantitative analysis. However, the computer offers today's historian a far greater range of possibilities than the analysis of structured or semistructured data. Above all, history is a textual discipline, and the use of computers as a tool for textual analysis is sorely underutilized. Seminal work such as Mosteller and Wallace's analysis of the *Federalist Papers* to try to resolve questions of authorship attribution are reminders of the potential for content analysis of historical texts.[22]

Nor does using computers for textual analyses require a great deal of innovation. There are a number of well-established applications, such as TACT and Wordsmith, that have been exploited to great effect by literary and linguistic scholars for many years. Part of the explanation for the underutilization of computer textual analysis programs is a belief that computer use forces upon the historian a quantitative methodology. This is no longer the case for structured data sources let alone free-flowing prose. Computer-aided textual analysis does not force any sort of methodology upon the historian or the history student.

For a number of years the computer analysis of the *Federalist Papers* was a significant component of Glasgow's MPhil in History and Computing. Here students spent a large part of their second term of study following in the footsteps of Mosteller and Wallace using the freely available TACT software. Once students overcame the shock at using a keyboard-controlled DOS interface, creating and analyzing their own electronic textbases was no more complicated than using databases. The ability to generate instantaneous word indexes and word frequencies, see selected keywords in context, and create collocations, concordances, and statistical measures of stylistic and vocabulary patterns provides students with new and meaningful insights into historical sources. Although the computer-assisted analysis of texts has infrequently permeated the undergraduate level, there is no reason why it should not. Arguably it has more relevance to historical inquiry than database management systems and statistical analysis.

So far, this section has concentrated on computer applications that have made the transition from historical research to history teaching. Beyond these, a range of other uses of the computer in the history classroom that has burgeoned in recent years. One such area is the use of computers to support student work with primary source material. The QAA's benchmarking statement for history makes the following recommendation in relation to course content:

> Opportunity for close work on source material originating in the period studied is essential. This will often comprise written documents, but when appropriate will include artifacts, visual evidence, etc. Students should carry out intensive critical work on such source material. This may take place in a "Special Subject" course, in other courses or in independent work. In many instances the work done by students approximates to historical research. We note that most students do not expect a career in research, but we nevertheless regard documentary work as a necessary part of learning some of the characteristics of the discipline.[23]

In relation to assessment, the QAA goes on to recommend that students "should be assessed in some way or another on their understanding of and their ability to handle primary source material."[24] This is one development that has been embraced by history teachers in the U.K., and students' working with primary sources is now a common component of the undergraduate history degree, whether this is provided as part of a sources and methods course or as a special subject.

Typically, sources in an institution's own library—special collections or archives—are used. In some cases facsimiles of research material held further afield are accessed—material held in local museums, archives, and libraries. In relation to the overall learning outcomes of history, the benefits of such work are clear. It provides another opportunity for students to develop critical and analytical skills and provides an invaluable insight into the processes and methods that shape the discourses in secondary historical literature. However, there are problems with this form of study. While students are generally excited at the prospect of handling primary sources, they can easily become frustrated. This frustration is not only with the challenges that the sources themselves present but also with the purpose of such work. As the QAA states, such work often approximates to historical research yet the majority of students do not go on to be professional historians. There are two ways one can respond to the question, "why are we doing this?" The first is that extracting, synthesizing, and forming conclusions on imperfect and incomplete information not only enhances historical understanding but also is a valuable transferable skill. The second is to further enhance the skills developed through working with primary sources by combining it with computing work.

The history department at Dickinson College, Pennsylvania, takes just such an approach. Over the past five years John Osborne has extended a long-running, entry-level historical-methods course to include students producing on-line digital collections in collaboration with James Gerencser, the university archivist.[25] As a result, students not only gain the benefits of working with primary sources but also acquire elementary skills in digitization, HTML markup, Web design, and on-line publishing, and a sense of investment in their work through the production of a tangible outcome. In this approach the historical skills are very much to the fore. Ultimately, the process and methods count, rather than the end product. The course does not pretend to teach students digitization or Web design but provides faculty and students alike with meaningful engagement in the topic while keeping pace with technical developments.[26]

Aside from these developments, the greatest expansion in the use of computers in the history classroom has been in the use of on-line and electronic resources, often in conjunction with on-line learning environments. The development of ever more sophisticated e-learning environments, production of digital history programs, and the growing number of historical sites and resources on the Internet have opened up the possibility for entire history programs to be delivered by computer. Although this last scenario is unlikely outside of distance education, there remain huge possibilities for enhancing student learning and catering to the ever more diverse student body. There is a vast array of on-line resources available to today's historian, and it is not possible here to even begin to scratch the surface. For those seeking on-line material for teaching there is no better starting point than Trinkle and Merriman's *The History Highway*.[27]

In relation to the learning outcomes identified here, the use of on-line resources can support almost any or all of them. What on-line resources do best is support learning that takes advantage of the inherent benefits of the Web, bringing together disparate and geographically dispersed material, comment, and opinion, and fostering debate, exchange, and interaction. Because on-line resources provide an excellent opportunity for students to work independently, they are particularly useful in fostering students' learning skills of self-discipline, self-direction, independence of mind and initiative, ability to work with others, respect for others' reasoned views, intellectual integrity, maturity, empathy, and imaginative insight.[28] What the use of on-line resources cannot claim to do is develop the "high level" ICT skills that the intensive use of database, spreadsheet, or text analysis programs does. There are ICT skills that are developed by using on-line resources, Web browsers, the Internet, and electronic discussion lists, but these should not be overstated.

Implementation

In seeking to introduce the use of on-line resources to the history classroom, the challenge lies not so much in finding the resources or acquiring the necessary technical expertise as in developing a strategy for incorporating them effectively into the teaching program. Is there a generically applicable pedagogy that can be used to ensure the use of computers in the classroom in a way that really does enhance students' learning outcomes? All too frequently, history courses provide students with lists of links to Web resources without any clear indication as to how these relate to course content, teaching methods, assessment, or learning outcomes. One project that sought to address these exact issues was the Courseware for History Implementation Consortium (CHIC), a phase-three project of the Teaching and Learning Technology Programme (TLTP) based at the University of Teesside.[29]

As part of phases one and two of TLTP, the History Courseware Consortium (HCC), led by the University of Glasgow, produced a series of twelve multimedia tutorials for teaching history in U.K. higher education.[30] Released on CD-ROM, the uptake of the material was encouraging. What was unclear was how effectively the materials were being used, if indeed they were being used at all. The CHIC project sought to examine various implementations of the tutorials and associated technology, such as electronic discussion groups, within different types of courses, levels of teaching, institutional contexts, and support services. Although the CHIC project started with an "off the shelf" set of resources, the lessons from its extensive evaluations are directly applicable to teachers seeking to effectively incorporate on-line resources.

One of the first and easiest steps to take is to provide course information on-line. While the vast majority of history department Web sites provide brochure-like descriptions of the course, times, and locations, far fewer detail the course aims and learning outcomes, lecture, tutorial or lab topics, methods of assessment, assessment criteria, grading scheme, bibliographies, Web resources, or lecture notes and slides. As the CHIC project concluded early on, "there is an almost overwhelming student acceptance of the principle that teaching materials should be available on-line, especially the linking of course bibliographies to university library catalogues and pointing up relevant Web resources."[31] The provision of such information is the first step in providing an open, supportive, and effective learning environment irrespective of any other form of computer use.

The next issue is that in spite of the vast range of on-line resources available, finding an exact match for course requirements can be frustrating, especially when seeking resources for an existing course rather than a new option. Sources may not be the exactly right period, type, genre, or best possible example. Alternatively, the commentary, secondary literature, reviews, or interpretations provided may not accord with those of the teacher. A solution to these problems is to customize the resources. This was another feature borne out by the CHIC project. Although designed to be flexible and easily incorporated into existing courses in practice, the majority of institutions desired to undertake some form of customization of the HCC tutorials. This involved various strategies from directing students to specific parts of the tutorials that best matched the existing content to using the tutorials' sources but authoring a new dialogue in which to situate them. This not only ensured that faculty felt their courses were not being compromised but that the "time devoted to preparing instructions and to customizing the tutorials by providing local pointers to particular resources was supported by a majority of students."[32]

In planning the use of computers in the history classroom and the use of on-line resources in particular, careful account of differentiated learning needs to be made. The context in which resources are provided for first-year students will need to be different from that for third-year students. In general, entry-level students respond best to a more structured and directed on-line environment that introduces them to a limited range of material. The more advanced the students, the less structure and direction required, and the greater the range and specialization of resources can be. The greater flexibility and freedom for higher-level students to independently explore on-line resources has been found to be "useful in developing those disciplinary skills of critical and independent thought."[33]

Nor does using on-line resources relegate the history teacher to a glorified Web master. On the contrary, such an approach can enhance learning, help satisfy the needs of a diverse student body, and make traditional face-to-face contact (between faculty and students and among the students) more productive. For example, interspersing traditional face-to-face tutorials with on-line discussion groups or e-mail distribution lists provides an opportunity for students who do not feel confident in expressing their opinions in front of their peers or tutor. The use of on-line discussion groups can also be an excellent medium for promoting group work and provides another means by which students can apply their knowledge and understanding. The CHIC project noted that, "there is potential for module Web sites to provide delivery platforms that can increase the quality of face to face and electronic contact between staff and students, and support differentiated and co-operative learning opportunities."[34] Using on-line resources does not, and indeed should not, replace traditional lectures, seminars, or tutorials. Rather they should run in parallel and be integrated with them as part of an effective learning environment.

Other CHIC project conclusions reinforce the critical role of taking a holistic approach to the use of computers in the history classroom emphasized here.

1. The alignment of learning outcomes, teaching processes and assessment criteria is best supported by integrated learning provision. This can be effectively delivered on-line.
2. Such an integrated provision promotes critical awareness, reflection and action amongst students. However, a robust, integrated approach is required.[35]

Notwithstanding the learning advantages that the use of on-line resources in the history classroom brings, effective integration is not without problems. Aside from the availability and quality of resources, the provision of on-line material can exclude students as easily as it can include them. Growing numbers of students have work and family commitments, and these students frequently have well-developed and specialized study patterns. Being able to read a book in the bath, on the train or bus, or prepare coursework during breaks at work, may not be ideal but reflects the reality of student life. One introduces extensive on-line resources at the risk of disrupting or preventing such learning patterns. One of the CHIC recommendations is to ensure that resources are available in a variety of locations on and off campus. In addition, it should be easy for students to print copies of the resources if they wish. This may be less of an issue for U.S. students, where laptop requirements and dorm room computer provision are increasingly common, but it needs to be borne in mind.

There are more practical issues that can also hinder effective implementation. One of the most common—and this applies to all uses of the computer —is the level of faculty technical skill. Where faculty do not have the requisite technical skills and/or the time to develop on-line resources, the provision of technical training, support, and communication is vital. Nor must one assume that all students are technical water babies. Even for relatively undemanding applications, the availability of technical training and support for students is essential. The CHIC project found that such support is particularly effective in developing the confidence and awareness of mature and part-time students.[36]

Finally, introducing computers into the history classroom can sometimes feel like ploughing a lonely furrow. Of particular importance in relation to promotion, tenure, and review is whether computer use accords with departmental and institutional objectives and practice. Is innovation encouraged, supported, and rewarded? Can one's practice be integrated with that of the department as a whole? Does a broader institutional cultural change need to take place before one can effectively integrate one's teaching with computers? None of these are reasons not to innovate, but may help temper expectations and ensure that innovative ideas translate into practice that is recognized and rewarded.

Evaluation

Earlier in this chapter the above pedagogical approach was described as a critically reflective process. Part of this critical reflection has already been described—the review of learning outcomes and the alignment of these with assessment, content, and teaching methods. An inseparable part of this critically reflective process is evaluation. Evaluation is vital for ensuring effective use of computers and for providing evidence for promotion, tenure, and review. Whereas alignment provides evidence of a pedagogical process, evaluation provides evidence of that pedagogy's outcome. It enables faculty to demonstrate that the use of computers is in response to learning needs, that these needs are being met, and that the provision is critically reviewed. Course evaluation is now common practice, particularly summative student feedback, and extending evaluation to provide evidence for promotion, tenure, or review need not be a massive undertaking.

By following the alignment process outlined above, the instructor will already have undertaken a significant amount of self-evaluation. Providing evidence of this need only takes the form of logging or describing the process of assessing course aims and outcomes, content, and teaching methods. This can take the form of a teaching diary, journal, or portfolio depending on how extensive the faculty member wants the documentation to be. Creating this type of evidence is not unique to using computers in teaching but is applicable to all forms of teaching development. The table that follows (Table 7.2) is an example from a standard review of an existing course on multimedia. This material complements and supports evidence provided by course documentation, lab and/or lecture notes, and assessments.

Table 7.2

Log of Teaching Review for Multimedia Analysis and Design

Process	Outcome
Review aims and outcomes	Renamed objectives to outcomes.
	Made a clear and consistent distinction between aims and outcomes.
	Reworded outcomes to better reflect the various intellectual processes required. In particular a progression through comprehension, application, analysis, and synthesis to evaluation.
Review assessment	Form of assessment unaltered, but clear marking criteria established and guidelines completely revised.
	Criteria and weighting of elements of assessment made available to students.
	Method of second marking revised.
Review content	Greater emphasis on design introduced to lectures.
	Choice of applications introduced to lab sessions and greater emphasis on evaluation.
	Course title altered to "Introduction to Multimedia Analysis and Design" to reflect changes above.

Ideally, evaluation would take three forms:

- Front-end evaluation—at the start of the alignment process
- Formative evaluation—during the development of course content
- Summative evaluation—at the end of implementing the course.

Providing evaluative evidence under each of these categories needs not add significantly to workloads, as many existing evaluation methods can be adapted and not all stages need to be repeated.[37]

Providing front-end evaluation is important to demonstrate that introducing or altering computer use is meeting a student need that is not adequately met elsewhere. Adding a question or two to end-of-year evaluation forms or raising the issue with class representatives in faculty/student meetings are two easy ways to undertake this evaluation. Less formal evaluation methods can also provide useful evidence. Faculty continually receive informal feedback from students, and it is entirely appropriate to use this to test reaction. E-mailing the class is another efficient way of conducting evaluation, particularly for these ad hoc issues. Course approval documentation, such as that required by boards of study in the U.K., can also provide evidence of front-end evaluation, as this is a form of peer review. Some of the potential questions that can usefully be asked by front-end evaluation are listed below.

Front-end Evaluation Checklist

- Would on-line resources be a useful addition to the course materials?
- How do you think these resources will help your study?
- In what way would you like to use these resources?
- Do you use computers in any of your other courses, and if so, how?
- Are there any computing skills that you cannot learn elsewhere that you would like to develop as part of this course?
- Would you prefer to use computers in supported sessions or independent study or a combination of both?
- Would you like your use of computers to be assessed in some form, and if so, how?
- Should this assessment form part of your final grade?

Formative evaluation is the most commonly conducted type of evaluation. When developing substantial new resources, such as new course Web sites or a collection of on-line resources, then a formal evaluation is worthwhile. This evaluation is most commonly conducted by a questionnaire that may be paper-based, electronic, or used in face-to-face interviews. This questionnaire is frequently complemented by focus group sessions. Designing appropriate questionnaires, organizing focus groups, and analyzing the results are time-consuming but not impossible activities. Students provide an excellent captive audience, and formative evaluation surveys can be incorporated as useful exercises in existing courses. Focus groups can be somewhat harder to arrange, but the lure of free pizza and soda should not be underestimated in the undergraduate psyche. Less formal methods can also be used for formative evaluation. Asking a few students for their comments can provide useful feedback. Peer review can often provide the most useful and critically informed responses. Some useful formative evaluation questions are provided below.

Formative Evaluation Checklist

- Is the amount of resources adequate?
- Are the range and type of resources appropriate for the level of study?
- Are resources relevant to the topic of study?
- Are the amount and depth of accompanying information appropriate for the level of study?

- Is the information accurate?
- Are instructions clear and informative?
- Are tasks or exercises clearly explained?
- Do students understand what they are supposed to do, why, and how?
- Can students navigate and locate material easily?
- Is the user interface consistent and appropriate to present the subject matter?

Summative evaluation is the most familiar type to history faculty. End-of-course questionnaires are a form of summative evaluation. Undertaking summative evaluation on the use of computers is particularly valuable for two reasons. It will demonstrate whether the intended learning outcomes and the provision and use of computers have met the needs and learning outcomes established earlier. Second, it demonstrates that faculty are engaged in a process of critical reflection. This is particularly so if evidence of action based on the feedback can be provided. It is a relatively simple task to add questions, asking if students thought the use of computers aided their understanding, developed new skills, or was more or less preferable to traditional learning and teaching formats. A set of evaluation instruments developed for the Contemporary and Historical Census Collection (CHCC) project asks the following summative questions regarding students' use of on-line learning materials about the nineteenth-century census. These questions can easily be adapted to different history courses and computer uses.

Summative Evaluation Checklist

Thinking about the learning and teaching unit/s you used please indicate your responses to these statements:

1. Using the material stimulated my interest in the subject matter (e.g., migration, ethnicity)
   Significantly   Somewhat   A little   Not at all

2. Using the material improved my understanding of the subject matter
   Significantly   Somewhat   A little   Not at all

3. Using the material enhanced my methodological skills
   Significantly   Somewhat   A little   Not at all

4. Using the material improved my all-round computer skills
   Significantly   Somewhat   A little   Not at all

5. Comparing the session/sessions using the CHCC learning and teaching materials with other forms of learning about you subject, were they
   More useful   As useful   Less useful

6. What do you feel you accomplished in using the CHCC material?

Conclusion

This chapter has sought to provide a pedagogic and evaluative framework for history teachers to make use of computers in the history classroom, to do so effectively and in ways that maximize benefits for students and faculty. Students should benefit from a clearer understanding of the learning outcomes they are expected to achieve and the skills they ought to develop for an enhanced learning experience. Above all, the use of computers in the history classroom should make for better history students. It is this, more than any other type of evidence, that will benefit faculty in the event of promotion, tenure, or review.

Notes

1. Donald A. Spaeth and Sonja Cameron, "Computers and Resource-Based History Teaching: A UK Perspective," *Computers and the Humanities* 34 (Dordrecht: Kluwer Academic, 2000), 326.

2. D. Laurillard, *Rethinking University Teaching: A Framework for Effective Use of Educational Technology* (London and New York: Routledge, 1993).

3. Spaeth and Cameron, "Computers and Resource-Based History Teachings," 327–28.

4. Evan Mawdsley and Thomas Munck, *Computing for Historians. An Introductory Guide* (Manchester: Manchester University Press, 1993), 3.

5. For an overview of the debate on computers in historical research see Daniel Greenstein, *A Historian's Guide to Computing* (Oxford: Oxford University Press, 1994).

6. Examples of such arguments can be found in Charles Tilley, "Computers in Historical Analysis" in *Computers in the Humanities*, ed. J.L. Mitchell (Edinburgh: Edinburgh University Press, 1973), 7:6; Lawrence Stone, "History and the Social Sciences," *Past and the Present* (Boston and London: Routledge & Kegan Paul, 1981); Konrad H. Jarausch, "Some Reflections on Coding" in *Datenbanken und Datenverwaltungssteme als Werkzeuge Historischer Forschung*, ed. M. Thaller (St. Katerinen: Scripta Mercaturae Verlag, 1986).

7. See Alan Booth's and Paul Hyland's *History Today* at: hca.ltsn.ac.uk/resources/ reviews/h2k_news2a.php and A. Booth and P. Hyland, eds., *History in Higher Education: New Directions in Teaching and Learning* (Oxford: Blackwell, 1996) for an excellent exploration of teaching issues, including the use of ICT.

8. The British Universities' Computer Board initially funded the DISH lab (Development and Implementation of Software for History). The in-house development of software was soon abandoned when off-the-shelf, commercial applications for PCs proved suitable for most historical applications. See www.arts.gla.ac.uk/History/DISH/ dish.htm.

9. The Computers in Teaching Initiative Centre for History (CTICH) and the Teaching and Learning Technology Programme's (TLTP) History Courseware Consortium were the first major initiatives, both with national remits. See www.gla.ac.uk/ ~histtltp/.

The Learning and Teaching Subject Network's (LTSN) Centre for History, Classics and Archaeology, a distributed network of teaching expertise, with the ICT expert based in Glasgow, has taken over from CTICH. See hca.ltsn.ac.uk/.

Glasgow continues the pioneering work of the History Courseware Consortium by developing on-line modules in historical census studies for the Contemporary and Historical Census Collection Project. See www.chcc.ac.uk for project information. Links to the resources are restricted to UK HE (Higher Education).

10. Booth and Hyland, *History in Higher Education.*

11. J. Garrison, M. Larochelle, and N. Bednarz, *Constructivism and Education* (Cambridge: Cambridge University Press, 1998), and Thomas M. Duffy and David H. Jonassen, eds., *Constructivism and the Technology of Instruction: A Conversation,* (Hillsdale, NJ: Lawrence Erlbaum Associates, 1992).

12. Higher Education Funding Council for England, *QO 3–95 Subject Overview Report—History. Quality Assessment of History 1993–94* (Bristol: HEFCE, 1995).

13. Ibid.

14. QAA—Quality Assurance Agency for Higher Education, *History Subject Benchmark Statement* (Gloucester: QAA, 2000).

15. Ibid.

16. I must acknowledge Professor Andrew Prescott of the Department of History at the University of Sheffield for the idea of using the Magna Carta.

17. QAA, *History Subject Benchmark Statement.* This is one of five assessment methods that include teamwork and collaborative activity, shorter written tasks, use of archival material, and IT for bibliographic and archival searches.

18. The RELN field in the database is the person's relationship to the head of the household. RELCOD is used only in the Sandyford data set and is a shorter, coded version of RELN. SHN is the unique ID field for each record in the Sandyford data set. ID is used in the Gorbals data set.

19. Scottish Higher Education Funding Council, *Quality Assessment in History: University of Glasgow* (Edinburgh: SHEFC, 1996).

20. See www.arts.gla.ac.uk/History/Honours/handbook/twentyone.htm.

21. Many thanks to Dr. Donald Spaeth of the Department of History, University of Glasgow, for his permission to use this material and his invaluable advice and insights about historical computing in general.

22. Frederick Mosteller and David L. Wallace, *Inference and Disputed Authorship: The Federalist Papers* (Reading, MA and London: Addison-Wesley, 1964).

23. QAA, *History Subject Benchmark Statement.*

24. Ibid.

25. See chronicles.dickinson.edu/ for the Dickinson Chronicles project.

26. John M. Osborne, Ian G. Anderson, and James W. Gerencser, *Teaching, Learning, and Digitizing Resources in the Humanities through the Cooperation of Educators and Archivists* (Edinburgh: Digital Resources for The Humanities 2002 Conference Abstracts, 2002), 162. See also www.drh2002.lib.ed.ac.uk/abstracts.html#162.

27. Dennis Trinkle and Scott Merriman, eds., *The History Highway 2000* (Armonk, NY: M.E. Sharpe, 2000).

28. QAA, *History Subject Benchmark Statement.*

29. See chic.tees.ac.uk/ for further information, case studies, and summary reports. [Incidentally, the project name is pronounced shēk as in smart, elegant, and fashionable, not as in baby chicken.]

30. See www.gla.ac.uk/~histtltp/ for details of the courseware and www.albany.edu/ jmmh/ for an explanation on the pedagogy behind the development of the courseware and initial evaluations of its use.

31. Richard Hall, *Evaluating the Context of On-line History Teaching: The First Year of the Chic Project* (Milton Keynes: IET: Open University, Proceedings of the 5th Humanities and Arts Network Conference, 1999).

32. Ibid.

33. Ibid.

34. Richard Hall and Derek Harding, "Driving Departmental Change through Evaluation: Some Outcomes and Problems," *Association for Learning Technology Journal* 8 (2000) part 1: 19–29.

35. Ibid.

36. Ibid.

37. See the Learning Technology Dissemination Initiative's Evaluation Cookbook at www.icbl.hw.ac.uk/ltdi/cookbook/contents.html for an invaluable guide to evaluation techniques.

Chapter 8

Teaching in a Classroom Without Walls

What It Takes to Cultivate a Rich On-line Learning Community

Daphne Jorgensen

Asynchronous Learning Networks

What do a schoolteacher from Italy, a university football coach from Pennsylvania, a high school business teacher from New York City, and a librarian from England have in common? They are all enrolled in the same course at the University at Albany, State University of New York, and as such, are part of a growing number of adult learners who are pursuing advanced degrees through distance education via asynchronous learning networks (ALNs). ALNs are an educational use of digital technologies with the potential to expand the four walls of the classroom to the four corners of the globe. This distance learning method, whereby with just a personal computer and Internet access students can be active members of rich, viable learning communities, is increasingly popular. Not only is it convenient, as students can attend class anytime and from anywhere, it also meets the needs of the changing composition of the college student population: mature students who juggle coursework with familial and professional obligations.[1] The proliferation of educational Web sites and Internet resources, as well as the advent of on-line university libraries and full-text databases, has facilitated this changing paradigm of "the classroom."

In his provocative treatise on the social construction of digital learning communities, Robert McClintock illuminates the challenges teachers encounter as they shift from a fixed classroom into a classroom without walls.

> Traditionally, the school and the classroom have been places where teachers and students are isolated from the general culture and where information and ideas have been relatively scarce—the textbook is a meager selection of what a field of knowledge comprises, a skilled teacher is a bundle of

ignorance relative to the sum of learning, and a school library a sparse collection at best. Networks reaching through the school into the classroom and to the desktop are ending the isolation and substituting a rule of abundance for that of scarcity.[2]

McClintock approaches this issue from the perspective of information networks leading into a physical classroom where students who are situated in one location have access to a dynamic array of resources outside that space. However, through the evolution of ALNs, the reverse scenario is taking place, as classroom walls are being knocked down and a class can consist of students who are geographically dispersed all over the world.

Many universities are embracing ALNs and offering courses in both traditional and distance formats. The State University of New York (SUNY) Learning Network (SLN), with the support of a generous grant from the Alfred P. Sloan Foundation, and in partnership with SUNY System Administration and 55 participating campuses, has been providing high-quality online courses since 1995. SLN course offerings have flourished from a sparse 8 in 1995 to more than 1,500 in the 2000–2001 academic year, with over 1,400 on-line faculty and 25,000 students.[3]

My foray into the world of on-line instruction began in spring 2002 when I was approached to teach an SLN course on the use of media in teaching and learning. Prior to that, I had experienced distance education as a student in several on-line courses and had spent many hours researching various issues in distance learning. Enthusiastically embracing the challenge, I had no idea where my journey would take me or of the amount of work that was ahead of me.

Subsequent to my being asked to teach on-line, I had initiated a series of conversations with several seasoned university faculty members about their perspectives on the teaching of asynchronous on-line courses and explored some of the issues that had surfaced through their experiences with this medium of course delivery. The professors with whom I spoke all had between 15 and 35 years of instructional experience, 3 to 5 years of which was online. I will share my story, as well as my colleagues' perspectives, in the hope of shedding light on the work that goes into creating a rich on-line class community.

The Course

Media in Teaching and Learning was a graduate-level course that explored pedagogically sound uses of computing technologies to enhance teaching and learning. Students read and discussed scholarly articles, critically analyzed issues involving instructional uses of graphics, audio, video, and computers, and developed lesson plans that incorporated each media. The 16–member fall 2002 class was composed of 12 teachers, 2 librarians, and 2 football coaches.

Originally created to be taught in a face-to-face format at the University at Albany, the course was redesigned for the on-line classroom by Professors Karen Swan and Carla Meskill.[4] Restructuring face-to-face courses to an effective on-line format is one of the challenges that many faculty members encounter as they transition to the distance classroom. Professors often have to completely rethink their courses and adopt a whole new approach to facilitate effective on-line course delivery.[5] This is discussed further in the section on Instructional Roles.

The fall 2002 version of the course was segmented into an orientation section, 4 comprehensive modules, and a culminating activity. The modules consisted of a total of 39 detailed hyperlinked lecture documents, an overview of the readings and assignments expected for each module, a page where students could construct or attach assignments, a place to ask the professor a public question, a personal folder in which students conferenced privately with the professor, and most important, the discussion boards. We will delve more into the discussion boards later.

Faculty Investment

Teaching on-line can be an exciting prospect as faculty explore the terrain of a different kind of learning environment, build relationships with students from all over the world, and engage in deep reflective scholarly discourse. However, it is also fraught with many challenges. The literature suggests that on-line faculty often contend with an increased workload and start-up time for course preparation, mastering more organizational skills, adapting to a student-centered instructional approach, undergoing technical and instructional design training, and facing the enormous demands of student-teacher interaction and constant feedback.[6] The investment of instructional time and effort, learning a new method of course delivery, and grappling with the technology can place tremendous burdens on faculty.

Start-up Time

In a 1998 survey of 48 faculty members at the University of Central Florida, "ninety percent of the instructors felt that on-line courses required more work than traditional versions of the same course."[7] Starr Roxanne Hiltz reported that on-line faculty at the New Jersey Institute of Technology experienced an increased workload and more start-up time than their traditional counterparts in order to fully prepare courses before the semester.[8] According to Hiltz, this has even spurred some debate about the issue of compensation, as faculty members invest much time between semesters preparing for their courses. It can take an exorbitant amount of time to prepare to teach on-line. After all, in a full-text environment, an enormous part of the preparation is the polishing and refining of a full semester's worth of lecture notes. It also involves a great deal of forethought in terms of course design in a hypertext environment. Issues like navigation, usability, ease of access, and consistency must be factored into the design of the course.

I began preparing for the course nearly four months before it was open. SLN is an established network with excellent support services and faculty development programs. In addition to 20 hours of hands-on training conducted by seasoned on-line faculty and multimedia instructional design professionals, where I learned to work with the Lotus Notes interface, I had access to an on-line Faculty Development Center. The center afforded me the opportunity to explore relevant resources, read instructional design tips, enter selected courses that were in progress, and even join in an asynchronous discussion with other instructors about the challenges and successes they experienced while preparing their courses to go live.

This was even before immersing myself in the course content. Although I was fortunate enough to have been asked to teach a course that had already been created, that summer Professors Karen Swan, Donna Rogers,[9] and I drastically revised it. Between training and the course revamping project, I documented 89 hours of course preparation even before I ever began interacting with students. Once the course opened, I spent between 10 and 17 hours polishing each module before I opened it. I checked my course daily, answered student messages that were left in my on-line office hours folders, graded papers, and kept up with the flow of discourse. Two weeks before the course officially closed, I had recorded, conservatively, a total of 241 hours of time devoted to the course, with final grading left to go.

Several colleagues revealed they too invested a huge amount of start-up time when instituting new courses, but once the courses were established and refined, their instructional activities took about the same amount of time as their more traditional, face-to-face courses. The time that would have been spent in a physical classroom was instead occupied with grading a larger quantity of written assignments, moderating discussions, and interacting with students. Professors who were not proficient with their course software, or who did not receive adequate technical support, contended with technical problems. The point is that teaching on-line does not take less time than face-to-face instruction, but often may encompass more of a time commitment. This is what some of my on-line instructional colleagues had to say:

Every semester I say, "I am not going to be on seven days. I am going to restrict myself to five days. I find, though, that I really need to be on to give my students that comfort feeling that I'm not way off and they're not way off, and that we are able to communicate much more so than in a regular classroom. (Professor Barbara Olsen)[10]

There are invisible costs to faculty who live in the electronic realm. A polished software, for example, is meant to be easy to use. The more effort one puts into it to make it user friendly, the less apparent the labor. The same holds true for on-line teaching. After hours and hours of preplanning and tinkering and getting all the text and interface to read just right, the student sometimes feels the instructor is "absent." (Professor Steve Harmon)

Discussion

As Jenny Preece declares, "People are the pulse of any community. Without them, there is no community. Vibrant discussion, new ideas, and continually changing content distinguish online communication from Web pages."[11] An essential underpinning to building a dynamic community of inquiry[12] is that authentic discussion must be factored heavily into the course design and into the grading. Students need to reflect upon and discuss the concepts and ideas introduced in the readings and by their instructor and peers. As students interact with one another, formulate and refine their opinions, challenge one another, process multiple perspectives, and possibly restructure their mental models, the community of inquiry is nurtured and developed. This is supported by a recent survey that found high levels of peer interaction produced higher levels of course satisfaction and high levels of perceived learning in on-line students.[13] As one colleague asserts: "There is no sitting in the back and nodding off. The socio-cognitive demands are much, much greater on individual students to read, think, articulate, and defend their positions."[14]

In my class, students were required to answer specific, open-ended questions related to the week's readings, drawing from their personal lives and professional experiences, as well as to respond to at least 2 of their peers on a weekly basis. This translated into a total of 39 required discussion postings per semester. At the time of this writing, 33 discussion pieces had been due from each student. However, students had each contributed to the class discussion from 18 to 68 times, with a median of 36, and a mean of 37.5 postings.

Several colleagues shared the techniques they have used to encourage discussion:

Sticks. Grades. I factor the discussion into the grading. I try to ask open-ended questions. I try to encourage multiple perspectives. In the beginning of the course, I try to model what I want to see in a discussion response. (Professor Flor Lugo-Smith)

Asking good questions. Assigning tasks for which there is no set recipe for acceptable responses. Stepping back from time to time and letting students answer one another. Having all students' written assignments public documents which classmates are required to read and comment on. Assigning pairs to work through specific tasks. (Professor Lars Peterson)

I foster interaction by trying to give students an issue to think about and discuss in each module. The quality of those discussions is dependent upon the kinds of questions asked. You can't just give them free reign. I need to constantly mold their behavior at the beginning of the course, as they mold the behaviors of students in their classrooms. You work in small increments from where they are to where you want them to be. To prevent babbling, you have to focus questions that are good things for them to respond to. And you have to interact, reinforce with the student whether or not they are meeting the objectives and where on the continuum they are. You are molding their responses. Give them the knowledge with which they can answer the question, make sure they have the information at their disposal through the lectures and the readings, and then ask them to do it. If they can't do it, then either the question isn't good, or they haven't done the reading. (Professor Barbara Olsen)

Management Skills

In addition to facilitating a vibrant discussion, the on-line instructor must also engage in a highly interactive discursive process with each student. The course template had a section where each student introduced himself to the class. Whenever a student created his or her profile, the platform that was used, Lotus Notes, automatically created a personal folder for the student. This personal folder was where students could confer in private with the instructor and was equivalent to a consultation in a faculty member's office. At the time of this writing, I had held 82 virtual office consultations. I had also created 562 other documents, most of which were detailed evaluations and correspondence with students. This did not include e-mail exchanges. In all, I had created over 690 course documents, with numerous updates and refinements, in a period of six months.

The management of such a high volume of course files increases the need for faculty to exercise strong organizational skills.[15] Once an on-line class was made public for the semester, it was active from day one until the closing date. Lotus Notes afforded the opportunity to view student attendance. Students had attended and contributed to the class every single day since the course opened on August 27, 2002. As the instructor, I needed to evaluate and interact with the students in a timely fashion. That meant I had to check into my course every day. In fact, three out of the four colleagues with whom I spoke revealed that they too signed on to their courses on a daily basis. Most experienced on-line professors adhere to the policy of checking their courses seven days a week: otherwise, as one colleague put it, keeping up with the course is like chasing after a moving conga line one cannot quite seem to join. It becomes a management nightmare.

I experienced this nightmare at certain crunch points in the semester when I barely had time to minimally interact with students and no time to grade assignments. Typically, the turnaround time for assignments in an on-line courses is much quicker than in a face-to-face class—generally 24 to 48 hours as opposed to one week in a face-to-face class. Students began to expect that quick turnaround and almost immediately started looking for their grades. Due to the volume of assignments and the ongoing discussions for which students got graded, even waiting a few days to grade papers and discussions was like watching snowdrifts accumulate during a blizzard.

Interaction

The concepts of instructional immediacy and social presence inform the kind of interaction that occurs in the on-line professor-student relationship. Instructional immediacy refers to the behaviors that bridge the distance of time and space between instructor and student. Social presence is the sense of affective and social contact in a digital world and is crucial to the establishment of a close on-line classroom community.[16] In face-to-face settings, physical cues like body language, tone of voice, eye contact, and facial expression promote social presence. The social and affective behaviors that enhance on-line intimacy, and foster instructional immediacy and social presence, include humor, using a student's first name, providing immediate feedback, sending encouraging comments, and sharing personal narratives about life outside the classroom.[17]

Professor Barbara Olsen related how instructional immediacy helped her novice on-line students to settle into her asynchronous classroom:

> Some of my students initially missed the interaction of being spoken to and they weren't sure of how they were going to react to this distance feeling. Once they saw that I answered their questions within a very short time frame, they began to feel that I was just around the corner. I wasn't visible, but I was very accessible. There was a lot of e-mail, a lot of asking questions. After the first module, and their journal reflection, they began to say that their perception of on-line courses was changing. It was not truly distant learning in terms of feeling isolated; they did feel like a member. And they didn't feel barriers to the teacher.

In a survey of 1,406 SLN students, Swan et al.[18] found that it was imperative that instructors provide frequent and constructive interaction with students, as this was critical to the formation of rich academic on-line communities. This interaction not only significantly affected students' perceived learning ($p < .01$), but also influenced their overall course satisfaction ($p < .01$). Although this interactive process is extremely time consuming, and sometimes tedious, I join the ranks of other on-line professors who claim that it is precisely this student-teacher interaction that brings the most joy and fulfillment in on-line instruction.[19] Making meaningful connections with students was absolutely the most rewarding aspect of teaching on-line.

One way I had tried to foster discussion with students was by making meaningful personal connections with them and by acknowledging significant events in their lives. One student went through a particularly devastating time when her cousin died. I wrote personal letters of condolence and tried to check up on her periodically, especially as she steadily fell behind. Another student asked for an extension of one week because his wife had just had an emergency C-section, and the baby was in a hospital one hour from his home. He gave me permission to announce the birth of his daughter, which I posted in the newsflash on the course front page. He was an active discussant and so by announcing his happy news, the rest of the class understood why he was "away" for the week. They also had the opportunity to congratulate him upon his return. When students brought in stories about their own students or children, I regularly drew upon stories from my personal life, including the antics of my own children. These expressions of warmth, personal feelings, congeniality, and appreciation supported community building in our on-line classroom.[20]

During conversations with three on-line faculty, it became apparent that they were concerned with keeping deep, rich, and ongoing connections with students and that interaction with their students seemed to bring them the most fulfillment. One colleague checked her e-mail and discussion boards immediately upon entering her course. She also made it a practice to respond to each and every posting so that the students regularly received prompt private feedback. A second colleague checked student folders, questions, and bulletin boards first. She said her students "can write to me 24/7 and I am back to them with expanded time to think through their queries." A third colleague looked forward to responding to her students' weekly learning journals, which she described as, "in-depth and more interactive" than the journals of her face-to-face students. All three professors heavily factored weekly discussion into the grading.

On-line faculty not only experience more frequency of interaction with their on-line students than with their face-to-face students, but the quality of the interaction is different. The communication is more personal, there is evidence of humor and caring, and the asynchronous method fosters reflection because students have time to digest and think about the class discussion before they reply. Following is what one colleague reported. This professor was concerned that her students view her as a real person and not, as she put it, a talking head. (Another faculty member voiced the same concern when she confided that sometimes she got the feeling her students thought she was a computer.)

> I tend to want to provide a lot of interaction with students, so I look for opportunities on-line that would allow that high interaction and that's why I like the discussion board. That's why I like the ability on every screen to ask questions, and I respond to those questions. I want to be viewed as a real person out there, and not as a talking head. I could never be a lecturer in a classroom where I talked and they just listened and then have a question period at the end. I want to be a person to them.

She went on to explain how she sometimes incorporates humor in her postings so that her students can get a glimpse of her as an individual.

> I want to model my cognitive thinking to them. I want to model my logic to them. I want to model my humor to them. I want them to know me as a real person. So, you do that on-line by the interaction, and by posting a humor here and there. When we were moving, I told them I would be AWOL for a couple of days and that we were moving. When I got back, I said, "I'm back. All went well. I'm still sane, but the jury is still out on that. [Laughter]." They all thought that was humorous. But, again, that's showing them a real person in me.

Later in the conversation, she recounted a poignant story of how her students demonstrated care for her during a very tragic week in our nation's history.

> If I am going to be absent, I tell them. I didn't tell them on September 11th that I was away at a conference. I had said that I was going to be away and that I wasn't sure if I could interact or not. When I came back, it had been three days. I had been inactive, and it had been three days, and of course, with September 11th, they were wondering where I was. They showed a caring that they were concerned if I had been in a place where I wasn't safe anymore. I had many e-mails, "Are you okay?" You know, maybe they sent those out to everyone that they knew, I don't know, but I interpreted it that they cared and that they considered me an individual and not a talking head. (Professor Barbara Olsen)

Instructional Roles

The professors with whom I dialogued all espoused a student-centered, constructivist, "social construction of knowledge" approach in their face-to-face classrooms, so it was not a stretch for them to do so when they transitioned to on-line instruction.[21] However, instructors who practice a lecture method in their face-to-face classrooms may encounter growing pains as they modify their teaching style for on-line course delivery. In on-line instruction, the professor fills a new role as facilitator: instead of the "sage on the stage," he is the "guide on the side," who is facilitating the flow of discussion rather than being at its epicenter.[22] The course becomes more student-centered and student-led within the framework laid out by the professor. Students must take more responsibility for their own learning. As one professor asserts: "Students have to be much more engaged and hands-on. They cannot rely upon absorption and recite back. They have to apply what they learn. Their role has changed to be an active engaged learner."

While teaching an educational Web site development course in a face-to-face digital classroom, I had the opportunity to immediately ascertain whether I effectively communicated a new concept to students by circling the room, answering student questions, and observing students as they attempted to apply the new skill or concept into their Web site design. When several students asked the same questions or committed similar errors, I got a clear indication that I needed to get the group's attention and present the new information more clearly. In an on-line classroom, I am not aware of ambiguous presentation until the students' assignments start pouring in. This could be a full two weeks after the reading was assigned. This occurred in the Audio Module's critical analysis assignment. Too many students had misunderstood the assignment, which alerted me to the fact that I needed either to revise the assignment or rephrase it for next time. One student alluded to this in his learning journal at the end of the module when he commented, "I just wanted to reaffirm that I thought the information was great but the assignment needed some work." (The beauty of having a bunch of teachers in the class was that I got evaluated all the time.)

When asked if her role as instructor changed in the on-line classroom, Professor Barbara Olsen responded:

> My function is to provide the learning environment to enhance the transfer of knowledge from all resources to meaningful understandings. In many ways the instructor's role is different on-line and many ways the same. Different in terms of you have to motivate students by your reactions and your interactions, versus in the classroom you have to motivate them by your energies, your personae, your mode of presentation, more personal

nature. Assessment is different. Assessment on-line is totally through projects. Assessment in face-to-face would be projects, class participation as an indicator of motivation, and tests. So the role is the same, but the methodology is different in terms of the assessment.

Technology

The literature suggests that one of the most daunting factors for on-line teaching faculty is overcoming the technology barrier.[23] Given my information science background, technology was not an issue for me. I had been a Webmaster for two years prior to teaching and was adept at manipulating a variety of computer software applications. What I did not know in terms of the Lotus Notes platform, I learned quickly through the SLN training or in e-mail consultation with my multimedia instructional designer. The faculty members with whom I spoke were all experts in instructional technology and reported the same experience. However, this is not always the case. It is very likely that a teacher from another discipline, for instance, a biology teacher with no instructional design or technology background, would probably report some frustrations in learning how to work with the technology.

This is not to say that there were no technical glitches. I discovered quite by accident that I had been editing my course documents directly on the SLN server instead of on my local computer. This was dangerous because by working directly on the uploaded original documents, there was the potential that irreversible errors could have been made during the editing process. I should have been working on my local computer and then replicated (or uploaded) the corrected documents to the server. If I made a mistake in my local computer, I had the option of just signing out of the course and not replicating the changes. This was not an option if I had made unwanted changes directly on the SLN server.

I also experienced the joys of broken URL links from ever-evolving Web addresses. One professor revealed she had problems with slow downloading of files. Another instructor related that whole sections of her courses had disappeared. One time she had set up a number of minilabs for her students and found that she was somehow disconnected from her students and not getting her material on the server. She had one view of the course, while her students saw something else entirely. She said that although she still encountered problems with the technology, they were easier for her to handle: "You know what has changed? Me. Things still happen, but I am calmer now and don't react the same way."

Since grappling with technology was relatively easy for my colleagues and me, we were able to get down to the business of teaching and to focus on the issues that all teachers care about: building a cohesive dynamic learning community, creating and maintaining relationships with students, and mentoring students as they produced real-world, authentic, quality work.

Old Policies—New Practices

As is customary whenever societal change occurs, often policy lags behind practice. Old rules are often applied to new practices, yielding the same effect as putting old wine into new wineskins: the seams burst. They do not fit. This has been the case with the traditional university tenure and review process. As an increasing number of university faculty members are incorporating digital technologies into their courses, and especially the on-line courses, some of these instructors are finding when they come up for promotion that their on-line instructional activities may not be valued the same as their other more traditional academic activities. Dr. Karen Swan, Professor at Kent State University, who leads a team of researchers from Kent's Research Center for Educational Technology, said,

> "Digital technology is becoming a primary means for creating, manipulating and disseminating knowledge in our society. That it is not valued in the tenure and review process just separates institutions of higher education even further from the rest of the world."[24]

Other on-line faculty chimed in:

> Part of going up for the stages of professorship involves the evaluation by students. If you wanted to move from step A to B up the ladder, or C to D, you can't without those evaluations. If you have been doing everything online or have been primary in the development of online courses, and online philosophy, you don't have those student interactions that you can use in support. I know of people who have said, "I can't move up the ladder here because I am teaching everything online and I have no student evaluations, which are necessary. (Professor Barbara Olsen)

Professor Lars Peterson claims the evaluation issue was resolved at his institution. When asked about his university support in the tenure and review process in relation to on-line teaching and technology in general, he responded:

> Things have changed so rapidly. When [another faculty member] and I went up for tenure, nothing counted. Absolutely nothing counted. It was like we were wasting our time. But I think things have changed since then because [my school], in particular, has gotten behind [the ALN] in a strong way.

Another on-line professor recounted the story of when she went up for tenure at her institution in the early 1990s. It had taken her two years to create an interactive video program for which she had successfully sold the rights to a commercial distributor. When she included it in her tenure portfolio, she initially encountered opposition because a software program was not a typical item for inclusion. However, she persisted because she held the position that someone who was coming up for tenure in a technology-related field should include this kind of valuable evidence of scholarly activity that reflected the quality of her work.

In spite of the frustrations and the difficulties encountered in the tenure and review process, the professors with whom I spoke were committed to the medium. Their satisfaction and enjoyment with on-line teaching hinged on sound pedagogical reasons. Professor Barbara Olsen wanted to experience this method of instruction, as well as interaction with students, while Professor Lars Peterson felt his course, which integrated technology with a specific discipline, was best modeled to his students through the on-line method. All the instructors reported a very high degree of satisfaction with their on-line course experience. When asked, "In what ways has teaching on-line courses been pleasurable or fulfilling?" their responses indicated a love of teaching, a higher quality of student output, empowerment of women (i.e., a voice in the classroom), and observing student growth in thinking and writing ability as the modules progressed. Here is what some of them said:

> I wanted the opportunity to expand my understanding of teaching and the components of teaching. I had taken an on-line course and I wanted to see what it is from the teacher's side. The on-line interaction with students is very fulfilling. (Professor Barbara Olsen)

> My motive was that I had a particular content and particular aims that seemed to fit the medium well. I have come to believe that there are certain content and certain aims that are appropriate for the medium, and what I had has proven to be best done on-line. (Professor Lars Peterson)

> I wouldn't keep teaching on-line if I didn't think it benefited student learning. In spite of the challenges of the media, I think the quality of student work has been better on-line than in-class. I find it fulfilling when students take fuller responsibility for their learning and use the opportunity to excel. (Professor Steve Harmon)

> I have had a number of personal messages from former students stating that the course had changed their lives. These were all women who had for the 16+ years of their educations been silenced in live classrooms and who had found voices (and powerful ones) in an on-line environment. This has been a tremendous reward. (Professor Lars Peterson)

Synergistic Effects

The cultivation of a dynamic on-line classroom can at once be both challenging and exciting. The challenges for faculty come in the forms of a possible increased start-up time, engaging in a different kind of workload, facilitating a stimulating flow of discourse, managing a large number of files and e-mails, nurturing a healthy field of interaction, adapting to instructional role changes, and grappling with the tools of technology. Additionally, online faculty may contend with outdated policies or perceptions by administrators or peers.

In spite of these challenges, teaching on-line can be enormously exhilarating. The formulation of a rich interactive learning culture where all members in the community contribute to the shared construction of knowledge is very rewarding. As students bring in their own personal and professional experiences, transacting with one another and the course material, a synergistic effect is created where knowledge and ideas flourish and where students are encouraged to think.

ALNs and classrooms without walls are now an important part of the institution of education. As educators embrace this changing paradigm of the classroom, they must continue to foster the practices and policies that augment a high-quality, on-line, scholastic experience. This includes taking a critical view of the kinds of practices and policies that would effectively enhance this method of course delivery. It also means supporting those instructors who are engaged in on-line instruction.

Notes

Many thanks to Karen Swan and Donna Rogers for their mentoring and support. Thanks to Annie Moore-Cox for her helpful critical feedback.

1. Rosalie J. Ocker and Gayle J. Yaverbaum, "Asynchronous Computer-Mediated Communication Versus Face-to-Face Collaboration: Results on Student Learning, Quality and Satisfaction," *Group Decisions and Negotiations* 8 (1999): 428.

2. Robert McClintock, "Renewing the Progressive Contract with Posterity: On the Social Construction of Digital Learning Communities" (1996), www.ilt.columbia.edu/mcclintock/renew/ren_main.htm (December 3, 2002): 7.

3. Eric Fredericksen et al., "Factors Influencing Faculty Satisfaction with Asynchronous Teaching and Learning in the SUNY Learning Network," *Learning Networks Effectiveness Research Web Center of New Jersey Institute of Technology* (2000), www.alnresearch.org/Data_Files/articles/full_text/fs-fredericksen.htm (October 6, 2002); see also sln.suny.edu/.

4. Karen Swan and Carla Meskill developed and co-taught Media in Teaching and Learning.

5. John R. Bourne et al., "Paradigms for On-Line Learning: A Case Study in the Design and Implementation of Asynchronous Learning Networks (ALN) Course,"

Journal of Asynchronous Learning Networks 1, No. 2 (August 1997), www.aln.org/alnWeb/journal/issue2/assee.htm (March 14, 2001).

6. Starr Roxanne Hiltz, "Impacts of College-Level Courses via Asynchronous Learning Networks: Some Preliminary Results," *Journal of Asynchronous Learning Networks* 1, No. 2 (1997), www.aln.org/alnWeb/journal/issue2/hiltz.htm (December 3, 2002); Mark H. Rossman, "Successful On-line Teaching Using an Asynchronous Learning Discussion Forum," *Journal of Asynchronous Learning Networks* 3, No. 2 (November 1999), www.aln.org/alnWeb/journal/Vol3_issue2/Rossman.htm (November 28, 2000); Bourne et al., "Paradigms for On-Line Learning."

7. Joel Hartman, Charles Dziuban, and Patsy Moskal, "Faculty Satisfaction in ALNs: A Dependent or Independent Variable?" *Learning Networks Effectiveness Research Web Center of New Jersey Institute of Technology* (2000), www.alnresearch.org/Data_Files/articles/full_text/fs-hartman.htm (October 6, 2002): 12.

8. Hiltz, "Impacts of College-Level Courses," 4.

9. Donna Rogers taught the other section of the course in fall 2002.

10. Pseudonyms were used for the professors who took part in conversations about on-line learning.

11. Jenny Preece, *On-line Communities: Designing Usability, Supporting Sociability* (New York: John Wiley & Sons, 2000), 82.

12. D. Randy Garrison, Terry Anderson, and Walter Archer, "Critical Thinking, Cognitive Presence, and Computer Conferencing in Distance Education," *American Journal of Distance Education* 15, No. 1 (2001): 7.

13. Karen Swan et al., "Building Knowledge, Building Communities: Consistency, Contact and Communication in the Virtual Classroom," *Journal of Educational Computing Research* 23, No. 4 (2000): 367.

14. Anonymous, private interview with author, November 2002.

15. Hiltz, "Impacts of College-Level Courses," 4.

16. Bourne et al., "Paradigms for On-Line Learning."

17. Liam Rourke et al., "Assessing Social Presence in Asynchronous Text-Based Computer Conferencing," *Journal of Distance Education* 14, No. 2 (1999), www.icaap.org/iuicode?151.14.2.6 (December 3, 2002); Robert LaRose and Pam Whitten, "Re-Thinking Instructional Immediacy for Web Courses: A Social Cognitive Exploration," *Communication Education* 49, No. 4 (2000): 324; Dawn M. Poole, "Student Participation in a Discussion-Oriented On-line Course: A Case Study," *Journal of Research on Computing in Education* 33, No. 2 (Winter 2000): 162.

18. Swan et al., "Building Knowledge, Building Communities."

19. Hartman, Dziuban, and Moskal, "Faculty Satisfaction in ALNs," 12–13.

20. Francoise Herrmann, "Building On-line Communities of Practice: An Example and Implications," *Educational Technology* (January–February 1998): 18; Jenny Preece, "Online Communities," 83.

21. Linda Harasim et al., *Learning Networks: A Field Guide to Teaching and Learning On-line*, 3d ed. (Cambridge, MA: MIT Press, 1997), 174.

22. Ibid., 188.

23. Thierry Volery, "On-line Education: An Exploratory Study into Success Factors," *Journal of Educational Computing Research* 24 (2001): 81; Linda Harasim et al., *Learning Networks*, 219; Eric Fredericksen et al., "Factors Influencing Faculty Satisfaction," 24.

24. Karen Swan, letter to author, November 23, 2002.

Chapter 9

Learning Together and Moving Toward Tenure

Special Collections and Teaching Faculty Collaboration in the Development of an On-line Sheet Music Exhibition

Jessica Lacher-Feldman

Digital Scholarship for the Archivist

Tenure and promotion positions for academic librarians and archivists are not ubiquitous, but for many librarians and archivists working in an academic setting throughout the United States, tenure and promotion are a matter of course. There are many exciting opportunities for tenure-track archivists working in academic special collections libraries. Opportunities exist to develop projects and products that contribute to building a strong body of creative work, while contributing to the academic community as a whole. The special collections librarian or archivist, especially within public service areas, has unique opportunities to work collaboratively with teaching faculty, learning about collections from a "subject specialist," contributing to the scholarly community, and increasing the impact of a project or event by bringing in a broader audience through this collaboration.

The use of digital technology as a tool and a vehicle to develop these projects and programs is becoming much more prevalent. Digital projects require new and specific skill sets—skills that have traditionally run counter to the range of expertise of the special collections librarian or archivist. But the archival profession, and the skills required or deemed favorable within the profession, are changing at a lightning pace. With the movement toward digital technology, with the use of Encoded Archival Description (EAD)[1] as well as the mounting of digital collections and exhibits on the World Wide Web, it is clear that we are in a watershed moment. Archival practice and the range of skills necessary to further the mission and goals of the archival repository are evolving in our digital age. Archivists have long been trained in the handling and preservation of fragile materials, of *provenance*,[2] *respect des fonds*,[3] and the principals of *original order*,[4] but more and more, new archivists are coming to the profession with an interest in and a knowledge of Web development, digitization techniques, and graphic design. Digital technology has completely changed the way that archivists do business.

Is digital scholarship being recognized as a strong contribution to the mission and goals of the repository? Is participation in digital scholarship furthering the tenure and promotion process for the library's faculty member? Is this work being recognized as adding a massive increase to the workload of the archivist? And, is the repository providing adequate support in terms of equipment, staffing, and training to allow for these new kinds of projects? These questions are critical to consider for the tenure-track archivist as well as the administrative bodies within the library and the college or university. At the same time, it is also critical to consider the countless opportunities for innovative outreach, creating new and unprecedented access via the World Wide Web, and in developing partnerships within the university community that will draw positive attention to the repository, the academic institution, and the participants in the project.

On-line Exhibits and On-line Collections: Understanding Differences

This chapter addresses specific issues relating to a collaborative project that resulted in the digital exhibition, *Over There! And Back Again: Patriotic American Sheet Music from the First World War*.[5] The exhibition can be seen at www.lib.ua.edu/libraries/hoole/digital/overthere/index.htm.

It is important to distinguish between an on-line collection and an on-line exhibition. There are excellent on-line sources for sheet music, most notably through the Library of Congress's American Memory Project at: memory.loc. gov/ammem/mussmhtml/mussmhome.html, the Historic American Sheet Music collection of Duke University, now part of the Library of Congress American Memory site at: memory.loc.gov/ammem/award97/ncdhtml/ hasmhome.html, and the Lester S. Levy Collection of Sheet Music at Johns Hopkins University at: levysheetmusic.mse.jhu.edu/.

An on-line collection most often attempts to be comprehensive in scope and does not necessarily present digital surrogates[6] in context. It most often provides an index to materials, or a searchable database, and is meant to be used for research purposes. While an on-line exhibition does also have potential for researchers because the materials are present in surrogate form, the exhibition is more selective in its presentation, and there is a level of curatorial practice that does not necessarily exist with digital collections being made available on-line. While digital collections also require a selection process, and materials are not necessarily scanned and made available wholesale, there is a more comprehensive view to a digital collection.

The on-line exhibit is quite different from the on-line collection. This exhibit put sheet music in context, creating several categories that helped the audience to better understand patriotism during World War I by giving them examples of specific genres of music. Categories for *Over There! And Back Again* included, "Wartime Hits," "Daddies and Daughters," "Sweethearts," "Novelty Songs," and "Miniatures"—smaller-format sheet music printed with the message to conserve paper for the war effort. These categories not only create a sense of structure for the viewer, but they also help to put this era into context.

Additionally, the development of on-line exhibits and projects through special collections repositories, museums, and other cultural institutions provides valuable resources and context to a broad audience. And with the involvement of scholars, using interesting and important cultural materials from their areas of expertise, this serves as a logical extension of the role of the exhibitions coordinator in any cultural institution.

Archivists and Scholars: A Logical Match

Scholars in a variety of areas rely upon the knowledge and skill of the special collections librarian or archivist. Oftentimes, the archivist does not have the opportunity to develop a relationship with the scholar that will help to further his knowledge of the collections and gain valuable background information about the collections. A collaborative project with a subject expert will allow the archivist to gain important knowledge of matters relating to the collections used in the project, including background information, as well as a better understanding of the physical items themselves. This type of collaboration will in turn better future reference service for library and archival collections.

Furthermore, a dynamic Web presence within the special collections repository is gaining increased importance. It is the World Wide Web that is often the initial, or perhaps only, contact that individuals might have with a repository. By creating a dynamic Web presence that not only informs the public of holdings but also seeks to educate, the Web archivist is contributing to the viability of her institution.

On-line Exhibit Projects and Collaboration

The greatest constraint regarding on-line projects lies within the abilities of the contributors. It is important that archivists interested in developing these kinds of projects seek out and be provided with the training and support necessary to complete them. It must also be recognized that these projects require time, software, and hardware to make them happen.[7] If there are expectations to create these kinds of projects, administration must be supportive of the efforts and must actively provide adequate facilities and support.

Any time a collaborative project is initiated, it is critical to initially address as many issues as possible before beginning and make certain that all parties involved have a complete understanding of their responsibilities. Discussion of the outcome and end goals should be approached immediately. If collaboration is already in place and a decision is made to make that project evolve into a digital project, the outcomes, permissions, and responsibilities should also be addressed upon initiating this second phase of the project. When work is being done collaboratively between two junior faculty members, it is critical to discuss how these end products will further both their positions within their departments and how they will be represented on each respective curriculum vita. Initiating this dialog and building upon it will best prepare all involved parties for the work and achievements ahead.

The Expanded Project

This sheet music exhibit was done as part of a larger event. The event involved a film screening, a lecture, an additional exhibition, and a reception. A "multitiered event," where projects and ideas can piggyback upon each other for maximum exposure and impact, is ideal not only in promoting the collections and repository, but also in allowing for the most community (both university community and general community) involvement.

Over There!" supported the primary exhibition entitled, *Poor Pilgrim, Poor Stranger: Remembering Alabama Author William March.* This exhibition focused on the published works and the manuscript materials of William March [Campbell], an Alabama author whose manuscripts are part of the collections at the W.S. Hoole Special Collections Library. Not only is William March (1894–1956) an internationally known author, he also has relatives living within the community. March is perhaps best known in literary circles for his book, *The Bad Seed,* which was turned into a Broadway play by Maxwell Anderson, and then into a film in 1956.

To further increase the impact of the event, arrangements were made to sponsor a screening of the film at the local historic theater, with a reception and an opening lecture by well-respected author and University of Alabama English professor, Dr. Philip Beidler. Dr. Beidler also wrote an introduction to the 1989 reprint of William March's work, *Company K*, published by the University of Alabama Press.

The inspiration and the idea for the second exhibition on World War I sheet music came partially from March's involvement in World War I, especially the fact that he was a decorated soldier, receiving numerous citations including the Croix de Guerre. The William March manuscript collection includes these World War I era artifacts, along with his dog tags, mess kit, canteen, pocketknife, and "diddy" bag. And while plans for the March exhibit were already in place, the effects of September 11, 2001 also made an exhibition of World War I American patriotic music both a logical and comforting choice. The sheet music exhibit supported the March exhibit, dovetailing to create a unified presence in the exhibition space in the Hoole Library lobby. While March was much more than a decorated soldier, his experiences in World War I shaped not only his writing but also his entire life.

The Sheet Music Virtual Exhibit

While this sheet music exhibit and the virtual project that came from it were relatively small, there was a great deal of work involved in the production of the site. Decisions such as the color, font, and overall appearance were fundamental elements of the site design. Issues such as functionality and searchability of the site were also addressed. Parameters were defined, such as the decision not to create a definitive on-line site for World War I patriotic American sheet music, but rather a reflection of the "physical" exhibition that was held in the repository in fall 2001. Additional decisions, such as not to create a searchable interface for the individual items, helped to further the progress of the site. Defining the overall objectives of the actual on-line project before beginning an endeavor such as this is essential to its success. The objective was to create an interest in Wold War I patriotic sheet music, and to highlight the collections, just as was done with the physical exhibition. An additional objective was to provide some useful and entertaining information about the *Wade Hall Sheet Music Collection*. Dr. Wade Hall is an important donor to the W.S. Hoole Special Collections Library, and his materials make up a significant percentage of its published holdings. They are also vital for creating exhibitions, as they are visually interesting and they capture some very important elements of Alabama, Southern, and American culture. These types of projects can also illustrate to donors that their materials are critical to the collections and are being used in innovative ways.

By providing links with each full image to the university libraries' catalog citation for each individual title, the user can then access the MARC record,[8] making the transition from entertainment to research. Those with further interest in the collections themselves are given the opportunity to reference the MARC record and to contact the repository for further information.

Collaboration with a Teaching Faculty Member

I made initial contact with Dr. Daniel Goldmark through a discussion of my position and role within special collections. Dr. Goldmark, a musicologist specializing in American popular music and an enthusiastic new faculty member who joined the university faculty in fall 2001, has a deep interest in libraries and primary-source materials, and had already identified some rich resources in the Hoole Library. We spoke and decided upon a longer meeting and tour of the repository. After having a "behind the scenes" tour with unprecedented access to the collections, we developed a rapport and began to discuss how we could work together using the collections.

At the University of Alabama, Dr. Goldmark and I had identified several hundred items from the *Wade Hall Sheet Music Collection* that pertained to World War I patriotic sheet music. The goal was to review the collections and to identify themes for the exhibition. Upon narrowing the selections, Dr. Goldmark and I selected six separate themes that would serve to capture the era and the genre of music and would provide the audience with an excellent overview of the history of World War I patriotic sheet music, while giving them a sample of some of the most interesting choices. Dr. Goldmark researched the era and created text to provide context to the selections. Through his own knowledge and expertise, he was able to provide brief but informative text to accompany each individual theme.

Translating Real to Virtual

Curating an exhibit within Special Collections requires a specific set of skills, including the knowledge and ability to handle rare materials. Beyond that, an understanding of the arrangement of these materials, putting the information in context and displaying it in a pleasing and interesting manner are all-important. A mind toward security is critical, as materials need to be protected from theft. An understanding of preservation principles, an adherence to proper handling, and limiting exposure to light, are all of critical importance as well.

It should be clarified that neither the virtual nor the physical version of this sheet music exhibition presents itself as a comprehensive guide to World

War I patriotic sheet music. These are not to be confused with a collection of photographs in the exhibit cases. The virtual exhibition of *Over There!* is a collection of digitized sheet music covers, presented thematically and put into context with commentary that explains the culture of the era and how it is reflected in the music presented. And while on-line collections of materials are incredibly valuable, the on-line exhibition, in presenting this cultural context, serves as a teaching tool both in an informal setting, such as for the casual Web user who comes across the exhibit either by searching for materials with a search engine that strikes his or her interest, or by a hyperlink from a related page; or for the user in the classroom or research setting who is exposed to the material either through the recommendation of a teacher or professor, or in his own course-related research, bibliography, or "webliography."

The Web Development Component: Creating the On-line Exhibit

Developing the site was an exciting challenge. The archivist completed the research needed for the development of the on-line exhibition. There was a need to determine how this information would best be presented and to make decisions on how best to represent the original exhibition, while simultaneously creating visual interest, user accessibility, and a true representation of the original exhibition.

Initial issues such as the basic structure and overall look were first considerations. The exhibit design is a simple one, using a pale blue background color (#7695B0), with white Arial 3-pt. font in the body of the text. While this choice is not ideal for heavily text-driven sites, the decision to use these colors further illustrates that this is an exhibition site, rather than an on-line collection. The visual appeal and ease of use were critical factors in making this site.

The first step in assembling the on-line version of the exhibit was to create digital surrogates of the sheet music to be used on-line. The original ("real") exhibit presented only the covers of the sheet music and not the written music itself. It was decided to create the exhibit using only covers since the covers themselves present interesting imagery and are attractive to the eye. The blue background, white and dark blue text, and the selection of one piece of sheet music (a 1917 version of *Over There* with a red, white, and blue motif featuring Nora Bayes in a patriotic costume) for the title page completed the initial design decisions.

The actual digitization of the sheet music was not done in Special Collections but off-site in the University of Alabama's department of Geography's

Cartographic Research Laboratory using their high-powered planetary scanner. Most of the sheet music for the exhibit was larger than what can be accommodated by a standard flatbed scanner, the only scanner available within Special Collections at that time. If the scanning had been done on-site, there would have been a great deal of extra work, as the music would have to have been scanned in two pieces and then carefully pieced together using Adobe Photoshop. These large format TIFF files were then saved to recordable compact disks. These compact disks serve as the master copies of the images. The sheet music was scanned at 600 dpi, and the file size for each image was between 30 and 86 megabytes.

After the digitization and recording of the images to compact disc, I created the exhibit using the images, as well as the text that was written for the initial "physical" exhibition. The images were digitized after the physical exhibition was taken off display. Much of the work for the on-line exhibit was done not within Special Collections but on a computer in my home. This was done for two reasons. The machine and software at home are more powerful than those in my office. I also chose to do the project at home because I viewed it more as a "creative product" (akin to research) and not specifically part of my primary job responsibilities. The on-line version of this exhibition was a project that I developed on my own time, rather than as part of my day-to-day activity. Projects such as this could certainly fall within the realm of primary job responsibility, but this endeavor was self-initiated and both a learning experience and a form of research. General responsibility for the W.S. Hoole Special Collections Library Web site is within my control, and exhibitions and outreach are part of my general job description (the first category of three areas addressed in the tenure and promotion process). The creative decisions on what types of exhibits and events to develop and with whom I develop collaborative relationships are largely my own. I created the site using a PC, Adobe Photoshop, and Macromedia Dreamweaver MX.

Upon beginning the development of the site, the file-naming structure was an important consideration. Although there is no search mechanism for this exhibit site, there is a need to be able to identify the overall exhibition, the categories within the exhibition, as well as the song title by the file name, and hence the URL. This is useful when building the Web site because it facilitates the sorting of the images. It is also of assistance to the end user who can identify an image with the intuitive file name if a copy of the image is made from the Web site and saved by the end user.

The total number of actual pieces of sheet music used in the exhibition was relatively small. We chose forty-six items in the six categories. One of the great impetuses for the project is the fact that it is a manageable opportunity to develop a workable process to create an effective on-line exhibit using a small number of images. As with any new project, it is always favorable to start with a manageable goal and expand on the project and processes from that point on.

The digital surrogates on compact disk were copied to the hard drive. Because of the file sizes and the number of images, it was necessary to have a relatively large hard drive and an efficient machine. The copies of the TIFF files placed on the hard drive were then converted from 600 dpi TIFF files to 96 dpi JPG, and then to optimized JPG files using Adobe Photoshop 6.0. Any images that are to be viewed on the Web should not be larger than 96 dpi compressed JPG files, unless those images are being made available for use in publication or for other purposes. When designing an on-line exhibit, the ultimate purpose is to have that Web site accessible and navigable to individuals using a 56k modem, and with a 640 x 480 screen resolution at a minimum.

Thumbnails, or small versions of each of the images, were also created for the main page of each individual category. This allowed the user to view the entire category in brief before going farther into each category and its identification. This also allowed for a more visually appealing exhibition and presented all of the materials within each category simultaneously.

The 96 dpi JPG served as the access copy and the one that was manipulated, leaving the original 600 dpi files unchanged. A decision was made to make all of the images of the sheet music one standard size, despite the fact that several of the pieces were the small format sheet music created to conserve paper as part of the war effort (Feist Miniatures). Making all of the images a uniform size for on-line viewing aided in the overall design of the site. An additional image, an enlarged view of the disclaimer regarding the small format, is featured in the final exhibit. A second decision was made to make all of the full-size images a 600 dpi height. The steps in resizing the images were:

1. First open the master image in Photoshop 6.0; rotate as necessary;
2. Crop the image; reduce/optimize to a 96 dpi image for the Web;
3. Reduce size to a standard 600 dpi height;
4. Convert to RGB mode; and
5. Save the file to a new folder as a JPG using the file structure "category_abbreviatedsongtitle.jpg."

Using Adobe Photoshop 6.0, the images were then converted to RGB color from indexed color. The images were saved as JPGs with medium compression (5). Each full-size image is about 160k for the full size on the Web site. The exhibit was designed for viewing with a 1024 x 768 resolution monitor, though it can be viewed with a higher or lower resolution in both Netscape and Microsoft Explorer browsers with no problems. The finished site was checked on four separate machines and with different browsers and versions of those browsers.

A second image was then created, namely a large thumbnail or small image for the main page within each subsection of the exhibition. The size that was decided upon was a height of 150 pixels, larger than a standard thumbnail, but ideal for this purpose. Using Photoshop 6.0 for all of this work, the function of "optimize for web" (default settings) was used to reduce the overall file size. This is useful for a graphically heavy on-line exhibition such as this.

Mid-Course Corrections

Because the development of the on-line project was research in and of itself, and a great learning experience, it was necessary to continually review the process and make decisions about the design, scope, appearance, functionality, and breadth of the site. Feedback was sought from a colleague who has a great deal of experience with Web development.

Unveiling of the Site

Initially, a version of the site was mounted to personal Web space to test. The URL was presented to Daniel Goldmark, and to a few knowledgeable individuals who could evaluate its appearance, accuracy, and functionality. This was necessary because there was a need to make certain that the on-line exhibit appeared properly on different machines using different Internet browsers, different screen resolutions, and different connection speeds. The site was then presented to the curator of Special Collections and to the associate dean responsible for Special Collections to gain their approval.

Upon receiving comments and feedback, corrections and alterations were made to improve the site and its functionality. The completed site was burned onto a CD and sent to the libraries' Web site manager. It was then mounted to the Hoole Library Web site under "Digital Resources and Exhibitions." A small explanation of the site is provided on the "On-line Exhibits at Hoole" page at www.lib.ua.edu/libraries/hoole/digital/overthere/index.htm.

This on-line exhibit is a permanent exhibit and will be part of the Hoole Libraries Web site indefinitely. For this reason, a MARC record will be created, and the site will also be accessible via the University of Alabama Libraries' on-line catalog.

Benefits

The benefits of working with Daniel Goldmark were manifold, not just to us as individuals building toward tenure, but also to the repository and to our respective professions. The most considerable benefit is that working together in developing these sheet music exhibitions will add to our body of creative work, and this should ultimately assist us in gaining tenure from the university. While this assertion may not necessarily be quantifiable, creative endeavors such as this certainly are noticed and appreciated by those involved in decisions relating to the tenure and promotion process, including department heads, deans, tenure committees, and universities.

Another great benefit of this level of exposure via the World Wide Web is the benefit in terms of donor relations. Dr. Wade Hall, the donor of the sheet music as well as many other important materials including books, photographs, and sound recordings that help to document the rich and varied history and culture of the American South, will be pleased to see that his collections are being well used and brought to a broader audience. While this was not the ultimate driving force behind creating the exhibit, there was the benefit of recognizing a donor and his gifts to the repository and indicating to him that this generous gift is being actively used both for research and for exhibition.

An additional benefit to the development of digital projects in Special Collections is that placing surrogates of these materials on-line acts as a possible collection development tool. Special collections libraries are often misunderstood, with the average person not always fully understanding the collecting scope of the repository or what kinds of materials may be of interest for donation.

When on-line exhibitions or digital collections appear on the World Wide Web, those who are interested, and those who may not have thought they were interested, become exposed to a new aspect of special collections librarianship. The realization that these materials are being preserved may lead to donations of both collections and funding. The creation of the on-line exhibit is a new form of publicity, and the proper publicity of the project can also lead to additional recognition and exposure. Further, using these projects and collaborative efforts as fodder for publication is an additional way to publicize these efforts.

Benefits to the Institution

On-line exhibitions and collections open the world of special collections to a much broader audience. They serve as long-term definitive proof of the collections being held at one particular repository. They also serve to promote the collections and the repository itself. The notion of "spontaneous learning" is the idea that one can become inspired to learn more from the initial exposure to something like a virtual or real exhibition. The repository and the institution benefit from this collaboration in many ways. The teaching faculty member in turn exposes the collections to colleagues within his or her department, and also to colleagues throughout the country and the world who are interested in the holdings of the repository. This is all based upon the initial contact and project with the teaching faculty member. Yet another benefit for creating this level of on-line exposure to collections is that potential donors, or those who might never even consider themselves donors, might see the exhibit and in turn contact Special Collections regarding the donation of their own materials. Certainly with materials such as sheet music, many may not realize the historical and cultural significance or the research potential they possess. Sheet music was the precursor to recorded music in American households and was the primary source of group home entertainment in the days before television and the broad use of radio. Many people have collections of sheet music as family possessions that would be of great informational and research value to a library and its patrons.

Digital technology and its applications have also had a noticeable impact on the volume of requests made for materials. They have also allowed for greater contact with a broader audience. Specialized scholars are no longer the primary users, and those with casual and avocational interest in a collecting area have unprecedented access thanks to a search engine and a few mouse clicks. Requests can now quite easily come to the repository from anywhere in the world via e-mail.

The ability to physically house and provide intellectual access and description to archival materials, whether they are rare books, manuscript materials, or artifacts, is an expensive and time-consuming responsibility of the archivist. Digital technology, while creating numerous additional opportunities for creative output, intellectual and virtual "physical" access to collections, not only requires this new skill set, but also exponentially increases the amount of work and responsibility that falls to the special collections faculty member. These issues raise many questions with respect to the evolving role of the academic special collections librarian in a tenure-track setting. These are questions that the archivist must address in collaboration with the unit heads, library administration, and college or university administration.

In this particular instance, because of this collaboration, two potential donors have contacted us, wishing to give large music-related collections to our repository. This was in direct response to this collaboration. Our next exhibit and the publicity it generates will allow for others within the university community to consider these kinds of collaborative partnerships with our repository, and with other repositories as well. It has added to the profile of Special Collections, and has already led to additional partnerships with other teaching faculty. And by having a URL that allows immediate access to this on-line exhibition, the opportunities to promote the exhibit, the collections, and the repository are endless, both within the university community and beyond, through Web site links, dynamic press releases, listservs, and e-mail lists.

Continued Contact and Collaboration

An additional benefit of this collaboration was that in exploring in depth the holdings in the *Wade Hall Sheet Music Collection*, Dr. Goldmark decided that his next monograph will be on the subject of American sheet music. And the energy and positive reaction to the first experience has already generated a second collaboration, an exhibition entitled, *Music Goes to the Movies: Sheet Music Reflected in American Cinema.* This exhibit will begin its life as a physical exhibit within special collections, but when it is dismantled from the exhibit cases, it will probably become an on-line exhibit as well. The research and structure of the first virtual exhibition is already in place, so this project will be easier, and more successful because of the experience generated through *Over There!*

Future Research and Related Projects

It is anticipated that the next on-line exhibition created for the Hoole Library will be done using the new state-of-the-art digitization laboratory now under development in Hoole. The University Libraries at the University of Alabama are currently participating in a large, statewide Institute of Museum and Library Services (IMLS) grant to digitize unique materials pertaining to the unique, diverse history and culture of the state of Alabama. This opportunity falls within the realm of primary job responsibility for the archivists in the Hoole Library and has allowed for numerous training opportunities that will help further skills in digitization and Web development. The University of Alabama and specifically the University Libraries are to serve as a digitization center to process our own unique materials, and also to assist other smaller institutions with the digitization of theirs. This grant, along with support from the University and University Libraries, will allow us to have the equipment, server space, and software to make this and future projects a reality. Because of the additional training and assistance, technical tasks such as the digitization and capture of these digital surrogates can be done with the assistance of students as well. This is also a unique and beneficial opportunity for students, most often graduate students in the University of Alabama's School of Library and Information Studies, to gain experience with this growing area of librarianship. Students will not only be able to participate in an exciting project but will also gain practical experience and will be able to reference the URLs for these projects on their own résumés when seeking out their first professional librarian or archivist position.

Conclusions

Tenure and promotion have a strict set of criteria and require recommendation for promotion and tenure by committees, department heads, and deans. These individuals make that decision by scrutinizing a faculty member's body of work. This body of work includes primary job responsibilities, professional activities and publication, and service to the institution. The decision to promote is based on the body of work in its entirety, evaluating all of the efforts put forth by the individual faculty member. While there may not be a direct impetus for library faculty to seek out teaching faculty for collaborative projects such as the creation of exhibitions or digital projects, the elements of these types of projects both typify and help to define the work that we, in fact, should be doing, and the kind of work that is expected of us. While Web development may not be a specific job duty or responsibility for individuals working in these areas, the added skills required to use an HTML editor, and to understand the theory and practice of digitization, only enhance the potential of the individual archivist. This additional skill set serves as a major component of the digital project and is necessary in order to further these efforts. The second component is the initiative, drive, and ability to seek out and work with faculty in developing interesting, viable projects that relate to the collections and mission of the repository. By merging these two areas and creating projects such as these, we are indicating clearly to those who are ultimately responsible for evaluating our body of work and either granting or denying tenure, that there is much to offer within this arena. By recognizing the added effort, and being rewarded for that effort not only will the candidate for tenure and promotion benefit, but the repository, the university, and the community will as well. Before taking on a project such as this, it is recommended that one gain support from systems and Web departments and seek out their input and advice, especially if this is a first project in this area.

For tenure-track special collections faculty working in a public service capacity, there are numerous opportunities to involve untenured, junior faculty in projects and programs that not only help further the mission and goals of the repository and the university as a whole but also help to develop strong relationships and allegiances with the junior teaching faculty. Since they will more than likely be at the college or university for many years, it is important to build these relationships early. The experience of working together, their added expertise, and the opportunity to add another project, publication, lecture, or exhibition to their vitae are of vital importance to them as well. This collaboration is also a form of outreach for the special collections faculty member, who is able to get the good name and good work of her repository out not just to the faculty member with whom she is working but also to the entire department of the faculty member and beyond.

Collaborators also need to be advocates for each other. They can ask their department chairs to send thank-you letters to their collaborators' departments. A letter sent to the faculty member through his department chair or dean, thanking him for his collaboration, will then appear in his dossier or tenure file. The tenure committee will also see the collaboration as evidenced in the tenure file. Advertising and promotion of the exhibition or other collaboration will also indicate that there is involvement from another department.

Tenure-track library faculty are at an advantage overall because of the use of technology in the delivery of information and the extent to which that technology has infiltrated the librarian's world. The academic librarian is expected not only to understand current technologies but also to use them in everyday interactions with collections and patrons. Traditionally, archivists have had less opportunity for this level of technological interaction because of the nature of their holdings and the methods of creating intellectual access. This is true for the processing archivist as well as the public service archivist.

The opportunity to create an exhibit that is housed physically within a special collections library, with limited access available to the public, is by definition a standard practice. To reach beyond the walls of special collections to create and mount an exhibit with access via the World Wide Web is not only beneficial to the promotion of the library but also expands the use of the collection and is beneficial to the world at large.

While it is impossible to determine the weight my involvement with technology will have in the tenure process, the administration of the university and the libraries appreciate and expect faculty to get involved with new technologies. One such example is the University of Alabama's *Innovative Instructional Technology Faculty Grants*. These grants encourage faculty to use technology to develop innovative teaching and learning methods, which can serve as a model to others. These grants not only make these projects possible, they also serve to allow others to recognize the importance of technology in an academic setting. Faculty are encouraged to seek out this funding, and their projects are presented at a university-wide forum each year. It would seem that a department head, associate dean, dean, and tenure committee would look favorably upon an untenured professor who sought out, received, and used a grant specifically put in place to implement technology in the classroom, with money specifically allocated by the provost of the university.

In reflecting upon the work done on this project, specifically the digital component, I recognize that there is a need for and will be a continued emphasis on digital scholarship, whether that be in the form of developing Web-based teaching tools, digital surrogates, or digital exhibitions. In my own conversations with those interested in developing on-line projects, it is evident that in some instances, the technological support, both in training and in equipment and software, does not match the desire to initiate and develop these projects.

In summation, this project and many of the on-line exhibitions planned for the future within special collections are building on the basic principles of outreach. While special collections traditionally cannot reach beyond their own walls with regard to collections because of the very nature of special collections librarianship and of the fragility and security of the collections themselves, the World Wide Web has changed that notion by bringing visitors to collections, albeit surrogates of the collections, via the World Wide Web. While our exhibition of World War I patriotic sheet music was timely, entertaining, and educational, and was a welcome accompaniment to the exhibition on William March, we will have multiplied the impact of the exhibition many times by placing digital surrogates of these titles on the World Wide Web. And while those visiting the repository Web site will see the materials in this context, they will also be accessible through search engines such as Google and AltaVista, alerting potential patrons and visitors to our sheet music collection and in turn to the repository and to other holdings as well. While this exhibition features just under fifty pieces of sheet music, introductory information within the exhibition will alert those interested in American sheet music to the extensive collection held in our repository and will also provide the audience access to the breadth of the collection through our on-line catalog.

The tenure and promotion process for academic librarians and archivists most often reflects that of the tenure-track teaching faculty. While the accomplishments of each individual are weighed separately, there is an overall need for productive, collegial activity that not only assists in representing the department and university as a whole in a positive light, but also illustrates that the faculty member is able and willing to participate in the broader collegial environment. The digital project is the ideal environment for such a project within the construct of the special collections environment. The very nature of the collections limits wide exposure to the outside world. Under ordinary circumstances—or rather in an era before widespread use of the World Wide Web, Web graphics, and large quantities of bandwidth and fast Internet connections—the visitor needed direct access to the repository in order to participate in the exhibit, unless a catalog was created for the exhibit. Publishing a catalog can be costly, and distribution will certainly be limited. The use of the digital medium to expose patrons to our work has completely changed the face of archives and special collections.

While a project such as completing a small on-line exhibition that closely follows the original makeup of an actual exhibit within special collections may not in and of itself be on a par with the publication of an article—in terms of weight within the tenure and promotion review, it does indicate to those reviewing the dossier a different set of skills used by a faculty member, often junior faculty, that can bring an added dimension of exposure to the collections and repository.

Actively seeking out projects in which to collaborate and taking the initiative to go beyond the familiar and expected walls of one's own repository illustrate an understanding of the need not only to work beyond the confines of one's own repository, but also to develop innovative and fulfilling partnerships with teaching faculty, community members, and other repositories. These relationships not only allow new uses of these unique materials but also, through the development of these digital projects, allow the materials to have a much greater impact that goes beyond the standard exhibit.

Teaching faculty should seek out the special collections library on their campus or a special collections library that holds collections that reflect their research interests and expertise. Possible collaborations with archival repositories can lead to long-standing productive relationships with an archivist. While not every repository has the facilities or the capacity for extensive exhibitions, there is certainly room for many different levels of collaboration. My partnerships have gone beyond those of the history faculty to include professors in music, human environmental science, English, psychology, library and information studies, and the book arts. Special collections faculty should also investigate opportunities to work with teaching faculty to develop projects and programs, especially digital projects and programs that work toward increasing access to collections and educating the public on many levels.

This is the first in what I hope will be several collaborative projects using the sheet music from the *Wade Hall Collection of Southern History and Culture*. There is much potential for expanding this project and others like it to incorporate music, both in its written form as images and in the form of .wav or .mpg files. This will only increase the value of the on-line exhibition as an educational tool.

Collaborative outreach efforts between special collections faculty and teaching faculty serve to develop and build upon numerous opportunities for creative and professional growth as well as for promotion of the repository and academic institution. These efforts should be both encouraged and recognized for their myriad contributions to the repository and institution as a whole, as well as for the initiative, skill, and creativity of the faculty members involved.

Notes

1. The EAD Document Type Definition (DTD) is a standard for encoding archival finding aids using the Standard Generalized Markup Language (SGML). The standard is maintained in the Network Development and MARC Standards Office of the Library of Congress (LC) in partnership with the Society of American Archivists.

2. *Provenance* refers to the organization or individual that created, accumulated, and/or maintained a collection of materials prior to their deposit in an archival repository.

3. *Respect des fonds* refers specifically to the principle that archival materials of the same provenance must not be intermingled with others of a different provenance.

4. *Original order* refers to the principal that archivists maintain the original arrangement of a collection to the best of their ability in order to preserve existing relationships and evidential significance.

5. The creation of this project stems from a long-developing interest in the display of historical resources information on the World Wide Web, starting with a seminar paper project completed for the fulfillment of the MLS from the University at Albany's School of Information Science and Policy in 1999. Interest and participation in the presentation of resources and information via the World Wide Web pertaining to archival materials and resources has continued to be a part of my work since graduate school. The findings for this first project were published in the *Journal of the Association for History and Computing* in August 1999 and are accessible at www.mcel.pacificu.edu/JAHC/JAHCII2/ARTICLESII2/LACHER-FELDMAN/Lacherindex.HTML.

6. A digital surrogate is a digitized (scanned or digitally photographed) copy of a physical item that has been made available electronically via the World Wide Web. While it is not meant to *replace* the original item, it is used in on-line collections or on-line exhibitions as a digital representation of an item or object. The digital surrogate can play an extensive role in the operations of a special collections library, by allowing for greater access, digital enhancement, and preservation, and by preventing damage caused by overhandling fragile items. In this instance, it refers specifically to digital images of physical items originally used for a physical exhibition to be used in an on-line or virtual exhibition.

7. I made the decision to complete the on-line version of this exhibition on my computer at home because of current conditions within my repository. I also was required to digitize the materials off-site because of the then technological constraints within my repository to scan larger-format materials such as sheet music.

8. MARC (Machine Readable Catalog) record, a communications format and descriptive standard for library materials was developed by the Library of Congress, and is used widely in the United States and abroad to describe materials and as a vehicle to provide access.

Part III

The Present and the Future

Deborah Lines Andersen

Past, Present, and Future

The chapters preceding this one have looked at the past from the point of view of studies about how the tenure, promotion, and review process have been influenced (or not) by digital scholarship. Additionally, the case studies present a view of the present, particularly of the kind of digital scholarship that academics are using to publish, do research, and teach their students. The future is left for the rest of this book.

Without a crystal ball, there are still ways to establish what the future might hold. Based upon trends that we see today in the university, in technology, and in the way people do business, there is no sure way to predict what will happen to digital scholarship, but there are indicators that might point the way.

The Changing Nature of Information Delivery

Influenced by distance education, the escalating cost of journal subscriptions, and the ubiquitous nature of computers and Internet connections, the information-delivery role of the academic library is undergoing major changes. Whereas once individuals came into the library for their research, spending hours using paper indexes and abstracts as guides to paper journals and monographs, the present library user might very well not come to the library at all. This is not just a phenomenon brought about by the World Wide Web. Even if one never uses the Web, one can access indexes and full-text journal articles on-line in a variety of fields from an ever-growing number of sources. Some paper-based journals have gone to dual formats, while others have licensed out their back issues to have them digitized and made available through Web-based library connections.

Library users now expect that they will be able to receive information over the conduit of their computers. This technology has moved from novelty to expectation for students in the university setting. My students expect that their reserve readings will be available on-line (and password-protected to meet copyright regulations) so that they can read articles in the convenience of their homes, whether or not the library is open.

This expectation extends to faculty members who receive current contents of pertinent journals, full-text articles, and answers to reference queries from the comfort of their offices or home desks. Both students and faculty have become experts at the use of e-mail to answer questions (through virtual office hours), contact colleagues, turn in papers, and work collaboratively on research. Although there will remain faculty who refuse to use digital technologies, it is impossible in today's university to be a student who manages to avoid all sorts of digital technologies and still survive.

New information-delivery mechanisms, and their acceptance by students as well as large numbers of faculty, must influence the way that academics view the products of digital scholarship. As it becomes more and more common for information to flow through their computers, scholars will identify with digital delivery mechanisms, understand their complexity, and credit the effort that it takes to create an on-line class, CD-ROM, or Web-based museum exhibition. These scholars will eventually become part of tenure, promotion, and review committees that credit assistant professors' digital work on the way toward tenure.

Trickle-down Effects of Sophisticated Technologies

There was a time when computers were only in the form of mainframes and so expensive that only the government or the military had access to them. The advent of the personal computer meant that many more individuals could have computing at their fingertips, but these computers were slow and could manipulate only small amounts of data. With the present state of computerization it is possible to run multiple applications on a laptop computer, working among documents like this one, spreadsheets, the World Wide Web, and e-mail at the same time. Miniaturization has reached a state where computers are lighter and lighter, performing more functions all the time, and inexpensive enough so that the average college student can afford one. Palm technologies and wireless technologies are also common on the average campus, or soon will be.

Advances in software over the past twenty years have also made information manipulation cheaper, faster, and easier. There are still individuals in academe who remember accessing the Web with "Archie," and "Veronica"—technologies that were UNIX-based and relied on the memories of users to know the right commands for the right situation. Menu-driven software has changed how much the user is required to remember, while search engines make information easily available to the average searcher.

The decreased cost of doing business—in time, talents, and funds—because of very powerful computing means that more individuals will be exposed to these technologies and expect them to be available at the university. As with library information, this expectation should cause tenure, promotion, and review committee membership to slowly shift, as older faculty members retire out of the system and younger faculty members consider digital technologies to be a part of their everyday academic lives.

Doing Business in the Twenty-First Century

The private sector plays a part in conditioning individuals to accept the role that digital technologies could play in their lives. The examples are countless. Banks offer Web-based banking that includes paying bills, transferring money between different accounts, checking balances, and making investments. Grocery stores use their cards to capture their customers' buying habits, but these same cards mean that it is possible to check out one's own groceries, never dealing with a grocery clerk again. E-ticketing on airlines has reached a point where one can swipe a credit card at the airport, be greeted by name, point to a computerized map to change seating for the flight, and be issued a boarding pass—all in a strictly digital transaction. More and more of the U.S. toll-road system is wired with fiber optic cable so that automobile drivers with transponders can pull through toll booths without fishing for change in their pockets or slowing down to pay.

These methods of doing business are a third example of indicators that would tend to predict that scholars of the not-so-distant future will be so comfortable with digital technologies that their ability to use them will be expected by individuals who work in academic settings. The only mechanism that might slow down this process is a dynamic effect brought about by tenuring today. If the individuals who sit on tenuring committees are not digital scholars and do not credit digital scholarship, then only traditionally based assistant professors will become tenured and go on to become the committee members of the future. Without some mechanisms in place today to credit the digital scholarship of tomorrow, it is very likely that junior faculty members will shy away, or at least be slowed down, from scholarship that might be good for their students or research but would be detrimental to continued appointment.

Changing Tenure and Promotion Policy
in a Digital Environment

One way of dealing with digital scholarship that follows from the above discussion is to create university policies that explicitly evaluate and honor the digital. The first chapter in Part III, by Dennis Trinkle, deals with specific guidelines for evaluating digital media activities. Ryan Johnson, in the chapter that follows, looks at exactly this method of change, citing the case of Washington State University. Rather than waiting for one or more test cases and then seeing how the junior faculty members fared, the university libraries decided to define the bounds of digital scholarship. The libraries allow newly minted library faculty members to make use of what they learned as students, rather than wait until after they are tenured and their digital abilities are no longer at the cutting edge.

Changing Copyright Policy in a Digital Environment

It would be impossible to write a book about digital scholarship without looking at how copyright owners will be affected in a digital environment. The music industry was shaken by the effects of MP3 files and Napster, realizing that with digitization, ownership of information was at times extremely tenuous. Videotapes, audio tapes, and easily copied computer files mean that information can be passed from one individual to another without compensating the original creator and owner of the work. Today, writable CD-ROMs provide copies of visual and auditory materials that are just as good as the originals.

Technology will always move faster than the law. The Napster case made the news not just because so many students were using MP3s and would be affected by the outcome of the court's decision, but also because there was no firm legal precedent for dealing with music files that were transferred across college campuses with this enabling software. For every password-protected or encrypted file there is the computer programmer who will be happy to spend hours breaking its code. It is very possible that tenuous ownership of digital materials will make some academics hesitant to be digital scholars. Although one can copy paper-based scholarship, digital scholarly works are simply easier to reproduce and distribute electronically. Terrence Maxwell's chapter looks at these issues in light of different stakeholder groups and the effects of digitization on legal doctrine.

Influencing the Future

The last chapter of this book looks at the future through a variety of possible scenarios. David Staley suggests that one cannot predict what will happen—there are too many variables to consider—but that one can posit a variety of ways in which academia might deal with products of digital scholarship. He discusses a continuum of possibilities from out-and-out rejection to total acceptance of the digital scholar, pausing along the way to discuss what differences these various scenarios will have in the tenure, promotion, and review process.

Staley's position as a historian gives an interesting flavor to his chapter. We cannot predict the future, but that does not mean that we cannot influence it. The purpose of this book is to inform scholars, administrators, and tenure committee members about the scope and depth of digital scholarship, in order to make better-informed decisions and policies about tenure at their universities. Our actions today have implications for the future.

Chapter 10

Guidelines for Evaluating Digital Media Activities in Tenure, Promotion, and Review

Dennis A. Trinkle

Creating Guidelines

The members of the Executive Council of the American Association for History and Computing (AAHC) worked with members of the Modern Language Association and the American Political Science Association in crafting guidelines for scholars who are facing tenure, promotion, and review where there is digital scholarship involved. The guidelines below are published here with the permission of AAHC, and were adapted with permission from the *MLA Guidelines for Evaluating Work with Digital Media in the Modern Languages.*

These guidelines provide a template for other institutions to develop their own written guidelines, so that faculty members engaged in research and teaching with digital media can be adequately, fully, and fairly evaluated and rewarded. This book contains an example of that adaptation in Ryan Johnson's example in the next chapter from the Washington State University Libraries. Written guidelines provide clear rationales for valuing digital scholarship. They are advocated in various ways in every chapter of this book and, with this book, should provide scholars as well as evaluators with methods and benchmark approaches for both creating and evaluating digital scholarship.

The pace of technological change makes it impossible for any one set of guidelines to account completely for the ways digital media and the work done with them are influencing historical research, teaching, and publication. The principle underlying these guidelines is that when institutions seek work with digital media and faculty members express interest in it, the institution must give full regard to this work when faculty members are hired or considered for reappointment, tenure, and promotion.

Guidelines for Appointment, Reappointment, Promotion, and Tenure Committees

1. Delineate and Communicate Responsibilities

When chairs and hiring committees seek candidates who have expertise in the use of digital media, explicit reference to such work should be included in job descriptions, and candidates should be apprised of their responsibilities relative to this work. When candidates wish to have work with digital media considered an integral part of their positions, the expectations and responsibilities connected with such work, and the recognition given to it, should be clearly delineated and communicated to them at hiring.

2. Engage Qualified Reviewers

Faculty members who work with digital media should have their work evaluated by persons knowledgeable about the use of these media in the candidate's field. At times this may be possible only by engaging qualified reviewers from other institutions. The American Association for History and Computing will help departments and review committees in search of appropriate expertise to locate and coordinate qualified outside evaluators whenever requested.

3. Review Work in the Medium in Which It Was Produced

Since scholarly work is sometimes designed for presentation in a specific medium, evaluative bodies should review faculty members' work in the medium in which it was produced. For example, Web-based projects should be viewed on-line, not in printed form.

4. Seek Interdisciplinary Advice

If faculty members have used technology to collaborate with colleagues from other disciplines on the same campus or on different campuses, departments and institutions should seek the assistance of experts in those other disciplines to assess and evaluate such interdisciplinary work.

5. Stay Informed About Disability Issues

Search, reappointment, promotion, and tenure committees have a responsibility to become and remain informed of technological innovations that permit disabled individuals to conduct research and carry out other professional responsibilities effectively. Information on this issue is available at, for example, the Adaptech Project.

Guidelines for Candidates and Faculty Members

1. Ask About Evaluation and Support

When candidates for faculty positions first negotiate the terms of their jobs, they should ask how credit for work with digital media in teaching, research, and service will be considered in the reappointment, tenure, and promotion processes. In addition, candidates and faculty members should confirm that they will have institutional support and access to facilities so that they can work creatively and productively with digital media.

2. Negotiate Roles and Responsibilities

Faculty members and job candidates should negotiate their responsibilities and departmental roles in the use, development, and support of information technologies in their teaching, service, and research. Faculty members and candidates for positions that combine administrative and faculty responsibilities, including the development and support of technological infrastructures, must have a clear understanding of how their work will be evaluated.

3. Document and Explain Digital Work

Faculty members who work with digital media should be prepared to make explicit the results, theoretical underpinnings, and intellectual rigor of their work. They should be prepared, to the same extent that faculty members in other fields are held accountable, to show the relevance of their work in terms of the traditional areas of teaching, research, and service. They should take particular care to

- Describe how their work may overlap or redefine the traditional categories.
- Describe the process underlying the creation of work in digital media (e.g., the creation of infrastructure as well as content).
- Describe new collaborative relationships with other faculty members and students required by their work in digital media.

Documentation of projects might include recording sources of internal or external funding, awards or other professional recognition, and reviews and citations of the work in print or digital journals.

Chapter 11

The Development of Criteria for the Inclusion of Digital Publications in the Tenure Process

A Case Study of the Washington State University Libraries

Ryan Johnson

Predicting the Demise of Print

The death of print has been predicted for many years. As each new techno-logical means of disseminating information has been developed during this century, some have proclaimed that the new technology, whether it be film or microform or now digital, would supplant the printed word. While the first two failed to expand appropriately for this to occur, the digital form has made some real inroads. This does not mean that print is surrendering without a fight. According to the Book Industry Study Group, the number of volumes sold annually between 1995 and 2000 remained relatively stable.[1] However, the number of titles published has gone down over this period with the reduction primarily in scholarly monographs.[2] Similarly, the *Gale Directory of Publication and Broadcast Media* reports that the number of newspapers and magazines published has also increased over the same time period.[3]

Many of the attempts to produce profitable electronic periodicals for the general public have been failures. Microsoft's *Slate*,[4] which has reverted to a free access policy, and *Suck*,[5] which went out of business, are just two ex-amples. While this may change over time, *Salon*,[6] for example, is surviving on a mixed model of free and fee-based content. For now, general on-line publishing has yet to prove itself a profitable enterprise. This is not true for more specialized types of information. Information providers in business, for example, have successfully adopted an on-line format for delivery of proprietary information in a timely fashion. This is not a recent development.

Lexis-Nexis™ has been providing this type of service for decades. They are beginning to get more specialized competitors entering the market place including Hoover's™ and Mergent™. These companies typically provide services to businesses or professionals who are in need of the timeliest information and are thus willing to pay for it. The general public has not yet shown a similar willingness to purchase intellectual content on-line.

The other area in which on-line publishing is proving profitable is scholarly journals.[7] Journal publishers have been converting their content into electronic format for a decade now. The majority of these are electronic versions of print journals. Most are still available in both formats. The primary market for these journals is academic libraries, which have had an ongoing budget crisis since the mid-1980s due largely to increases in the cost of what librarians refer to as STM (science, technology, and medicine) journals.[8] While the subscription costs for electronic journals are often not less than the cost of their print counterparts, libraries are able to find savings with electronic journals over print from the reduced staff and other operational costs as fewer and fewer journals need to be marked, shelved, bound, and claimed. The many varied pricing models and the development of regional and other library consortia have allowed for cooperative purchasing as well as bundled purchasing of electronic journals. While this model allows a library or library consortia to subscribe to an increased number of journal titles at a reduced cost per title, many of these arrangements have clauses that limit a library's flexibility in reducing these titles in the face of future budget shortfalls, and they have also led libraries to add titles they would not have otherwise purchased simply because they are part of the package. Kenneth Frasier, university librarian at the University of Wisconsin-Madison, has called bundled acquisition of journals the "Big Deal" and has predicted that libraries will regret having entered into these contracts over time.[9]

While electronic journals have been increasing in number, electronic books have not done as well. There have been several attempts to set up e-book publishing and distribution, both original monographs and electronic versions of print titles, none of which has succeeded financially. This is largely due to the fact that most people do not read a great deal of text on a screen, and there is no single reader standard that consumers can adopt.[10]

For academics, the publication of articles in scholarly journals or monographs is essential to obtaining tenure and promotion. However, with the changes in publishing, the ability of all scholars to publish their research findings is becoming more difficult, particularly in monograph-length works. Technological change has also increased the ways in which information can be presented, moving beyond the traditional text format, sometimes augmented with charts or other images. The development of on-line instruction has also expanded the ways university faculty can present information aimed at students. While there are more opportunities available for faculty to be creative, the rules by which they are evaluated often do not recognize these efforts.[11]

Some academic organizations have attempted to bring this issue to light by developing sample guidelines for the incorporation of new nontraditional publications in the tenure, promotion, and review process for faculty. One such set of guidelines was developed by the American Association for History and Computing.[12] These association-level efforts serve to inform members of the issues. They have been augmented by an ongoing discussion among academics in the literature[13] as well as by independent organizations such as the Multimedia Educational Resource for Learning and Online Teaching (MERLOT).[14] These organizations seek to provide a way for faculty to get on-line information peer reviewed, to help establish best practices—particularly with on-line teaching modules—and to encourage standards by which materials can be evaluated.

The world of scholarly communication, in particular, and publishing, in general, is changing because of the technologies that have been developed with the Internet. While print is not dead, nor will it die any time soon in the opinion of this author, there are more ways to create and distribute information than there have been at any time in the past, and the ability to do so without having to go through any intermediary such as an editorial board or a publisher has led to a vast array of sources of information of varying quality. In this environment, university faculty need to find a way for their more creative efforts to be acknowledged in the formal evaluations conducted by their universities, or they risk being left behind in this new environment. Failure to obtain tenure will discourage other faculty from participating in the development of materials to be presented in new and innovative ways. If the expansion of the world of information within the academy is to continue to move forward rapidly, there must be an acknowledgment of the new models of publishing in the standards by which faculty are judged, and the means to evaluate these materials must be clearly defined. While professional associations can suggest guidelines, they are not binding on the institutions or their faculties. Universities and departments can, on the other hand, adopt guidelines that will make the process of evaluation more transparent in the university setting.

In May 2001, the faculty of the Washington State University Libraries took the step to establish a policy and incorporated "Guidelines for the Evaluation of Electronic Publications" into the criteria by which library faculty would be evaluated for tenure, promotion, and annual review.[15] These guidelines provide the faculty the opportunity to be creative in current and future technologies by establishing a method of evaluating the quality of those publications that are produced outside of the traditional avenues of peer-reviewed journals or monographs.

While members of the library faculty had been interested in the changing nature of scholarly communication both from a research standpoint and in terms of collecting and making information in new formats available to students and faculty, the formulation of these guidelines was the effort of the Libraries' Faculty Affairs Committee, of which the author was a member. The discussion on inclusion of materials published outside of existing avenues began when the author sent a copy of the newly adopted guidelines created by the American Association for History and Computing (AAHC) to the other members of the committee as an information item. The committee as whole, in February 2001, decided that the issue was of sufficient importance to attempt the creation of a document that would facilitate the incorporation of scholarly information published in nonprint formats. The committee assigned Joel Cummings, Electronic Resource Librarian for the Owen Science and Engineering Library at WSU, and this author to draft a set of guidelines using the AAHC document as a guide while looking to the Association for Research Libraries and the Association for College and Research Libraries for similar examples of such policy statements and other materials that would be of assistance in this effort.[16]

As the draft guidelines began to take shape, there were three distinct sections that developed. The first was to be a framework, or introduction, to provide structure to the specific guidelines and to suggest what types of publications are and are not covered by the document. This portion of the document remained basically unchanged from the first draft until formal adoption. The final version reads:

> With the advent of digital publication and all of the varied opportunities that it allows, it is important that these materials be fairly evaluated in a manner consistent over time and across format as part of Category II in the tenure, promotion and review process. Standards for the evaluation of printed materials are well established within the academy, with peer-review as the primary standard for quality. If the peer-review process is applied to digital publications, then those publications should be treated in the same manner as print publications that have received peer-review. However, it is possible to publish materials electronically without any type of formal peer or editorial review. In these cases it is essential that materials be judged consistently over time in order to insure a fair tenure and promotion process.[17]

As a point of clarification, in the WSU tenure, promotion, and review process there are three distinct categories. Category II is entitled "Research/

Scholarly/Creative and Professional Achievements and Activities."[18] Category I is professional competence, and Category III is service to the university, the profession, and the world.

There were two premises incorporated in this paragraph. The first was that publications that followed an established process of peer review would be considered equally regardless of format of publication and were thus beyond the purview of these guidelines. While this statement was not troubling to the members of the library faculty at WSU, within academia at large, the format of the journal has at times been an issue in some review decisions.[19] This statement was the first *de jure* statement authorizing the inclusion of nonpeer-reviewed digital publications fully into the tenure and review process. There had been a *de facto* policy in place, and at least two faculty members had created on-line searchable bibliographies, one covering scientific research on Yellowstone National Park and the other on women and the workplace.[20] This statement formalized the policy, ensuring consistency over time.

Once the introductory framework was established, creating the criteria for evaluation was the next task. LFAC (Library Faculty Affairs Committee) had decided in the February meeting to follow the pattern of the AAHC guidelines, and include instructions for both the institution and the faculty member.[21] These sections underwent a good deal of change prior to final approval, while retaining certain central principles. The first draft, dated March 15, 2001, included the following instructions for institutional review:

1. *Engage Qualified Reviewers.*
   Faculty members who work with digital media should have their work evaluated by persons knowledgeable about the use of these media in the candidate's field. At times this may be possible only by engaging qualified reviewers from other institutions.
2. *Review Work in the Medium in Which It Was Produced.*
   Evaluative bodies should always review faculty members' work in the medium in which it was produced. For example, Web-based projects should be viewed online, not in printed form.
3. *Seek Interdisciplinary Advice.*
   If the work in question is multidisciplinary in nature or in a subject area other than librarianship, then the assistance of experts in the other disciplines should be acquired to assess and evaluate such interdisciplinary work unless such subject expertise is available within the libraries.[22]

The intent of this section was to provide for an evaluative process that would ensure that each publication was judged fairly by someone with the appropriate qualifications to provide input on both the content and the use of the media. Because librarians often publish in their disciplines of specialization as well as on the practice of librarianship, the recruitment of reviewers from outside the libraries, if needed, was provided for as well.

Another important standard included in this section was that these publications were to be evaluated in the media in which they were created. While fairly simple Web pages can appear similar when printed, the dynamic, interactive, and nonlinear resources that digital technology now allows do not translate well to the printed page and often do not print at all. Thus, for these publications to be accurately evaluated, particularly in the use of the media itself, they would have to be judged in their original form.

This section was simplified significantly in the discussions with the faculty as a whole. The primary principles were retained, however. By the time the final version was approved, it had been reduced from three points to two and was in a clearer and more easily understood form.

1. *Engage Qualified Reviewers.*
   Faculty members who work in non-print media should have their work evaluated in two areas:
   - The intellectual content of the work
   - The efficacy of the use of the media (this could be usability, appearance, innovation, etc.).
   If the necessary expertise to evaluate a faculty member's work is not available among the tenured faculty, then outside reviewers should be engaged.
2. *Review Work in the Medium in Which It Was Produced.*
   Evaluative bodies should always review faculty members' work in the medium in which it was produced (e.g., Web-based projects should be viewed online, not in printed form).[23]

When an article is published in a journal, it becomes part of a body of literature and is placed within a certain broad context. Since journals tend to publish within rather specific topical areas, where an article is published is partially defined by the subject matter. Furthermore, most articles contain a literature review that further places the article more specifically within the context of previous research. A project published on the World Wide Web and not in an electronic journal often does not possess this type of context to help readers, or evaluators, judge the quality of the arguments contained therein.

This need for a context was a part of the requirements for the faculty member's portion of the evaluation process. The initial draft included the following language:

Guidelines for Candidates and Faculty Members:

Document and Explain the Work.

Faculty members who work with digital media should be prepared to:
- Make explicit the results, theoretical underpinnings, and intellectual rigor of their work.
- Describe how the work is related to a spectrum of previous research.
- Describe the process underlying the creation of the work including design activities required to deliver the content in the particular media employed.
- Describe collaborative relationships with other faculty members and students required by the work in digital media.[24]

In addition to the context and intellectual framework of the publication, the faculty member was required to describe the process of creation especially in terms of the design and development of the media used to deliver the content as well as any collaboration with other faculty or students in the development of the publication and its design. Giving credit where it is due is part of the reason for this requirement. It is also so that the evaluators can understand what the actual scope of the project is and how much effort was required to complete it.

In the discussions on this topic, one of the issues that was clarified was to clearly state how this report was to be made. At WSU, faculty members prepare a Professional Activity Report each year as part of their formal evaluation. The faculty member's supporting materials are to be included as part of this review process. If the faculty member were submitting materials for third-year review, tenure, or promotion, this material would also include explanatory information about publication. The rest of the section remained relatively unchanged in the final draft.

Guidelines for Candidates and Faculty Members:

1. Document and Explain the Work.

   In the faculty activity report and/or tenure documentation, it is incumbent upon faculty members who work with digital media to:
   - Make explicit the results, theoretical underpinnings, and intellectual rigor of their work.
   - Describe how the work is related to a spectrum of previous research, scholarly/creative or professional achievements and activities.
   - Describe the process underlying the creation of the work including design activities required to deliver the content in the particular media employed.
   - Describe collaborative relationships with other faculty members and students required by the work in digital media.[25]

The discussion in the faculty meetings and the Faculty Affairs Committee about these proposed guidelines was lengthy and extended. The Faculty Affairs Committee decided to begin this process in its meeting in February 2001.[26] The first draft was submitted to the committee on March 15 and after revisions was put before the faculty for its meeting on March 27.[27] It was debated at length in both the March and April meetings and was passed unanimously on May 22, 2001.[28] The discussion included more than just the particulars of the guidelines; it also included the larger issue of what constitutes scholarship and how scholarship should be disseminated and archived. While these questions were not fully answered, it was acknowledged that with the changing nature of communication and ever increasing means of publishing information, the WSU Libraries needed to have a system in place to encourage faculty members to be creative and innovative in their scholarship. That creativity should reach beyond the topics examined, to the ways they are examined and the means of presenting the results to their colleagues and to the larger academic communities. These guidelines accomplish this by providing for the inclusion of innovative and new forms of scholarly communication in the tenure and review process so that those faculty members who choose to go outside the traditional journal model of publishing will not be punished for it but rather can be rewarded if their work is deemed to have sufficient merit and quality in both its content and presentation.

Notes

The author would like to acknowledge his colleagues on the Washington State University Libraries' Faculty Affairs Committee, Lynn Chmelir, Joel Cummings, Sharon Walbridge, and Leslie Wykoff, for their efforts on this committee in general and in the development of the guidelines discussed here in particular. I would also like to acknowledge the Berglund Center for Internet Studies at Pacific University and its staff for their supporting me as one of their 2002 Fellows.

1. "Quantity of Books Sold and Value of U.S. Domestic Consumer Expenditures: 1995–2000" in U.S. Department of Commerce, *Statistical Abstract of the United States: 2001* (Washington, D.C.: Government Printing Office, 2001), Chart No. 1134.

2. "American Book Title Production: 1998 and 1999" in U.S. Department of Commerce, *Statistical Abstract of the United States: 2001* (Washington, D.C.: Government Printing Office, 2001), Chart No. 1135.

3. "Newspapers and Periodicals–Number by Type: 1980–2000" in U.S. Department of Commerce, *Statistical Abstract of the United States: 2001* (Washington, D.C.: Government Printing Office, 2001), Chart No. 1126.

4. msn.slate.com.

5. www.suck.com.

6. www.salon.com.

7. Brendan J. Wyly, "Competition in Scholarly Publishing? What Publisher Profits Reveal," *ARL Newsletter* Issue 200, October 1998, www.arl.org/newsltr/200/wyly.html.

8. Julie Nicklin, "Libraries Drop Thousands of Journals as Budgets Shrink and Prices Rise," *Chronicle of Higher Education*, December 11, 1991, A29.

9. Andrea Foster, "Second Thoughts on 'Bundled' E-Journals," *Chronicle of Higher Education*, September 20, 2002, A31.

10. For an overview of the issues involved with electronic books and the possibilities for the future see Francis Bry and Michael Kraus, "Perspectives for Electronic Books in the World Wide Web Age," *Electronic Library* 20, No. 4 (2002): 275–87.

11. Lisa Guernsey, "Those that Publish Online Fear They Suffer in Tenure Reviews," *Chronicle of Higher Education*, June 6, 1997, A21–22.

12. "Guidelines for Evaluating Digital Media Activities in Tenure Promotion and Review," American Association for History and Computing, www.theaahc.org/tenure_guidelines.htm. Another example of these guidelines is: Modern Language Association, "Guidelines for Evaluating Work with Digital Media in the Modern Languages," www.mla.org/reports/ccet/ccet_guidelines.htm.

13. Jeffrey R. Young, "Ever So Slowly, Colleges Start to Count Work With Technology in Tenure Decisions," *Chronicle of Higher Education*, February 22, 2002, chronicle.com/weekly/v48/i24/24a02501.htm.

14. www.merlot.org.

15. Washington State University Libraries Faculty Manual 3.b.1.a.1, "Guidelines for the Evaluation of Electronic Publications," www.wsulibs.wsu.edu/faculty/faculty-handbook/Guidelines-For-Evaluation-of-Electronic-Publications.html.

16. Minutes of the Library Faculty Affairs Committee, Washington State University, February 19, 2001. Other materials examined include: Association of College and Research Libraries, Academic Librarianship and the Redefining Scholarship Project, www.ala.org/acrl/ipfr.html. Teresa Y. Neely, "Leading Ideas: The Impact of Electronic Publications on Promotions and Tenure Decisions," www.arl.org/diversity/issue10/tneely.html.

17. "Guidelines for the Evaluation of Electronic Publications."

18. Library Faculty Manual, Washington State University, 3.b.1 "Criteria for Merit Increases, Promotion and Granting of Tenure," www.wsulibs.wsu.edu/faculty/faculty-handbook/Promotion-Granting-Tenure.html.

19. Blaise Cronin and Kara Overfelt, "E-Journals and Tenure," *Journal of the American Society for Information Science* 46, No. 9 (1995): 700–703.

20. These databases can be accessed at lib4.wsulibs.wsu.edu/ris/risWeb.isa.

21. Minutes of the Library Faculty Affairs Committee, Washington State University, February 19, 2001.

22. "Draft of Guidelines for the Evaluation of Electronic Publications," e-mailed

to Library Faculty Affairs Committee, Washington State University by Ryan Johnson, March 15, 2001.

23. "Guidelines for the Evaluation of Electronic Publications."

24. "Draft of Guidelines for the Evaluation of Electronic Publications."

25. "Guidelines for the Evaluation of Electronic Publications."

26. Minutes of the Library Faculty Affairs Committee, Washington State University, February 19, 2001.

27. Minutes of the Library Faculty Meeting, March 27, 2001.

28. Minutes of the Library Faculty Meeting, May 22, 2001.

Chapter 12

Scholars, Digital Intellectual Property, and the New Economics of Publication and Preservation

Terrence Maxwell

The Future of Copyright

Recently, there has been much speculative literature about the future of copyright in a world dominated by digital documents. In general, the discussions involve two extremes, characterized by Borgman as continuous and discontinuous.[1] Scholars and other commentators who take the continuous view see the future of copyright as similar to its past, only more so. In contrast, many discontinuarians view copyright's future as severely constrained, if not downright moribund.

In order to answer questions about the future of copyright, however, it is important to realize that the history, future, and utility of this legal mechanism for control of intellectual assets is different for different media formats and genres of intellectual works. For instance, the value and structure of copyright for novels are different than for music, movies, or scholarly works. As such, it is important to discern not only legal trends, but also the technical, social, and economic systems that the legal doctrine reflects.

In the case of scholarly literature, five main stakeholders inhabit this environment: scholars, publishers, lawyers, government, and educational institutions, including academic librarians and the academic leadership of universities. Each has different motivations and constraints, and, as a result, each has a different view of the value and future of copyright in the academic arena.

Academic Copyright's Past

The relationship among academic endeavors, the doctrine of copyright, and the history of publishing provides a fascinating perspective from which to understand the current condition of copyright and its probable future. This is because the rise of our contemporary view of academic scholarship during the Enlightenment occurred at the same time as the formation of the modern system of copyright law and the structure of the publishing industry as we know it today.

The invention of movable type and the development of printing unleashed several forces in Europe from the sixteenth through the eighteenth centuries. From the perspective of scholarship, the proliferation of presses led to several benefits, including a rapid expansion of the number of texts and copies, a corresponding acceleration of intellectual communication and information diffusion, and a cross-fertilization of ideas that allowed for rapid advances in fields like geography, astronomy, medicine, and other physical sciences, as well as a proliferation of alternative religious and philosophical worldviews epitomized by the rise of Protestantism in northern Europe.[2] On the other hand, the rise of printing presses brought academics problems of attribution, information quality control, and capitalization challenges, particularly for works requiring large investments in graphics and uncommon typefaces.[3] Scholars responded to the opportunities of better information exchange, the challenges of lack of capital and unauthorized, unreliable printing of their scholarship with several mechanisms. Probably the most important innovation to meet the new challenge was the development of national institutions for intellectual exchange like England's Royal Society, which brought together scholars and well-off gentlemen to promote information exchange and mechanisms for printing capitalization and established methods for quality and attribution control for new discoveries and scientific advances. In such an environment, the romantic notion of individual genius was often subordinated to the demands of gentlemanly modesty and pressure to encourage a "republic of letters."

Early publishers were under no such constraints with regard to deference to others. In fact, the preprint costs (e.g., typesetting and graphic design) and the small market for academic works made protection of investments in new works critical. At the same time, the demand for new works drove publishers to seek and support new authors and ideas, while attempting to protect investments and control in older texts. They responded through craft protection, demands for import control, and efforts to strengthen legal protections for intellectual assets, by development of a property-based rationale for legal control over books and ideas.[4] In doing so, they often drove a Faustian bargain with governments concerned with censorship control over a potentially dangerous printing and bookselling industry.

In the early years of publishing, the concerns of academic institutions intersected with the other stakeholders in interesting ways. For example,

English universities like Oxford and Cambridge shared a concern for the advancement of learning with scholars, wishing to command easy and cheap access to the latest intellectual discoveries. As seats of religious learning, they often joined governments in a desire to protect orthodoxy. In addition, the major universities possessed their own printing facilities, and as such were jealous of both their prerogatives over certain texts and protection of new works they published. Their response to these challenges was to demand mechanisms for cost-free deposit of new works in their libraries, while supporting publishers' protections against piracy and low-cost imports.[5]

The Statute of Anne,[6] the first copyright law in English jurisprudence and the exemplar for the U.S. Constitution's protection of intellectuals' works, can be seen as a legislative compromise balancing the demands of the various stakeholders in the early years of academic publishing. Proclaiming its purpose as "the encouragement of learned men to compose and write useful books," it provided limited-term protection against piracy underwritten by legal mechanisms of the state, as opposed to imperfect systems of craft protection, while forestalling a theory of intellectual property that would have provided a means for perpetual monopoly over texts and ideas. In addition, it mandated delivery of free copies of books to nine university libraries in England, Scotland, and Ireland, and prohibited importation of books written in English, while permitting importation of volumes written in other languages.

The Statute of Anne, while acknowledging the author's role in the creation of intellectual works, did little to change the dynamics among authors, publishers, governments, and academic institutions. The legislation was primarily a rationalization of trade practices, replacing the trade conception of control of publications via "propriety" (trade custom) with a limited form of property.[7] Later court decisions and eighteenth-century copyright legislation, including the U.S. Constitution's intellectual property clause (Art. 1, Section 1, Clause 8), solidified authorial centrality in the legal scheme.

The movement toward legal centrality for authors had little practical effect on academic works, however, since the majority of scholarly communications continued to struggle with capitalization problems. An example of this difficulty can be found in the communication between Matthew Carey, one of the first major U.S. publishers, and the American Philosophical Association, in which he complained that, due to capital woes, academic authors in America could expect to wait an average of four years for publication of their papers, in contrast to six months if they sent their papers to London, Dublin, or Edinburgh.[8] In general, scholars seeking to publish theses or monographs paid for the costs of publication themselves, a situation which led several of the larger universities to establish their own presses.[9] At the same time, the system of peer review and intellectual quality control pioneered by the Royal Society melded with scholastic craft traditions imported from Britain to form the philosophical underpinnings of the scholarly publication practice and the system of academic review and promotion.

Publishers moved away from books of "learned men" toward novels and educational titles, where the market was both larger and more organized. While the stated purpose of copyright protection in the U.S. Constitution was to "promote the Progress of Science and useful Arts," the thrust of publishing in the United States was away from university-level scholarship and toward elementary education and entertainment.

Whatever voice the academic community brought to bear on the legal environment of copyright, it focused more on issues of international copyright protection for literary authors, the protection of operatic and classical music, and the protection of libraries from import controls of foreign works.[10] Although legislative and intellectual leaders during the early years of the American republic were most interested in supporting the development of a national culture and intellectual capacity,[11] this concern gave way, particularly under the leadership of Noah Webster, to ensuring the financial legacy of American authors[12] and by the end of the nineteenth century to the goals of ensuring low prices for consumers, protecting American industries and workers from foreign competition, and providing new formats for information production and dissemination.[13]

During the twentieth century, the area where copyrights and scholarship intersected once again was not one in which scholars were directly involved. For many years, publishers were concerned by exemptions to import controls guaranteed to libraries as a negotiated compromise prior to the passage of the 1891 Copyright Act.[14] During the negotiations over passage of what would become the Copyright Act of 1909, publishers attempted first to abolish the library import exemption, and then to decrease it from two copies to one copy per library.[15] Their rationale was that every imported copy of academic works, for which there was a small market, diminished the size of the domestic market, making publishers less able to profit from academically oriented books. Publishers' dislike of library practices expanded over the twentieth century and included discontent over the practice of lending to people who might otherwise be paying customers, and the practice of interlibrary loan, which also affected potential market share.

In 1935, the National Association of Book Publishers, the American Council of Learned Societies, and the Social Science Research Council forged an informal agreement that allowed academic research libraries to provide photographic copies of books or periodicals provided that the researcher was given notice that he or she was not exempt from liability for any copyright infringement and if the reproduction was furnished without profit by the institution. However, the parties to the agreement did not represent all stake-holders in the issue, and as a result the compromise proved ineffective, especially given the later proliferation of photocopying machines. By 1960, at the beginning of the process to forge a new, comprehensive copyright statute that culminated in the passage of the 1976 U.S. Copyright Act, the issue of library duplication of journal articles was significant enough to warrant a special study to be commissioned on the topic.[16]

The conflict over library photoduplication played out in legal terms as a conflict between the theory of exclusive copying rights for copyright owners and two legal doctrines, "fair use" and "first sale," designed to provide some balance between private control over intellectual assets and the social goals of supporting intellectual advancement and free speech. Fair use, as first enunciated by Justice Story in 1841,[17] supported the free use of portions of a prior work for purposes of research and commentary. The first-sale doctrine legalized the principle that once a buyer purchased a book or other item covered by copyright protection, he was free to dispose of that good as he saw fit. This ruling by the Supreme Court arose from early twentieth-century attempts by publishers to control the retail prices of their books in discount department stores,[18] but was also used by libraries as the rationale to support the practice of book lending to patrons and interlibrary borrowing.

At core, however, the dispute over library photocopying practices was not a legal one, but rather a clash of two cultures, a market-based worldview that saw scholarly documents as commodities embodying costs for production and distribution, and a communitarian view that saw scholarly articles, in particular, as part of an ongoing community-driven process of information sharing, critical analysis, and recombination that drove innovation and new research.[19]

It is important to note that prior to and immediately following the 1976 U.S. Copyright Act, the major forces in the dispute over library photocopy-ing were not the scholars, but rather the institutions that relied on their works and those that supported their research. For scholars, copyright had tradi-tionally been an inadequate, even irrelevant, mechanism for achieving their goals, since direct income enhancement through book sales was very rarely seen as likely or even necessarily desired. This explains the practice of pro forma assignment of copyright as a condition of publication. Instead, schol-ars' motives for publication were to support research, tenure, and promotion; hence, the assignment of copyright was viewed as a necessary administra-tive step in the process of publication. Scholars were far more concerned with concepts of proper attribution and quality control of findings and had developed alternative mechanisms to police these goals, including peer re-view and cultural and administrative strictures regarding plagiarism.

Attempts to define the relationships among scholars, publishers, and the institutions that support scholarship and research in the post-1976 period have focused on nonlegally binding agreements around specific technologies.[20] In some areas, such as the use of electronic reserves and electronic interlibrary loan document delivery, no agreements could be reached. In areas where the parameters of fair use in scholarly works have been tested in the legal arena, the courts have moved away from broader protection for libraries engaged in interlibrary loan[21] toward a greater degree of protection for publishers' copyrights.[22] This shift has occurred as administrative mechanisms of payment for photocopies have evolved. However, even within this sphere, the courts have tended to differentiate between nonprofit educational and research institutes, and those operating under the aegis of for-profit corporations.

A System Out of Balance

Late twentieth-century technological advances, particularly the continued falling costs of photocopying, the expansion of telecommunications networks, the digitization of documents, and the rise of the World Wide Web, have caused both an exacerbation of the economic problems in the publishing marketplace related to widespread photocopying and the potential for new streams of income for scholarly works, particularly in the areas of distance learning and digital rights management. Taken together, these advances have pushed the system of scholarly publishing out of equilibrium. They have exacerbated the gulf between the scholarly culture and the legalistic market-driven structure of intellectual property laws, and have challenged all stakeholders to search for new methods of achieving individual goals, while in turn placing strains on their relations with other players.

Given the new technological conditions, scholars have been intrigued by the possibilities of reengineering the scholarly network, including decreasing the time to publication, redesigning peer review, and decreasing journal costs through electronic rather than paper-based delivery.[23] They are also motivated to change their publishing practices because of a perception that journal publishers are charging inordinately high subscription prices and generating large profits from work they receive at little or no cost. With the promise of "every person a publisher" brought on by the development of the World Wide Web and its attendant tools, some scholarly communities have moved toward scholar-based e-journals and archives.[24]

The potential of other revenue streams for scholarly works, particularly distance learning, and also the potential for direct e-payments for copies through systems such as Rightslink and iCopyright are redefining the scholar's view of copyright.[25] Academics are beginning to recognize that copyright is not a single right of control over scholarly work, but a bundle of rights that can be separated. In such an environment, the scholar might sign over first-publication rights to a for-profit publisher, but retain the rights to use the work in distance-learning classes, or contractually establish that electronic reprint revenues accrue directly to him.

The danger for scholars of this commodification of scholarly communication is twofold. First, it could threaten the culture of open scholarly communication. Second, it could drive the institutions of which scholars are a part to view such revenues as rightfully theirs under "work-for-hire" provisions of the copyright law.[26] While this has not, to date, proved to be a major issue with respect to journal publications, the potential market for patentable discoveries is such that on some university campuses the general issue of intellectual property is becoming a topic in administration/scholar negotiations.

Another important challenge for academics caused by the realignment of the scholarly publication environment is perceptual. Academic promotion and tenure have traditionally relied on a system that places much of its emphasis on publication, where the relative perceived value and merit of different journals are recognized among a community of scholars. The rapid rise of new journal titles and a shift from print-based to electronic-based publication systems, where the quality control and reputation of publications in the new format is untested, are causing a temporary dislocation in the scholarly cultural system. This uncertainty could slow the adoption of newer, more flexible, and less expensive systems of scholarly communication.[27]

Publishers face different challenges. The development of alternative publishing sources has the potential to seriously damage their serials publication trade, traditionally one of the most lucrative sectors of the publishing industry.[28] Even if the scholastic community does not supplant publishing houses with peer-based publications and electronic archives, many scholarly publishers will be forced to support two formats for publication, print and electronic, increasing rather than decreasing costs. In addition, the continued erosion of journal purchasing due to improvements in electronic delivery of articles both within and among educational and research institutions will place greater pressures on the publishers' bottom lines.

To date, the responses of publishers to the technological challenges inherent in cheap copying machines has been to develop different pricing strategies for different classes of users in both the print and electronic media.[29] The most common practice has been to charge institutional rates to libraries to offset expected losses due to photocopying. However, this escalation of journal prices comes at a time when research library budgets have remained stagnant, forcing libraries either to expend larger proportions of their acquisition budgets for serials or cancel subscriptions to less regularly used journals.

The copyright strategy being used by publishers is to support development of effective digital rights management systems like Rightslink and iCopyright and to decrease the potential for copying of digital journal articles through development of copy-protection systems. One of the most controversial provisions of the Digital Millennium Copyright Act of 1998 was a provision that made it illegal to circumvent technological protection systems such as digital watermarks and encryption. While on its face this provision seems reasonable enough, the practical implications of full deployment of these technologies will be to undermine the first-sale doctrine, making it difficult for purchasers of digital works to dispose of their copies as they see fit, and replace the outright purchase of information goods with licenses.[30] As Lawrence Lessig points out, the implications for information diffusion and the advancement of knowledge could be substantial.[31] In addition, the aggressive tactics of some publishers in litigating this provision of the law has raised freedom-of-speech issues.[32]

Universities, and particularly their research libraries, have borne much of the brunt of the shifts in scholarly publishing brought on by technological change. Increasing journal costs in an era of decreasing real budgets, demands by scholars for access to electronic journals and for mechanisms to support teaching and research, as well as concerns about the legality of mechanisms and practices related to photocopying, electronic copying, and interlibrary loan all present significant challenges.

Another critical issue related to electronic journals that is of lower visibility but equal importance is the university research library community's role as the repository of accumulated knowledge. Through journal storage, access policies, preservation activities, and interlibrary loan, research libraries have traditionally provided the infrastructure necessary for scholarly communication.[33] This archiving role, which has also relieved publishers of any responsibility for ensuring long-term access to their publications, has become significantly more difficult in an electronic environment, where issues like authentication, version control, ongoing preservation of media and formats, metadata for multimedia documents, and maintenance of hyperlinks all make the librarian's and archivist's role more difficult.[34]

Although there have been some suggestions that copyright and digital rights management may help to alleviate some of these issues, other commentators suggest they raise as many questions as answers, particularly with regard to the legal, technological, and management processes used to secure and manage ownership through permissions and licensing.[35]

Uncertainty regarding the changed nature of documents in a digital environment is not, however, limited to scholars, publishers, and the university community. Governments and the legal profession are also struggling with the shift from paper-based to digital documents, and with the impact of this change on copyright practices. The structure of the traditional copyright legal regime is based on the fixity and tangibility of a limited number of documents that can be monitored and controlled through known distribution systems. Digitization, with its attendant capacity for rapid copying, modification, and recombination of textual and other elements, multidimensionality of texts through the use of hyperlinks, combination of communications and application tools leading to dynamic and interactive documents, and rapid international distribution via an open communications infrastructure present a serious and dramatic challenge to this system. Due to the inherently conservative and incremental culture of the legal system, as well as pressure by traditional information-processing industries for protection, the initial reaction of many legal and legislative decision makers has been to treat digital documents as if they were both fixed and tangible, and in doing so to constrain the potential for more flexible, dynamic, and efficient means of communication. Scholars, like other producers of information, will in turn be affected by such legal decisions and legislation.

Forging a New Equilibrium

What can scholars expect from intellectual property systems and publishing in the coming years? Although we can be aware of the variety of pressures operating on the system, we do not yet know the outcome of four key questions.

First, what will be valued by the scholarly community?

Will the perceived quality of electronic journals equal or exceed that of print-based journals, and will the development of Web-based instruction systems and techniques be seen as a valued intellectual activity? Will a new process of peer review based on preprinting of articles, continual community feedback, and iterative revision of documents come to be viewed as a more or less effective means of communication of findings and intellectual quality control? Will the scholarly community accept the more mutable nature of electronic documents, and relax expectations that their research-support libraries have the capacity to ensure authenticity and access to all relevant documents?

Second, who will pay for the new electronically based scholarly communications system and what management and revenue mechanisms will they use?

To date, many of the experiments in digital publishing, access, storage, and archiving (e.g., JSTOR, PEAK) have been underwritten by a combination of university libraries, government funding, foundation grants, and corporate experiments. Is there a likelihood or necessity, as some commentators have suggested,[36] for a national or international body to coordinate the management and preservation of scholarly works? Can the system be developed through cooperative agreements and activities,[37] or should we rely on market-based systems for payment and financing, as embodied in digital-rights management systems and traditional publishing firms? Who will bear the responsibility for and costs of ongoing assessment and archiving of electronic documents, and where will the funding for these activities originate? Will publishers assume long-term responsibility for access to their digital publications consistent with implementation of licensing and digital rights management systems, or will they expect libraries and archives to continue their traditional functions?

Third, what will a scholarly work look like?

Will we continue to conceive the scholarly article as an essentially two-dimensional and static document in the tradition of print media? What will the scholarly community's expectations be regarding hyperlinked citations and other means of turning documents into more multidimensional and interactive vehicles for communication? Will we have new expectations for dynamic documents? Will we expect, for instance, that papers reporting on simulation-modeling experiments include runtime versions of the model as part of the document, or that findings taken from collected data include links to public-use data sets?

And finally, how will the intellectual property system be reconfigured?

Will it rely on the traditional model of scholarly documents as static, two-dimensional objects, thus constraining the development of dynamic, linked scholarly communications? Will it succeed in underpinning new systems of copy payment and authentication in such a manner as to shift revenue streams from publishers to authors, causing a realignment of the notion of academics as independent bodies within universities? Will the development of new encryption and authentication schemes protected by copyright laws change the traditional system of information access via libraries and interlibrary loans to a system of use-based licensing and direct payments by users, in which the library's role is made redundant?

Scholars should realize that answers to these questions will be hammered out in the coming years through a variety of mechanisms, including: negotiated processes surrounding copyright and trade legislation; communitarian decisions by professional, legislative, international, and scholarly institutional bodies; corporate decisions of publishing firms; and legal interpretation by courts. The longstanding marginal intersection between scholarly communications and copyright laws, embodied in the scholar's traditional contractual relationships with publishers, is gone. It has been replaced at least for the foreseeable future by a necessity for scholars to become active participants in the current debate over intellectual property in the digital world, articulating their vision of the future of their community and its system of communication and advancement of knowledge. This is especially critical because of the progressive marginalization of authorship in successive iterations of national copyright laws, and the fact that while scholars may have natural allies in various aspects of the process of formation of new laws, each party is most concerned with its own interests, and will, when push comes to shove, subordinate others' needs to its own.

To the extent that scholars can both visualize and articulate their requirements for scholarship in the electronic environment, they will be more likely to succeed in nurturing an evolving identity for their community in the new, confusing, and often contentious environment of intellectual property law for digital works.

Notes

1. Christine L. Borgman, *From Gutenberg to the Global Information Infrastructure: Access to Information in the Networked World* (Cambridge, MA: MIT Press, 2000), 3.

2. Elizabeth L. Eisenstein, *The Printing Revolution in Early Modern Europe* (Cambridge: Cambridge University Press, 1983), 273–75.

3. Adrian Johns, *The Nature of the Book* (Chicago: University of Chicago Press, 1998), 445.

4. John Feather, *Publishing, Piracy and Politics: An Historical Study of Copyright in Britain* (London: Mansell, 1994), 50–63.

5. Ibid, 112–114.

6. *An Act for the Encouragement of Learning, by Vesting the Copies of Printed Books in the Authors or Purchasers of Such Copies* (8 Anne, c. 19, 1709).

7. Ibid., 189.

8. Earl L. Bradsher, *Mathew Carey: Editor, Author and Publisher* (New York: AMS Press, 1966), 35–36.

9. John Tebbel, *A History of Book Publishing in the United States,* Vol. 2 (New York: R.R. Bowker, 1972), 169.

10. See Thorvald Solberg, *Copyright in Congress: 1789–1904* (Washington, D.C.: Government Printing Office, 1905), 240–89; E. Fulton Brylawski and Abe Goldman, *Legislative History of the 1909 Copyright Act* (Hackensack: Fred B. Rothman, 1976), J71–73; and Aubert J. Clark, *The Movement for International Copyright in Nineteenth Century America* (Washington, D.C.: Catholic University of America Press, 1960), 158–75.

11. See Solberg, *Copyright in Congress*, 10–26; James Morton Smith, *The Republic of Letters* (New York: W.W. Norton, 1995), 512; Edward C. Walterscheid, *The Nature of the Intellectual Property Clause: A Study in Historical Perspective* (Buffalo: William H. Hein, 2002), 139–51; and William E. Channing, *The Works of William E. Channing* (Boston: Munroe and Company, 1848).

12. Harlow Giles Unger, *Noah Webster: The Life and Times of an American Patriot* (New York: John Wiley & Sons, 1998), 315–16.

13. See James A. Barnes, *Authors, Publishers and Politicians: The Quest for an Anglo-American Copyright Agreement 1815–1854* (London: Routledge & Kegan Paul, 1974), 49–74; and Representative [William] McAdoo, "What Congress Has Done," *North American Review* 151 (1890): 526–30.

14. *Copyright Act of 1891* (1891).

15. Ibid., 240–289.

16. *Photoduplication of Copyrighted Material by Libraries* (Washington, D.C.: United States Senate Committee on the Judiciary, Subcommittee on Patents, Trademarks, and Copyrights, 1960).

17. *Folsom v. Marsh* (1841).

18. *Scribner v. Straus et al.* (Supreme Court of the United States, 1908).

19. Ibid., 96–101.

20. Dwayne K. Buttler, "CONFU-sed: Security, Safe Harbors, and Fair Use," *Journal of the American Society for Information Science* 50 (1999): 1308–12.

21. *Williams & Wilkins Co. v. United States* (Supreme Court of the United States, 1974).

22. *American Geophysical Union, et al. v. Texaco* (United States Court of Appeals, Second Circuit, 1994).

23. See Andrew Odlyzko, "The Economics of Electronic Journals," *First Monday* 2 (1997): 8; and Mike Sosteric, Yuwei Shi, and Olivier Wenker, "The Upcoming Revolution in the Scholarly Communication System," *Journal of Electronic Publishing* 7 (2001).

24. William Y. Arms, "Preservation of Scientific Serials: Three Current Examples," *Journal of Electronic Publishing* 5 (1999), www.press.umich.edu/jep/05-02/arms.html.

25. See "CCC's Rightlink Goes Live on InformationWeek.com," *Information Today* (December 2001), www.copyright.com/PDFs/CCC'sRightslink.pdf; and "Primedia Business Announces Partnership with iCopyright," iCopyright.com Instant Clearance Service (2002), www.icopyright.com/news/pr20020423.html.

26. Margreth Barrett, "Intellectual Property: Patents, Trademarks, and Copyright," *Emanuel* (2000): 259–62.

27. Michael Day, "The Scholarly Journal in Transition and the PubMed Central Proposal," *Ariadne* 21 (September 1999), www.ariadne.ac.uk/issue21/.

28. Albert N. Greco, *The Book Publishing Industry* (Boston: Allyn and Bacon, 1997), 24–29.

29. Brian Kahin and Hal R. Varian, *Internet Publishing and Beyond: The Economics of Digital Information and Intellectual Property* (Cambridge, MA: MIT Press, 2000), 1–4.

30. Pamela Samuelson, "Intellectual Property and the Digital Economy: Why the Anti-Circumvention Regulations Need to Be Revised," *Berkeley Technology Law Journal* 14 (1999): 519.

31. Lawrence Lessig, *The Future of Ideas* (New York: Random House, 2001), 15–16.

32. Siva Vaidhyanathan, *Copyrights and Copywrongs* (New York: NYU Press, 2001), 177–84.

33. Gail M. Hodge, "Best Practices for Digital Archiving: An Information Life Cycle Approach," *D-Lib Magazine* 6 (2000).

34. Stewart Granger, "Digital Preservation and Deep Infrastructure," *D-Lib Magazine* 8 (2002).

35. See Henry M. Gladney, "Digital Dilemma: Intellectual Property," *D-Lib Magazine* 4 (1999); and Daniel J. Gervais, *E-Commerce and Intellectual Property: Lock-it-up or License?* (2002), www.copyright.com/News/AboutArticlesIntellectualProp.asp.

36. David Haynes and David Streatfield, "A National Co-ordinating Body for Digital Archiving?" *Ariadne* 15 (1997), www.ariadne.ac.uk/issue15/main.html.

37. Hilary Berthon, Susan Thomas and Colin Webb, "Safekeeping: A Cooperative Approach to Building a Digital Preservation Resource," *D-Lib Magazine* 8 (2002).

Chapter 13

Stories of the Future

David J. Staley

Futurists and Scenarios

Twenty years from now, will digital scholarship occupy an important position in academia? Will professors earn tenure and promotion on the basis of their digital work? Or will digital scholarship be confined to the margins of academic life, interesting and inventive perhaps, but insufficient for promotion and tenure? Will scholars produce radically new forms of scholarship, or will digital tools merely facilitate traditional forms of scholarship such as monographs and conference presentations? Is digital scholarship the wave of the future or a fad that will eventually fall out of fashion? The essays in this volume each recount stories of the current state of digital scholarship and its place in the promotion and tenure process. The goal of this concluding essay is to inquire into the future of digital scholarship by telling five stories of the future.

Futurists refer to stories of the future as scenarios. Over the past twenty years, there has been a revolution in the study of the future. Where they once offered one prediction, futurists today are more likely to think in terms of three or four scenarios. According to Peter Schwartz, a pioneer in the use of scenarios in business planning, scenarios are "stories of equally plausible futures."[1] Where a prediction confidently asserts the one "true" path to the future, scenarios begin with the assumption that the future cannot be predicted with certainty since it might follow one of several mutually plausible paths. Especially in the realm of human affairs, predictions are inherently difficult because of the many complex variables that define human societies. Because human affairs are sensitive to initial conditions, altering one variable only slightly may result in a wholly different future. The scenario method seeks to account for "surprise," those deviations from the trend line that often frustrate predictions.[2] Scenarios are, therefore, something like counterfactual arguments in reverse.[3] A counterfactual in history, for example, explores the different outcomes that might have resulted when one alters a significant variable in a familiar historical event. Had Booth not shot Lincoln, what might have been the effects on Reconstruction? Had Kennedy lived, would America have become more deeply involved in Vietnam? Futurists ask similar types of "what if?" questions, only thinking forward. Scenarios are, in effect, answers to those questions.

In describing the future as a story, the scenario writer seeks to describe the environment in which future activity will occur. A prediction lists a linear procession of events: this will happen, then this, then this. A scenario, however, is a nonlinear account describing—as the root of the word suggests—a "scene." Often written in the present tense, a scenario reads like an anthropological "thick description." Each scenario describes a set of variables and conditions that will structure individual action at some future point. For each of the scenarios below, I have also taken the step of including a small vignette at the beginning that imagines an individual whose choices are shaped by the variables and conditions described in the scenario.

Although written as stories, scenarios are not like science fiction or other types of utopian literature. That is, they are not simply fanciful stories or visions of our dreams of the future. Rather, scenarios are grounded in evidence and reasoned analysis. As the scenario writer Daniel Yergin asserts, scenarios must be built from both imagination and discipline.[4] In many ways, scenario writing is very similar to history writing, in that both are disciplined ways of using language to create narratives based on the rigorous analysis of the available evidence.[5] The goal of a scenario is to imagine realistically plausible future states, even those states that may not be to our liking. If scenarios are stories, then they are a particular type of disciplined story.

A scenario writer builds scenarios by examining the "driving forces" of the present.[6] Driving forces refer to the most significant trends that are likely to shape future actions. The scenario writer then explores the different ways in which these forces might interact, accounting for as many alternative scenes as seems plausible. When considering the future of digital scholarship, the most significant—and least predictable—driving force is the reaction of the academy and the resulting institutional settings in which such scholarship will be produced. This conclusion stems from my belief that the most important factor in assessing the future of technology is not the tool but the ways in which people will use those tools.[7] Tools are "revolutionary" only if they are used, by people, for revolutionary ends. Conversely, tools lead to superficial change or no change at all if people use them superficially or conservatively. Human decisions—and not the inexorable logic of the machine—determine the impact of technology.

Thus, in each one of the scenarios I have written below, the variable that has been altered in each case is the degree to which the institutions of the academy—hiring and tenure committees, professional societies, the administrative bodies of the university—accept or reject digital scholarship. In each case, digital technologies are assumed to be a given; what changes are the ways in which people decide to use the technologies. Contemplating these scenarios allows us to "[rehearse] the implications,"[8] as Schwartz describes it: imagining the future consequences of choices we make in the present.

Scenario 1: What If Computers Fall Out of Fashion?

The workmen have just finished removing the last of the monitors from the lab. Stuart, the recently selected chair of the sociology department, watches over the proceedings with a satisfied look. This computer lab had been created from a converted classroom some twenty years ago. Stuart's predecessor approved the funding of the computer lab, for at the time digital classrooms were the wave of the future. This decision seemed perfectly reasonable to Stuart; and if he had been chair, he might have made the same choice. Twenty years later, that decision seemed ill-advised. For although the department kept up with the latest upgrades, over the years fewer and fewer professors actually used the lab for teaching or research. Sociology, as Stuart well knows, has largely remained a field where interviews, participant observation, and theory are the main tools of research. Computers aid this process, but they serve a supporting role, much the same way that pencils and typewriters did two generations ago. By this time tomorrow, the long-abandoned and underused computer lab will be converted into a small classroom with a lectern at the front, chairs arranged in rows throughout the room, and blackboards lining the walls.

In this scenario, academic work has changed very little, if at all, because of digital technology. Some academics use digital tools to more efficiently facilitate the production of dissertations, monographs, and articles, but only to process the words or calculate the numbers. While some graduate students employ digital tools in their work, their dissertation committees still require a written paper document before granting the degree. Graduate advisers distrust digitized sources and look unfavorably at seminar papers that cite too many on-line resources; they insist that their students actually travel to archives or consult books in libraries. Hiring and tenure committees continue to value traditional types of scholarship when making their decisions, paying no attention to the technology used to produce them. These committees disregard on-line scholarship as little more than vanity publishing. As a result, on-line journals, which at one time seemed to be a vital new venue for scholarly publication, have declined in number. Paper journals remain the norm. E-books, once touted as the savior of the academic monograph, are very popular with readers of mass-market pop fiction, but tenure boards have long rejected these as serious forms of scholarship. In many disciplines, the creative use of computers is limited to a subfield, of interest to a small segment of the discipline but not the entire profession. Many academics use electronic tools to supplant older technologies—the overhead projector has long since given way to the digital projector—but technology has not fundamentally altered their teaching or scholarship. In fact, many professors said that digital technology did little to facilitate teaching and learning and have since returned to more traditional media such as textbooks and face-to-face lectures. Like cable-TV classrooms of a generation ago, or the elaborate recording systems that were supposed to transform foreign language education, digital technologies now sit unused, many having fallen into disrepair, eventually needing to be disassembled.

Some observers at the end of the twentieth century claimed that many everyday activities would be decentered and fragmented, carried out over long distances in cyberspace.[9] This included predictions that the activities of the university—from teaching to scholarship—would similarly be performed in cyberspace. These predictions never came to pass, for once the novelty of the technology wore off, succeeding generations began to covet, once again, physical presence. Rather than being made obsolete, universities continue to provide a "real" place for those who desire physical presence, not digitized "telepresence." Students demand face-to-face contact with professors, and professors want to lead discussions with students located in the same physical space. On-line courses, once considered the wave of the future, have fallen out of fashion, with students, professors, and administrators, as well as with business leaders, who look with suspicion at a résumé that includes too many on-line courses. Despite the fact that football games can be easily accessed from home by television, people still pay to sit in the cold to experience the game; similarly, while much information can be accessed on-line, students continue to flock to universities for the physical presence they enable.

Computers, digital technologies, and networked information systems are ubiquitous in the culture at large, but they are viewed by academics as technologies of mass culture and lowbrow entertainment, like television or video games. They are not technologies of serious scholarship.

Scenario 2: What If Digital Work Becomes Invisible and Routine?

Adam is preparing for the upcoming academic year. He must still post his syllabi sometime this week, and he has already received messages from some of his autumn semester seminar participants. He is finishing up the links to

the course packet for his Western Political Theory class. He must also light a
fire under a student who has an incomplete project from the spring semester
that he has still failed to attach. Once these matters are attended to, he will
finally e-mail the call for papers for this spring's regional political science
conference. If only he had more time to work on that journal article!

In this scenario, faculty members produce digital products and engage with digital technology as a regular part of their work. In a similar manner as their colleagues a generation ago, they design digital multimedia "Kinko's readers" for their classes. They engage in asynchronous on-line discussions with their students as a regular part of instruction. They oversee student Web-based projects. They make their syllabi and other course materials available on-line. In their professional work, in addition to sending e-mail and video-mail, faculty maintain listservs and contribute to their professional society's Web page. Where they once consulted bulky volumes, scholars access finding aids and other digitized information resources on-line before they venture off to the archives. Scholars rely on the technologies of print-on-demand to publish their books. Technology has become so integrated into teaching and scholarship that it has become "invisible," that is, the use of technology is now routine and unremarkable.

Digital work is a part of every faculty member's workload and is comparable to selecting textbooks or writing a syllabus. That is, a faculty member is not rewarded for these efforts; these activities constitute part of the minimum requirements for continued employment. At teaching colleges, these activities very rarely influence tenure decisions, and only in that they are viewed as part of teaching or service to the college. At larger research institutions, where research is the major component of any hiring, promotion, and tenure decision, the use of digital technology is not regarded as "scholarship" any more than talking on the telephone with a colleague or driving an automobile to a conference are considered scholarship. Digital technology supports routine academic work.

Digital work is so ordinary and unremarkable that conferences, collected essays, and professional societies that deal with "Computers and Scholarship" are no longer viewed as relevant. The American Association for History and Computing, which was a cutting-edge professional society two decades ago, has all but disbanded. A conference discussing computers and scholarship seems about as useful and important as a conference on teaching with paper and pencil or a film projector, although it may one day be of interest to historians of technology. Where at one time academics were discussing new forms of digital scholarship as a challenge to traditional articles and monographs, these now appear to be as quixotic as early twentieth-century utopian science fictions. Digital technology is like a plumbing system: it is necessary to ease the flow of information in academic life but goes largely unnoticed (except when it breaks down).

Scenario 3: What If Digital Scholarship Migrates Out of Universities?

Larry had long had an interest in virtual reality and its application to military history. He had approached his graduate adviser about an idea to recreate the Battle of Vicksburg in a virtual reality (VR) environment, in lieu of a traditional written dissertation. While sympathetic, his adviser knew that he could not expect such a radical proposal to be accepted by the department. Moreover, Larry's adviser knew that if he had any hope of landing a job he would need to produce "real" scholarship: a paper read at a conference, an article, or a book. Larry complies and finishes his degree. He continues to pursue his interest in VR military history outside of his real professional work. He lands a job at a large midwestern university, and is told that, while he is certainly free to explore the possibilities, his virtual reality project will not get him tenure.

After three years in his job, Larry is approached by a software firm that is quite interested in his ideas of recreating military history in VR environments. The company expects to make huge profits selling the re-creation as an attraction to history buffs who will be willing to pay to "make the past come to life." Larry leaves his academic post and joins the growing list of former academics, frustrated by the conservatism and inertia of the academy, who explore digital scholarship in the private sector.

In this scenario, digital scholarship is produced not by members of the academy but by those loosely allied to it or even outside of it entirely. The academy was slow to decide the status of digital scholarship; and when it finally did reach a consensus, many of the most creative people had left their positions to work for software companies and other content providers. As a result, an increasing number of graduate students who are interested in multimedia or other forms of digital scholarship have begun to track themselves toward a path in the private sector rather than a career in academia.

There is a ready and appreciative audience for these digital forms of information. Publishers produce digital "textbooks" that are being adopted by more and more school boards. (Indeed, when they reach college, students ask their professors if they can "look at the multimedia for this class," in the same way the generation before them asked to watch a movie.) In the same way they watched the Learning Channel, the Discovery Channel, and the

History Channel a generation before, the general public is fascinated with multimedia software dealing with zoology, geography, history, and a wide variety of other subjects. Virtual reality re-creations of famous historic scenes—*Gladiator* has been especially popular—are a big hit with audiences. The authors of these multimedia products received their training in graduate school and then formed their own educational software companies, rather than accept a career at a university where such work would be undervalued.

The academy, already lukewarm to digital scholarship, hardens its attitudes against technology. "Digital scholarship is not true scholarship," many claim. It is acceptable for the general public or for schoolchildren, these skeptics maintain, but "real" scholarly work is still recorded on paper, in books, and at face-to-face conferences. Digital scholarship is not as accurate, is overly simplistic, fails to address theoretical concerns, and is thus inferior to the work produced by faculty at universities. There are some academics who wish to treat these creations as legitimate forms of scholarship. They press journals to include reviews of multimedia products and articles dealing with digital creations. The critics themselves, however, choose not to produce their own digital scholarship, since this would do nothing to ensure their tenure or promotion.

Scenario 4: What If Technology Enables a Virtual University?

Alexa awakes one morning and consults her schedule for the day. At 8:00 she has to teach her Virginia Woolf class. At 12:00 she is delivering a paper on English radio in India at the MLA. She must also find time to access sources to help finish her study of Caribbean English and the literature of Trinidad, which she hopes to send off to a prestigious journal by the end of the semester. She is a professor of English at Harvard, but lives and works in Greenville, Ohio, in the home formerly owned by her grandmother. She is able to make it to Boston three or four times a year, but she spends most of her time in her office at home. Her class meets virtually in a 3-D chat room; the MLA now meets via videoconference. Her article will appear in one of several on-line journals.

In this scenario, scholarship is carried out almost exclusively in digital form. Despite its digital appearance, however, this scholarship remains basically the same as traditional scholarship. Professors still write papers and attend conferences and teach seminars, only these activities have migrated into a digital environment.

Most scholarly articles appear in on-line journals, which have long since replaced their paper counterparts as the preferred medium of scholarly communication. Many critics at one time were concerned that the apparent lack of "barriers to entry" to electronic publishing would mean that digital scholarship would simply be a form of vanity publishing, since they believed anyone could be published on-line. These fears never came to pass, since professional societies established standards for electronic publication that were just as rigorous as traditional paper publications. Because of the flexibility of electronic media, the author of an article, rather than publishing in one single journal, publishes his article in numerous on-line sites. The appearance of the article in several sources is a testimony to its quality and importance, the journal title acting as an imprimatur or seal of approval. Thus, while journals lose their monopoly over intellectual content, they retain their role, via peer review, as quality-assurance filtering mechanisms.[10]

Archivists continue to digitize increasing numbers of documents and artifacts, making these sources available on the World Wide Web. Digitized data make the scholar's research more productive, easier, less expensive, and free from time-consuming travel. One need not leave his personal workstation in order to access library and archival material. Students have access to the same materials as their professors, making hands-on research—rather than lecture and recitation—the preferred method of undergraduate instruction.

Now that archives, libraries, and museums are fully digitized and accessible from any location, the physical structures that used to house that information have become irrelevant. The "university" is no longer defined as a physical place. The old buildings that defined the university as a place continue to exist, but their function is quite different; the physical place of the university is where students go to pick up diplomas, as one makes a special journey to a church for important ceremonies. While institutions are not physically located in one place, they continue to exist as an electronic network, an archipelago of virtual residents. "Universities" are now defined as virtual networked associations of scholars and students. Membership in these associations remains restricted to those meeting certain criteria, thus ensuring intellectual rigor and maintaining the prestige of the name of the association, even if the physical structure is made irrelevant. These digital inhabitants are physically rootless, as itinerant scholars and students were in medieval Europe, but electronically tethered together. One's avatar in this placeless space is determined by his institutional affiliations; scholars define their identity by the network to which they belong. To say that one attends or teaches at Harvard, for example, means that he has been admitted into this restricted network association.

Increased use of distance learning, video conferencing, and other technologies of "telepresence" means that academics and students float in physically decentered institutions. Professors instruct students in virtual chat rooms and in shared virtual reality spaces. Scholarly conferences are held almost exclusively through video networks and virtual reality. Most of the participants do not have to venture far from their homes to read their papers or to engage in a panel discussion. In this scenario, "scholarship" is indistinguishable from "digital scholarship."

Scenario 5: What If the Academy Accepts Radically New Forms of Scholarship?

Owen paces back and forth as he awaits the decision of his PhD committee. The members are currently experiencing his immersive model of "The Costs of NAFTA." It is a three-dimensional virtual reality display that models the flow of goods, services, people, capital, and information during the first decade of NAFTA. Each variable is represented in the model either by a symbol, a color, or a sound; the dissertation committee is "experiencing the data" by moving among the numbers, listening to the sounds as the data change, and watching for shifts in color that represent significant economic and social trends. Some on the committee are concerned because Owen's model calls into question many of the standard interpretations of the effects of NAFTA; in fact, Owen's display challenges the conclusions reached by one of his committee members in her own virtual display that she presented at a conference three years ago. Nevertheless, the quality of the work is sound, his interpretation of the data is convincing, and the committee agrees to award him the degree. Now, after finding a job, he will need to send out his display to a suitable venue in order to be published. [11]

In this scenario, digitized sound, images, and movement increasingly crowd out written expression. A diminishing number of academics base their scholarly work on the silent verbal "text" alone. Where they once depended upon textual monographs and journal articles as the "coins of the realm" of academic life, scholars in this scenario favor visual, associative, and maplike displays of scholarship. These new scholars are not writers, but are more like artists and musicians, that is, those who think through images or sound. Visually oriented scholars create their displays in multimedia imagescapes, rather than in silent books or journals. They use sound, image, and movement as ways to embody their data and to communicate their findings to the rest of their colleagues. These scholars place greater emphasis on associative, multidimensional, and spatial links between elements of information, rather than the linear, one-dimensional links found in printed writing. This new form of digital scholarship is welcomed by tenure and promotion committees, and is accorded the same status as a written text. [12] Large research universities have earmarked significant resources for digital scholarship and are spending large amounts of money to lure leading practitioners to their campuses.

Virtual reality technology offers a venue for this style of scholarship. More and more academic work is carried out in "immersive environments." Historians, for example, create "virtual historical spaces," where one can navigate through a recreation of Renaissance Florence. Rather than being "poor relations" to the "real history" historians used to believe was codified in books and articles, virtual spatial displays have become an important and highly valued form of scholarship in history.

In addition to being able to "climb around" a virtual recreation of a historic place, scholars also "climb around" and immerse themselves in "habitable models." Political scientists, economists, sociologists, and quantitative-minded historians present their numerical data as three-dimensional immersive images. Three-dimensional visual displays of information—similar to graphs, the periodic table, the Mandelbrot set, or non-Euclidean surfaces—are wedded to virtual reality tools, allowing academics to surround themselves and to navigate through abstract three-dimensional "datascapes." Such "visual mathematics" change the way scholars think about quantitative analysis, allowing one to "experience the data" as a concrete object.[13] And not just numbers are so represented; scholars also create "text visualizations," which convert text into multidimensional immersive information spaces.[14] Rather than being presented as a page of prose, scholarship is now just as likely to be abstract shapes of data. Digital scholarship of this type does not appear that different from sculpture or architecture, in the same way that elegant "history" was once indistinguishable from literature.

The medieval scriptorium was a noisy place, where monks read aloud from books, as opposed to the quiet reading rooms of modern university libraries or Victorian parlors.[15] The digital environment in which scholarship is now carried out is as "noisy" as the scriptorium. In this scenario, the written word—the heretofore still and silent foundation of academic discourse—has been overwhelmed by other media.

Models for the Future

None of the above scenarios are predictions; each scenario should instead be read as a provisional model of the future. A model is a simplification of a more complex system, a simplification that nevertheless yields insight and understanding. I use the word "model" here in the way the physicist Freeman Dyson has used it. Dyson distinguishes between scientific models and scientific theories. Scientists create theories out of logic and mathematics to describe physical systems that are well known; a theory is "supposed to describe the actual universe we live in." A model, on the other hand, is a simplified version of the universe the scientist is describing, in that it leaves out much of that actual universe. Dyson believes that theories work well in describing those systems already well understood, whereas models are needed to explore systems that are not yet fully understood. "Models are essential tools for understanding nature in regions beyond the reach of observation," he writes. "Later, when more details can be observed, models will be replaced by theories."[16]

Dyson penned these words in a book about the future of technology, a "region" that is, by definition, beyond the reach of direct observation. "Accurate prediction is not my purpose," Dyson contends. "The purpose of model-building in the realm of the future is not to predict, but only to draw a rough sketch of the territory into which we might be moving."[17] In fact, any statement about the future must be viewed as a model, a simplified version of the actual system, since so much of the actual system is left out (because it has yet to occur). Since models give way to theories as more information becomes available, our expectation for a model of the future is that it should be revised, rewritten, even jettisoned as we observe the actual events unfold. A scenario is like a rough draft of the future. The final draft will be composed as the events play themselves out, to be written by contemporary observers or by historians with the benefit of hindsight. Until that day arrives, we must rely on these provisional heuristic statements.

These statements nevertheless can provide us with much insight about the future. As Peter Schwartz maintains, writing and reflecting upon scenarios allows us to rehearse the future. Scenarios provide us with a tool for placing decisions made in the present into a larger context. Having considered many of the alternatives, we now have a means for assessing the implications of actions made in the present. If tenure committees decide today that digital scholarship is insufficient for tenure and promotion, we can reflect upon the implications of that decision. If dissertation committees begin right now to accept digital scholarship in lieu of traditional written dissertations, we have already considered what that choice could mean for the academy as a whole. Because we have already "run through" many of the implications, we are less likely to be caught off guard by or be unaware of the effects of our actions. "Having considered all of the possibilities before the fact," writes one advocate for the use of scenarios, we "will immediately recognize the evolving future in terms that are familiar and significant."[18]

If scenarios can help guide the decisions we make in the present, they can also be used as tools to plan for the future. If we had a choice, which of these models of the future would we prefer to see happen? I imagine that advocates of digital scholarship would be distressed with the outcomes in the first three scenarios, where digital scholarship is either ignored by the academy, services unremarkable routine work, or is forced out of the university entirely. Their actions might therefore be guided in directions that lead away from these implications. They might instead favor the final two scenarios, where digital scholarship plays a vital and important role in academic life, and adjust their actions and decisions accordingly. Scenarios allow us a means of articulating our goals for the future and provide a map to guide our choices.

I cannot state with complete certainty how the academy will treat digital scholarship in the future. Academic deans, hiring and tenure committees, professional organizations, and dissertation advisers could view computers simply as fancy word processors, and thus digital scholarship would play a minor role. In the past, the academy has proved it can be resistant to change, especially with regard to technology. Witness how relatively little impact television has had on the presentation of scholarship, despite its ubiquity in the culture at large. The academy could just as easily see computers as a digital canvas with which to paint a new type of scholarship. In the past, the academy has also proved to be open to change and innovation; consider how the social turmoil of the 1960s changed the intellectual landscape of the university. The future role of digital technology in scholarship will depend largely on the resolution of this tension between stasis and change. This future is neither predetermined nor inevitable; the complexities inherent in the behaviors and actions of human institutions mean that the future will unfold in any one of several directions. The disciplined imagination afforded by scenarios best prepares us to make or adapt to these multiple possibilities, for to imagine is to be ready.

Notes

1. Peter Schwartz, *The Art of the Long View: Planning for the Future in an Uncertain World* (New York: Currency/Doubleday, 1996), xiii.

2. The version of the scenario method that I am employing here is known as the Shell method, or the intuitive method, and is the one championed by Schwartz. On other methods and uses of scenarios, see the special issue on scenarios in *Futures Research Quarterly* 17 (Summer 2001).

3. On the relationship between historical counterfactuals and future scenarios, see David J. Staley, "Digital Historiography: Subjunctivity," *Journal of the Association for History and Computing* (April 2000), mcel.pacificu.edu/JAHC/JAHCIII1/P-REVIEWS/staleyIII1.html (August 21, 2002).

4. Daniel Yergin and Thane Gustafson, *Russia 2010, and What It Means for the World* (New York: Vintage Books, 1995), 8–9.

5. On the relationship between history writing and scenario writing, see David J. Staley "History and the Future," *History and Theory, Theme Issue* 41 (December 2002), 72–89.

6. Schwartz, *The Art of Long View*, 101–8.

7. Three books that study how users of technology shape the "definition" of the technology include Abigail J. Sellen and Richard H.R. Harper, *The Myth of the Paperless Office* (Cambridge, MA: MIT Press, 2002); Kathryn Henderson, *On Line and On Paper: Visual Representations, Visual Culture, and Computer Graphics in Design Engineering* (Cambridge, MA: MIT Press, 1999); Bonnie A. Nardi and Vicki L. O'Day, *Information Ecologies: Using Technology with Heart* (Cambridge, MA: MIT Press, 1999).

8. Schwartz, *The Art of Long View*, xiv.

9. See, for example, William J. Mitchell, *City of Bits: Space, Place, and the Infobahn* (Cambridge, MA: MIT Press, 1995).

10. James J. O'Donnell, *Avatars of the Word: From Papyrus to Cyberspace* (Cambridge, MA: Harvard University Press, 1998), 60.

11. The idea for this vignette derives in part from an idea in Richard Powers, *Plowing the Dark* (New York: Farrar, Straus and Giroux, 2000).

12. I explore this scenario in David J. Staley, *Computers, Visualization, and History: How New Technology Will Transform Our Understanding of the Past* (Armonk, NY: M.E. Sharpe, 2003; and in David J. Staley, "From Writing to Associative Assemblages: 'History' in an Electronic Culture" in *Writing, Teaching, and Researching History in the Electronic Age*, ed. Dennis A. Trinkle (Armonk, NY: M.E. Sharpe, 1998), 3–13.

13. See Mary Anne Moser, ed., *Immersed in Technology: Art and Virtual Environments* (Cambridge, MA: MIT Press, 1996).

14. For interesting examples of text visualizations, see George Chang, "Explanation of Text Visualization," n.d., www.jupiterstar.com/lunarscribbles/visualization/explanation/ (August 21, 2002).

15. Ivan Illitch, *In the Vineyard of the Text: A Commentary to Hugh's Didascalicon* (Chicago: University of Chicago Press, 1993), 1–5.

16. Freeman J. Dyson, *The Sun, the Genome, and the Internet: Tools of Scientific Revolutions* (New York: The New York Public Library and Oxford University Press, 1999), xiv–xv.

17. Dyson, *The Sun, the Genome, and the Internet*, xv.

18. The Arlington Institute, "Scenarios," n.d., www.arlingtoninstitute.org/products_services/scenario_dev.html (August 21, 2002).

Bibliography

All Web addresses were active as of December 16, 2002 (with the exception of *Slate*, used as an example of a defunct Web address).

Act for the Encouragement of Learning, by Vesting the Copies of Printed Books in the Authors or Purchasers of Such Copies, An. (8 Anne, c. 19, 1709).

American Association for History and Computing. "Guidelines for Evaluating Digital Media Activities in Tenure Promotion and Review." *Journal of the Association for History and Computing*. www.theaahc.org/tenure_guidelines.htm.

American Association for History and Computing. "Suggested Guidelines for Evaluating Digital Media Activities in Tenure, Review, and Promotion—An AAHC Document." *Perspectives* 39, No. 7 (October 2001): 33–34.

American Geophysical Union et al. v. Texaco. United States Court of Appeals, Second Circuit, 1994.

American Historical Association, Gutenberg-e Prizes. www.theaha.org/prizes/gutenberg/Index.cfm.

American Political Science Association, Section on Computers and Multimedia. "IT Guidelines." www.public.iastate.edu/~sws/apsa%20guidelines/itguidelines.htm.

Andersen, Deborah Lines. "Academic Historians, Electronic Information Access Technologies, and the World Wide Web: A Longitudinal Study of Factors Affecting Use and Barriers to That Use." *Journal of the Association for History and Computing* 1, No. 1 (1998). mcel.pacificu.edu/JAHC/jahcindex.htm; also in *History.edu: Essays on Teaching with Technology*, ed. Dennis A. Trinkle and Scott A. Merriman, 3–24. Armonk, NY: M.E. Sharpe, 2001.

Andersen, Deborah Lines, and Dennis A. Trinkle. "'One or Two Is Not a Problem' or Technology in the Tenure, Promotion, and Review Process: A Survey of Current Practices in U.S. History Departments." *JAHC: Journal of the Association for History and Computing* 4, No. 1 (2001). mcel.pacificu.edu/JAHC/JAHCIV1/ARTICLES/Anderson-Trinkle/Anderson-Trinkle.html.

Arlington Institute. "Scenarios." N.d. www.arlingtoninstitute.org/products_services/scenario_dev.html.

Arms, William Y. "Preservation of Scientific Serials: Three Current Examples." *Journal of Electronic Publishing* 5 (1999). www.press.umich.edu/jep/05-02/arms.html.

———. "What Are the Alternatives to Peer Review? Quality Control in Scholarly Publishing on the Web." *Journal of Electronic Publishing* 8 (2002). www.press.umich.edu/jep/08-01/arms.html.

arXiv.org (e-Print archive). arxiv.org/list/hep-ex/0208.

Association of College and Research Libraries. "Academic Librarianship and the Redefining Scholarship Project." March 1998. www.ala.org/acrl/ipfr.html.

Auer, Nicole. *Bibliography on Evaluating Internet Information.* www.lib.vt.edu/research/evaluate/evalbiblio.html.

Babbie, Earl. *The Practice of Social Research.* 6th ed. Belmont, CA: Wadsworth, 1992.

Barnes, James A. *Authors, Publishers and Politicians: The Quest for an Anglo-American Copyright Agreement 1815–1854.* London: Routledge & Kegan Paul, 1974.

Barrett, Margreth. "Intellectual Property: Patents, Trademarks, and Copyright." *Emanuel* (2000): 259–262.

Berners-Lee, Tim. *Weaving The Web: The Original Design and Ultimate Destiny of the World Wide Web.* New York: HarperCollins, 2000, 28–29.

Berthon, Hilary, Susan Thomas, and Colin Webb. "Safekeeping: A Cooperative Approach to Building a Digital Preservation Resource." *D-Lib Magazine* 8 (2002).

Bolter, Jay David. *Writing Space: The Computer, Hypertext, and the History of Writing.* New Jersey: Lawrence Erlbaum Associates, 1991, 10.

Booth, Alan, and Paul Hyland. *History Today.* hca.ltsn.ac.uk/resources/reviews/h2k_news2a.php.

———, eds. *History in Higher Education: New Directions in Teaching and Learning.* Oxford: Blackwell, 1996.

Borgman, Christine L. *From Gutenberg to the Global Information Infrastructure: Access to Information in the Networked World.* Cambridge, MA: MIT Press, 2000.

Bourne, John R. et al. "Paradigms for On-Line Learning: A Case Study in the Design and Implementation of an Asynchronous Learning Networks (ALN) Course." *Journal of Asynchronous Learning Networks* 1, No. 2 (August 1997). www.aln.org/alnWeb/journal/issue2/assee.htm.

Bradsher, Earl L. *Mathew Carey: Editor, Author and Publisher.* New York: AMS Press, 1966.

Bry, Francis, and Michael Kraus. "Perspectives for Electronic Books in the World Wide Web Age." *Electronic Library* 20, No. 4 (2002): 275–87.

Brylawski, E. Fulton, and Abe Goldman. *Legislative History of the 1909 Copyright Act.* Hackensack: Fred B. Rothman, 1976.

Buchanan, Walter. "A Survey of Creative Endeavor Criteria for Promotion and Tenure of ET Faculty." *Journal of Engineering Technology* (Spring 1996): 30–36.

Budd, J.M. "Research in the Two Cultures: The Nature of Scholarship in Science and in the Humanities." *Collection Management* 11 (1987): 1–21.

Butler, H. Julene. "Research into the Reward System of Scholarship: Where Does Scholarly Electronic Publishing Get You?" In *Filling the Pipeline and Paying the Piper: Proceedings of the Fourth ALA/AAUP Symposium, Scholarly Publishing on the Electronic Networks,* ed. Ann Okerson, 67–77. Washington, D.C.: Office of Scientific and Academic Publishing, Association of Research Libraries, 1995.

Buttler, Dwayne K. "CONFU-sed: Security, Safe Harbors, and Fair Use." *Journal of the American Society for Information Science* 50 (1999): 1308–12.

Campus Computing Project. w,ww.campuscomputing.net/.

Carlson, Scott. "Student and Faculty Members Turn to On-line Library Materials Before Printed Ones, Study Finds." *Chronicle of Higher Education,* October 3, 2002. chronicle.com/free/2002/10/2002100301t.htm.

Carnegie Foundation. *Carnegie Classification of Institutions of Higher Education.* Table #1. 2002. www.carnegiefoundation.org/Classification/index.htm.

Cartwright, G. Philip. "Information Technology: Considerations for Tenure and Promotion." *Change* 26, No. 5 (September/October 1994): 26–28.

Carver, K.W. *Using Internet Primary Sources to Teach Critical Thinking Skills in History*. Westport, CT: Greenwood Press, 1999.

Case, Donald O. "The Collection and Use of Information by Some American Historians: A Study of Motives and Methods." *Library Quarterly* 61 (1991): 61–82.

CCCC (Committee on Computers and Composition). "Promotion and Tenure Guidelines for Work with Technology." *College Composition & Communication* (September 1999): 139–42. www.ncte.org/positions/promotion.shtml.

"CCC's Rightlink Goes Live on InformationWeek.com." *Information Today 18* (December 2001). www.copyright.com/PDFs/CCC'sRightslink.pdf.

CD HotList: New Releases for Librarians. www2.library.unr.edu/anderson/cdhl/index.htm.

Center for Excellence in Teaching and Learning. University at Albany. www.albany.edu/cetl.

Chang, George. "Explanation of Text Visualization." N.d. www.jupiterstar.com/lunarscribbles/visualization/explanation/.

Channing, William E. *The Works of William E. Channing*. Boston: Munroe and Company, 1848.

Clark, Aubert J. *The Movement for International Copyright in Nineteenth Century America.* Washington, D.C.: Catholic University of America Press, 1960, 158–75.

"Collaborations for Learning and Teaching at the University of Iowa." Ed-Media/Ed-Telecom 98 World Conference on Educational Multimedia and Hypermedia & World Conference on Education Telecommunications. Proceedings 10th, Freiburg, Germany, June 20–25, 1998. Charlottesville, VA: Association for the Advancement of Computing in Education, ERIC Document Reproduction Service, ED 428 659, 1998, 268–73.

"Communication Versus Face-to-Face Collaboration: Results on Student Learning, Quality and Satisfaction." *Group Decisions and Negotiations* 8 (1999): 428.

Computing Research Association (CRA). www.cra.org/.

Copyright Act of 1891. 1891.

Courseware for History Implementation Consortium. chic.tees.ac.uk/.

Crabb, Don. "Is Information Technology Work Force Adequate?" *Chicago Sun-Times*, September 29, 1999, 73.

Crawford, Walter. "Free Electronic Refereed Journals: Getting Past the Arc of Enthusiasm." *Learned Publishing* 15 (2002): 117–23.

Cronin, Blaise, and Kara Overfelt. "E-Journals and Tenure." *Journal of the American Society for Information Science* 46, No. 9 (October 1995): 700–703.

Day, Michael. "The Scholarly Journal in Transition and the PubMed Central Proposal." *Ariadne* 21 (September 1999).

———. "Teachers at the Crossroads: Evaluating Teaching in Electronic Environments." *Computers and Composition* 17, No. 1 (2000): 31–40.

Delgadillo, R., and B. P. Lynch. "Future Historians: Their Quest for Information." *College & Research Libraries* 60 (1999): 245–60.

DeLoughrey, Thomas J. "Professors Report Progress in Gaining Recognition for Their Use of Technology." *Chronicle of Higher Education* 39, No. 26 (March 3, 1993): A19, 21.

Dewey, Barbara I. "Beyond the Information Arcade ™: Next Generation Collaborations for Learning and Teaching at the University of Iowa." Ed-Media/Ed-Telecom 98 World Conference on Educational Multimedia and Hypermedia & World Conference on Education Telecommunications. Proceedings 10th, Freiburg, Germany, June 20–25, 1998. Charlottesville, VA: Association for the Advancement of Computing in Education, ERIC Document Reproduction Service, ED 428 659, 1998, 268–73.

Dickinson Chronicles Project. chronicles.dickinson.edu/.

D-Lib Magazine. www.dlib.org/.

Duffy, Thomas M., and David H. Jonassen, eds. *Constructivism and the Technology of Instruction: A Conversation*. Hillsdale, NJ: Lawrence Erlbaum Associates, 1992.

Dyson, Freeman J. *The Sun, the Genome, and the Internet: Tools of Scientific Revolutions*. New York: The New York Public Library and Oxford University Press, 1999.

Eastgate Systems, Inc. www.eastgate.com/catalog/Afternoon.html.

Eisenstein, Elizabeth L. *The Printing Revolution in Early Modern Europe*. Cambridge: Cambridge University Press, 1983.

Elbert, Mary-Hilda. "Contrasting Patterns of Specialized Library Use." *Drexel Library Quarterly* 1 (1971): 13–27.

Ellis, David, Deborah Cox, and Katherine Hall. "A Comparison of the Information Seeking Patterns of Researchers in the Physical and Social Sciences." *Journal of Documentation* 49 (1993): 356–69.

Ethington, Philip J. "Los Angeles and the Problem of Urban Historical Knowledge." *American Historical Review* 105 (December 2000). cwis.usc.edu/dept/LAS/history/historylab/LAPUHK/index.html.

Feather, John. *Publishing, Piracy and Politics: An Historical Study of Copyright in Britain*. London: Mansell, 1994.

First Monday (peer-reviewed journal of the Internet). www.firstmonday.dk.

"First Monday Basics." www.firstmonday.dk/idea.html.

Flecker, Dale. "Preserving Scholarly E-Journals." *D-Lib Magazine* 7, No. 9 (2001). www.dlib.org/dlib/september01/flecker/09flecker.html.

Folsom v. Marsh. 1841.

Foster, Andrea. "Second Thoughts on 'Bundled' E-Journals." *Chronicle of Higher Education*, September 20, 2002, A31.

Fountain, Kathleen Carlisle. "Perceptions of Acceptance: Evaluating World Wide Web Projects in Performance Reviews." *College & Research Libraries* 62 (May 2001): 260–68.

Fredericksen, Eric, William Pelz, and Karen Swan. "Factors Influencing Faculty Satisfaction with Asynchronous Teaching and Learning in the SUNY Learning Network." *Learning Networks Effectiveness Research Web Center of New Jersey Institute of Technology* 2000. www.alnresearch.org/Data_Files/articles/full_text/fs-fredericksen.htm.

Freeman, Peter. *The Supply of Information Technology Workers in the United States*. Washington, D.C.: Computing Research Association, 1999.

Futures Research Quarterly, special issue, 17 (Summer 2001).

Garrison, D. Randy, Terry Anderson, and Walter Archer. "Critical Thinking, Cognitive Presence, and Computer Conferencing in Distance Education." *American Journal of Distance Education* 15, No. 1 (2001): 7.

Garrison, J., M. Larochelle, and N. Bednarz. *Constructivism and Education*. Cambridge: Cambridge University Press, 1998.

Gervais, Daniel J. "E-Commerce and Intellectual Property: Lock-It-up or License?" Copyright Clearance Center (2002). www.copyright.com/News/About Articles IntellectualProp.asp.

Gladney, Henry M. "Digital Dilemma: Intellectual Property." *D-Lib Magazine* 4 (1999).

Goldman, Jerry. *The Oyez Project* 2002. oyez.nwu.edu.

Google. www.google.com.

Granger, Stewart. "Digital Preservation and Deep Infrastructure." *D-Lib Magazine* 8 (2002).

Greco, Albert N. *The Book Publishing Industry.* Boston: Allyn and Bacon, 1997.

Greenstein, Daniel. *A Historian's Guide to Computing.* Oxford: Oxford University Press, 1994.

Guernsey, Lisa. "Scholars Who Work with Technology Fear They Suffer in Tenure Reviews." *Chronicle of Higher Education*, June 6, 1997, A21–22.

Haines, Annette. "Librarians' Personal Web Pages: An Analysis." *College & Research Libraries* 60, No. 6 (November 1999): 546.

Hall, Richard. *Evaluating the Context of On-line History Teaching: The First Year of the Chic Project.* Milton Keynes: IET: Open University, Proceedings of the 5th Humanities and Arts Network Conference, 1999.

Hall, Richard, and Derek Harding. "Driving Departmental Change through Evaluation: Some Outcomes and Problems." *Association for Learning Technology Journal* 8 (2000): 19–29.

Harasim, Linda et al. *Learning Networks: A Field Guide to Teaching and Learning On-line*, 3d. ed. Cambridge, MA: MIT Press, 1997.

Hardy, Charles Hardy III, and Alessandro Portelli. "'I Can Almost See the Lights of Home—A Field Trip to Harlan County, Kentucky." *Journal for MultiMedia History* 2 (1999). www.albany.edu/jmmh/.

Harter, Stephen P. "Scholarly Communication and Electronic Journals: An Impact Study." *Journal of the American Society for Information Science* 49, No. 6: 507–16.

Hartman, Joel, Charles Dziuban, and Patsy Moskal. "Faculty Satisfaction in ALNs: A Dependent or Independent Variable?" *Learning Networks Effectiveness Research Web Center of New Jersey Institute of Technology.* 2000. www.alnresearch.org/Data_Files/articles/full_text/fs-hartman.htm.

Haynes, David, and David Streatfield. "A National Co-ordinating Body for Digital Archiving?" *Ariadne* 15 (1997).

Henderson, Kathryn. *On Line and On Paper: Visual Representations, Visual Culture, and Computer Graphics in Design Engineering.* Cambridge, MA: MIT Press, 1999.

Herrmann, Francoise. "Building On-line Communities of Practice: An Example and Implications." *Educational Technology* (January–February 1998): 18.

Higher Education Funding Council for England. *QO 3–95 Subject Overview Report - History. Quality Assessment of History 1993–94.* Bristol: HEFCE, 1995.

Hiltz, Starr Roxanne. "Impacts of College-Level Courses via Asynchronous Learning Networks: Some Preliminary Results." *Journal of Asynchronous Learning Networks* 1, No. 2 (1997). www.aln.org/alnWeb/journal/issue2/hiltz.htm.

Hodge, Gail M. "Best Practices for Digital Archiving: An Information Life Cycle Approach." *D-Lib Magazine* 6 (2000).

Illitch, Ivan. *In the Vineyard of the Text: A Commentary to Hugh's Didascalicon.* Chicago: University of Chicago Press, 1993.

Jarausch, Konrad H. "Some Reflections on Coding." In *Datenbanken und Datenverwaltungssteme als Werkzeuge Historischer Forschung*, ed. M. Thaller. St. Katerinen: Scripta Mercaturae Verlag, 1986.

Johns, Adrian. *The Nature of the Book*. Chicago: University of Chicago Press, 1998.

Jonscher, Charles. *The Evolution of Wired Life: From the Alphabet to the Soul-Catcher Chip—How Information Technologies Change Our World*. New York: John Wiley & Sons, 1999.

Journal for MultiMedia History. www.albany.edu/jmmh/.

Journal of the Association for History and Computing. mcel.pacificu.edu/JAHC/jahcindex.htm.

Journal of the Association for Information Systems. jais.aisnet.org/.

Joyce, Michael. *Of Two Minds: Hypertext, Pedagogy, and Poetics*. Ann Arbor: University of Michigan Press, 1995.

Kahin, Brian, and Hal R. Varian. *Internet Publishing and Beyond: The Economics of Digital Information and Intellectual Property*. Cambridge, MA: MIT Press, 2000.

Kairos: A Journal for Teachers of Writing in Webbed Environments. english.ttu.edu/kairos/2.1/index_f.html.

Katz, Richard N., and Julie A. Rudy. *Information Technology in Higher Education: Assessing Its Impact and Planning for the Future*. San Francisco: Jossey-Bass, New Directions for Institutional Research, No. 102 (Summer 1999).

Katz, Seth R. "One Department's Guidelines for Evaluating Computer-Related Work." *Kairos: A Journal for Teachers of Writing in Webbed Environments* (Spring 1997). english.ttu.edu/kairos/2.1/coverWeb/katz/art2.html.

Kiernan, Vincent. "Rewards Remain Dim for Professors Who Pursue Digital Scholarship." *Chronicle of Higher Education*, April 28, 2000, A45–A46.

King, Jack B. "History Research into the 21st Century." *Reference Librarian* 47 (1994): 89–108.

Kling, Rob. "Academic Rewards for Scholarly Research Communication via Electronic Publishing." Available on the Center for Social Informatics Working Paper site, number 02–13. www.slis.indiana.edu/csi/papers.html.

Kling, Rob, and Ewa Callahan. "Electronic Journals, the Internet, and Scholarly Communication. *Annual Review of Information Science and Technology* 37, ed. Blaise Cronin.

Kling, Rob, and Lisa Covi. "Electronic Journals and Legitimate Media in the Systems of Scholarly Communication." *Information Society* 11 (1995): 261–71.

Kling, Rob, and Geoffrey McKim. "Scholarly Communication and the Continuum of Electronic Publishing." *Journal of the American Society for Information Science* 50 (August 1999): 890–906.

Kling, Rob, Geoffrey McKim, and Adam King. "A Bit More to It: Scientific Multiple Media Communication Forums as Socio-Technical Interaction Networks." *Journal of the American Society for Information Science* 51, No. 1 (December 2002): 47–67.

Kling, Rob, Lisa Spector, and Geoff McKim. "Locally Controlled Scholarly Publishing via the Internet: The Guild Model." *Journal of Electronic Publishing* 8 (2002). www.press.umich.edu/jep/08–01/kling.html.

Lacher-Feldman, Jessica. "Presenting Historical Resources Information on the World Wide Web: A Case Study of the Development of the New York State Office of Cultural Education's Web site and the OCE History Advisory Council History Resources Web Pages." *Journal of the Association for History and Computing* 2, No. 2 (August 1999). www.mcel.pacificu.edu/JAHC/JAHCII2/ARTICLESII2/LACHER-FELDMAN/Lacherindex.HTML.

Landow, George P. *Hypertext: The Convergence of Contemporary Critical Theory and Technology.* Baltimore: Johns Hopkins University Press, 1992.

Langston, Lisbeth. "Scholarly Communication and Electronic Publication: Implications for Research, Advancement, and Promotion." In *Untangling the Web: Proceedings of the Conference Sponsored by the Librarians Association of the University of California, Santa Barbara, and Friends of the UCSB Library,* April 26, 1996. www.library.ucsb.edu/untangle/langston.html ERIC, ED 403892.

Lanham, Richard A. *The Electronic Word: Democracy, Technology, and the Arts.* Chicago: University of Chicago Press, 1993.

LaRose, Robert, and Pam Whitten. "Re-Thinking Instructional Immediacy for Web Courses: A Social Cognitive Exploration." *Communication Education* 49, No. 4 (2000): 324.

Larson, Mary A. "Potential, Potential, Potential: The Marriage of Oral History and the World Wide Web." *Journal of American History* 88, No. 2 (September 2001): 600–601.

Laurillard, D. *Rethinking University Teaching: A Framework for Effective Use of Educational Technology.* London and New York: Routledge, 1993.

Lawrence, Steve. "Free Online Availability Substantially Increases a Paper's Impact." *Nature Webdebates* (May 2001). www.nature.com/nature/debates/e-access/Articles/lawrence.html.

Lawson, Karen G., and Nancy L. Pelzer. "Assessing Technology-Based Projects for Promotion and/or Tenure in ARL Academic Libraries." *College & Research Libraries* 60 (September 1999): 464–76.

Learning and Teaching Subject Network (LTSN). Centre for History, Classics and Archaeology. hca.ltsn.ac.uk/.

Learning Technology Dissemination Initiative. "Evaluation Cookbook." www.icbl.hw.ac.uk/ltdi/cookbook/contents.html.

Leidner, Dorothy E., and Sirkka L. Jarvenpaa. "The Use of Information Technology to Enhance Management School Education: A Theoretical View." *MIS Quarterly* (September 1995): 265–91.

Lessig, Lawrence. *The Future of Ideas.* New York: Random House, 2001.

Librarians' Index to the Internet. www.lii.org.

Literary Movements. www.gonzaga.edu/faculty/campbell/enl311/litfram.html.

Lowry, Anita K. "The Information Arcade at the University of Iowa." *Cause/Effect* (Fall 1994): 38–44. www.educause.edu/ir/library/text/CEM9438.txt.

Lynch, Dianne. "Professors Should Embrace Technology in Courses. . . ." *Chronicle of Higher Education,* January 18, 2002, 1.

Mackey, Thomas. ISP301 Class Web site (Fall 2002). www.albany.edu/~mackey/isp301.

Malloy, Thomas E., and Gerard L. Hanley. "MERLOT: A Faculty-Focused Web Site of Educational Resources." *Behavior Research Methods, Instruments, & Computers* 33, No. 2 (2001): 274.

Martinez, Ignacio, and George P. Richardson. "Best Practices in System Dynamics Modeling." In *Proceedings of the 19th International Conference of the System Dynamics Society.* Atlanta, GA, 2001.

Mawdsley, Evan, and Thomas Munck. *Computing for Historians. An Introductory Guide.* Manchester: Manchester University Press, 1993.

McAdoo, Representative [William]. "What Congress Has Done." *North American Review* 151 (1890): 526–30.

McClintock, Robert. "Renewing the Progressive Contract with Posterity: On the Social Construction of Digital Learning Communities," 1996. www.ilt.columbia.edu/
mcclintock/renew/ren_main.htm.

McCollum, Kelly. "Colleges Urged to Use Technology to 'Promote Lifelong Learning.'" *Chronicle of Higher Education*, September 24, 1999, A39.

McMillian, Gail. "Viewing Results for Assessing Technology-Based Projects for Faculty Evaluations." Digital On-line Archives 2000. lumiere.lib.vt.edu/surveys/results/.

MERLOT (Multimedia Educational Resource for Learning and On-line Teaching).
www.merlot.org.

Mitchell, William J. *City of Bits: Space, Place, and the Infobahn*. Cambridge, MA:
MIT Press, 1995.

Modern Language Association. "Guidelines for Evaluating Work with Digital Media
in the Modern Languages." May 30, 2000. www.mla.org/reports/ccet/ccet_
guidelines.htm.

Morecroft, John, and John D. Sterman, eds. *Modeling for Learning Organizations*.
Portland, OR: Productivity Press, 1994.

Moser, Mary Anne, ed. *Immersed in Technology: Art and Virtual Environments*. Cambridge, MA: MIT Press, 1996.

Mosteller, Frederick, and David L. Wallace. *Inference and Disputed Authorship: The
Federalist Papers*. Reading, MA and London: Addison-Wesley, 1964.

Murphy, J. "Technology Training for Faculty." *Converge* 2 (1999): 30–31.

Nahrwold, Cindy. "'Just' Professing: A Call for the Valuation of Electronic Scholarship," *Kairos* 2, No. 1 (1997). english.ttu.edu/kairos/2.1/index_f.html.

Nardi, Bonnie A., and Vicki L. O'Day. *Information Ecologies: Using Technology
with Heart*. Cambridge, MA: MIT Press, 1999.

National Public Radio. www.npr.org.

Neely, Theresa Y. "The Impact of Electronic Publications on Promotion and Tenure
Decisions." *Leading Ideas* (October 1999): 1–6. www.arl.org/diversity/leading/
issue10/tneely.html.

"Newspapers and Periodicals—Number by Type: 1980–2000." In U.S. Department
of Commerce, *Statistical Abstract of the United States: 2001*. Washington, D.C.:
Government Printing Office, 2001, Chart No. 1126.

Nicklin, Julie B. "Libraries Drop Thousands of Journals as Budgets Shrink and Prices
Rise." *Chronicle of Higher Education*, December 11, 1991, A29.

Nielsen, Jakob. *Designing Web Usability: The Practice of Simplicity*. Indianapolis,
IN: New Riders Publishing, 2000: 15.

North Carolina State University, Department of Accounting. "Retention, Promotion, and Tenure Guidelines." 1999. www.ncsu.edu/provost/academic_affairs/rpt/
guidelines/ACC.html.

Ocker, Rosalie J. and Gayle J. Yaverbaum, "Asynchronous Computer-Mediated Communication Versus Face-to-Face Collaboration: Results on Student Learning, Quality and Satisfaction," *Group Decisions and Negotiations* 8 (1999): 428.

O'Connell, Heath B. "Physicists Thriving with Paperless Publishing." *High Energy
Physics Libraries Webzine* (March 2002). library.cern.ch/HEPLW/6/papers/3/.

Odlyzko, Andrew. "The Economics of Electronic Journals." *First Monday* 2 (1997): 8.

O'Donnell, James J. *Avatars of the Word: From Papyrus to Cyberspace*. Cambridge,
MA: Harvard University Press, 1998.

Okerson, Ann. "Are We There Yet? On-line E-resources Ten Years After." *Library
Trends* 48 (2000): 671–94.

Osborne, John M., Ian G. Anderson, and James W. Gerencser. *Teaching, Learning, and Digitizing Resources in the Humanities through the Cooperation of Educators and Archivists.* Edinburgh: Digital Resources for the Humanities 2002 Conference Abstracts, 2002, 162.

Oxford English Dictionary. 2d ed. Oxford and New York: Oxford University Press, 1989.

Palmer, Carole L., and Laura J. Neumann. "The Information Work of Interdisciplinary Humanities Scholars: Exploration and Translation." *Library Quarterly* 72 (2002): 85–117.

Patterson, David, Lawrence Snyder, and Jeffrey Ullman. "Evaluating Computer Scientists and Engineers for Promotion and Tenure," Computing Research Association Best Practices Memo in *Computing Research News* (September 1999) www.cra.org/reports/tenure_review.pdf.

Photoduplication of Copyrighted Material by Libraries. Washington, D.C.: United States Senate Committee on the Judiciary, Subcommittee on Patents, Trademarks, and Copyrights, 1960.

Poole, Dawn M. "Student Participation in a Discussion-Oriented On-line Course: A Case Study." *Journal of Research on Computing in Education* 33, No. 2 (Winter 2000): 162.

Powers, Richard. *Plowing the Dark.* New York: Farrar, Straus and Giroux, 2000.

Preece, Jenny. *On-line Communities: Designing Usability, Supporting Sociability.* New York: John Wiley & Sons, 2000.

"Primedia Business Announces Partnership with iCopyright." iCopyright.com Instant Clearance Service. 2002. www.icopyright.com/news/pr20020423.html.

QAA—Quality Assurance Agency for Higher Education, *History Subject Benchmark Statement.* Gloucester: QAA, 2000.

Randers, Jørgen. "Guidelines for Model Conceptualization." In *Elements of the System Dynamics Method.* ed. J. Randers, 117–39. Cambridge, MA: MIT Press, 1980.

Reagan-Cirincione, P. et al. "Decision Modeling: Tools for Strategic Thinking." *Interfaces* 21, No. 6: 52–65.

Rogers, Everett. *Diffusion of Innovations.* 4th ed. New York: Free Press, 1995.

Rogers, Sally A. "Electronic Journal Usage at Ohio State University." *College & Research Libraries* 62, No. 1 (January 2001): 33.

Rossman, Mark H. "Successful On-line Teaching Using an Asynchronous Learning Discussion Forum." *Journal of Asynchronous Learning Networks* 3, No. 2 (November 1999). www.aln.org/alnWeb/journal/Vol3_issue2/Rossman.htm.

Rourke, Liam et al. "Assessing Social Presence in Asynchronous Text-Based Computer Conferencing." *Journal of Distance Education* 14, No. 2 (1999). www.icaap.org/iuicode?151.14.2.6.

Salon, (on-line magazine). www.salon.com.

Samuelson, Pamela. "Intellectual Property and the Digital Economy: Why the Anti-Circumvention Regulations Need to Be Revised." *Berkeley Technology Law Journal* 14 (1999): 519.

Schauder, Don. "Electronic Publishing of Professional Articles: Attitudes of Academics and Implications for the Scholarly Communication Industry." *Journal of the American Society for Information Science* 45 (March 1994): 73–100.

Schmidt, Steffen W. et al. "Ad hoc Committee on Information Technology in Political Science." September 1, 1999 1–4. www.public.iastate.edu/~sws/apsa%20guidelines/itguidelines.htm.

Schwartz, Peter. *The Art of the Long View: Planning for the Future in an Uncertain World.* New York: Currency/Doubleday, 1996.

Scottish Higher Education Funding Council. *Quality Assessment in History: University of Glasgow.* Edinburgh: SHEFC, 1996.

Scribner v. Straus et al. Supreme Court of the United States, 1908.

Sellen, Abigail J., and Richard H.R. Harper. *The Myth of the Paperless Office.* Cambridge, MA: MIT Press, 2002.

Seminoff, Nancy E., and Shelley B. Wepner. "Are Technology-Based Projects Valued as Scholarship for Tenure and Promotion?" *Journal of Computing in Teacher Education* 11 (Spring 1995): 5–10.

———. "What Should We Know about Technology-Based Projects for Tenure and Promotion?" *Journal of Research in Computing in Education* 30, No. 1 (Fall 1997): 67–82.

Slate (on-line journal—no longer available). msn.slate.com.

Slatella, Michelle. "Building Web Pages Is Child's Play." *New York Times,* May 7, 1998, G11.

Smith, James Morton. *The Republic of Letters* New York: W.W. Norton, 1995.

Soderdahl, Paul A., and Carol Ann Hughes. "That's My Bailiwick: A Library-Sponsored Faculty Research Web Server." *Information Technology and Libraries* 19, No. 1 (March 2000): 29–34.

Solberg, Thorvald. *Copyright in Congress: 1789–1904.* Washington, D.C.: Government Printing Office, 1905.

Sosteric, Mike, Yuwei Shi, and Olivier Wenker. "The Upcoming Revolution in the Scholarly Communication System." *Journal of Electronic Publishing* 7 (2001).

Spaeth, Donald A., and Sonja Cameron. "Computers and Resource-Based History Teaching: A UK Perspective." In *Computers and the Humanities* 34. Dordrecht: Kluwer Academic, 2000.

Speier, Cheri et al. "Faculty Perceptions of Electronic Journals as Scholarly Communication: A Question of Prestige and Legitimacy." *Journal of the American Society for Information Science* 50 (May 1, 1999): 537–43.

Staley, David J. *Computers, Visualization, and History: How New Technology Will Transform Our Understanding of the Past.* Armonk, NY: M.E. Sharpe, 2003.

———. "Digital Historiography: Subjunctivity." *Journal of the Association for History and Computing* (April 2000). mcel.pacificu.edu/JAHC/JAHCIII1/P-RE-VIEWS/staleyIII1.html.

———. "From Writing to Associative Assemblages: 'History' in an Electronic Culture." In *Writing, Teaching and Researching History in the Electronic Age.* ed. Dennis A. Trinkle, 3–13. Armonk, NY: M.E. Sharpe, 1998.

———. "History and the Future." *History and Theory,* 41, No. 4 (December 2002), 72–89.

State University of New York. "SUNY On-line Courses and Degree Programs." sln.suny.edu/.

Sterman, John D. *Business Dynamics: Systems Thinking and Modeling for a Complex World.* Boston: Irwin/McGraw-Hill, 2000.

Stone, Lawrence. "History and the Social Sciences." *Past and the Present.* Boston and London: Routledge & Kegan Paul, 1981.

Strathclyde University, Glasgow. BUBL Information Service. bubl.ac.uk/.

Suck (on-line journal). www.suck.com.

"Survey Sees Demand Returning for Information-Tech Workers." *AP Worldstream,* May 6, 2002.

Swan, Karen et al. "Building Knowledge Building Communities: Consistency, Contact and Communication in the Virtual Classroom." *Journal of Educational Computing Research* 23, No. 4 (2000): 367.

Sweeney, Aldrin E. "E-Scholarship and Electronic Publishing in the Twenty-First Century: Implications for the Academic Community." *Education Media International* 38, No. 1 (March 2001): 25–38.

———. "Tenure and Promotion: Should You Publish in Electronic Journals?" *Journal of Electronic Publishing* 6 (2000). www.press.umich.edu/jep/06–02/sweeney.html.

Sylva, Kathryn, and Robin Lasser. *Eating Disorders: Disordered Culture*. March 3, 2000. www.eating.ucdavis.edu.

Tal, Kali. "Divisions Between Old and Young Professors Could Be Dangerous to Academe." *Chronicle of Higher Education*, October 1, 1999, B3.

Tebbel, John. *A History of Book Publishing in the United States*. Vol. 2. New York: R.R. Bowker, 1972.

Tilley, Charles. "Computers in Historical Analysis." In *Computers in the Humanities* ed. J.L. Mitchell. Edinburgh: Edinburgh University Press, 1973.

Tomlins, Christopher. "Don't Mourn, Organize! A Rumination on Printed Scholarly Journals at the Edge of the Internet." *Perspectives* (February 1998).

Townsend, Robert B. "All of Tomorrow's Yesterdays: History Scholarship on the Web." *Perspectives* (May 2002). www.theaha.org/Perspectives/Issues/2002/0205/0205pub3.cfm.

Trinkle, Dennis, and Scott Merriman, eds. *The History Highway 2000*. Armonk, NY: M.E. Sharpe, 2000.

Trinkle, Dennis A. and Scott A. Merriman, *History.edu: Essays on Teaching with Technology* (Armonk, NY: M.E. Sharpe, 2001).

Ulrich, Laurel Thatcher. *A Midwife's Tale: The Life of Martha Ballard Based on her Diary 1785–1812*. New York: Random House, 1990. Interactive Web site at www.dohistory.org/.

Ulrich's Periodicals Directory. New Providence, NJ: R.R. Bowker, 2002.

Unger, Harlow Giles. *Noah Webster: The Life and Times of an American Patriot*. New York: John Wiley & Sons, 1998.

University at Albany. "Computing at UAlbany." www.albany.edu/computing/.

University at Albany, University Libraries. *"Internet Tutorials."* library.albany.edu/internet/.

University of Arizona. "College of Humanities—Promotion and Tenure: Criteria." 2000. www.coh.arizona.edu/COH/facinfo/pandtcriteria2000/pandtcriteria2000.htm.

———. Mathematics Division. "Annual Performance Review Processes, Criteria, and Measures." January 1998. www.math.arizona.edu/overview/perf.html.

University of California. Office of the President. "Point 210–1 D. Academic Personnel Manual 210, d.," Page 5. 1992. www.ucop.edu/acadadv/acadpers/apm/apm-210.pdf.

University of Florida, College of Health Professions. "Guidelines for Tenure and Promotion." 2002. www.hp.ufl.edu/overview/ptguidelinesjuly2002.doc.

University of Glasgow. "Design and Implementation of Software for Historians (DISH)." www.arts.gla.ac.uk/History/DISH/dish.htm.

University of Glasgow. History Courseware Consortium. www.gla.ac.uk/~histtltp/.

University of Glasgow. School of History and Archaeology. "Honours Handbook 2002–3." www.arts.gla.ac.uk/History/Honours/handbook/twentyone.htm.

University of Michigan, "College of Literature, Sciences and the Arts—Tenure Proceedings: Principles." July 2001. www.lsa.umich.edu/dean/acad/promotions/principles.html.

"Useable Information Technology. Jakob Nielsen's Web site." www.useit.com.

U.S. Department of Commerce. "American Book Title Production: 1998 and 1999." *Statistical Abstract of the United States: 2001*. Washington, D.C.: Government Printing Office, 2001, Chart No. 1135.

————. Newspapers and Periodicals–Number by Type: 1980–2000." *Statistical Abstracts of the United States: 2001* (Washington, DC: Government Printing Office, 2001, Chart No. 1126.

————. "Quantity of Books Sold and Value of U.S. Domestic Consumer Expenditures: 1995–2000." *Statistical Abstract of the United States: 2001*. Washington, D.C.: Government Printing Office, 2001, Chart No. 1134.

Vaidhyanathan, Siva. *Copyrights and Copywrongs*. New York: NYU Press, 2001.

Valley of the Shadow. www.iath.virginia.edu/vshadow2.

Van Orsdel, Lee, and Kathleen Born. "Doing the Digital Flip: Has the Advent of the E-Journal Finally Turned the Periodicals Industry Upside Down?" *Library Journal* (April 15, 2002): 51–52.

Vennix, Jac A.M. *Group Model Building: Facilitating Team Learning Using System Dynamics*. Chichester, UK: John Wiley & Sons, 1996.

Vennix, Jac A.M., George P. Richardson, and David F. Andersen, eds. 1997. "Group Model Building." Special issue of the *System Dynamics Review* 13, No. 2.

Vigen, Jens. "New Communication Channels: Electronic Clones, but Probably the First Steps Towards a New Paradigm." *High Energy Physics Libraries Webzine* 6 (March 2002). library.cern.ch/HEPLW/6/papers/2.

Volery, Thierry. "On-line Education: An Exploratory Study into Success Factors." *Journal of Educational Computing Research* 24 (2001).

W3C, World Wide Web Consortium. www.w3.org/Consortium/#background.

————. "Cascading Style Sheets." www.w3.org/Style/CSS/.

————. "Contemporary and Historical Census Collection Project." www.chcc.ac.uk.

————. "MarkUp Validation Service." validator.w3.org/.

————. "User Agent Web Accessibility Guidelines 1.0." www.w3.org/TR/UAAG10/.

————. "Web Accessibility Initiative (WAI)." www.w3.org/WAI/.

Walker, Janice R. "Fanning the Flames: Tenure and Promotion and Other Role-Playing Games." 2, No. 1 *Kairos* (1997). english.ttu.edu/kairos/2.1/index_f.html.

Walterscheid, Edward C. *The Nature of the Intellectual Property Clause: A Study in Historical Perspective*. Buffalo: William H. Hein, 2002.

Washington State University. Library Faculty Manual, 3.b.1. "Criteria for Merit Increases, Promotion and Granting of Tenure." www.wsulibs.wsu.edu/faculty/faculty-handbook/Promotion-Granting-Tenure.html.

————. Libraries Faculty Manual, 3.b.1.a.1. "Guidelines for the Evaluation of Electronic Publications." www.wsulibs.wsu.edu/faculty/faculty-handbook/Guidelines-For-Evaluation-of-Electronic-Publications.html.

WebCT. www.Webct.com.

Westney, Lynn C. Hattendorf. "A Trivial Pursuit? Information Technology and the Tenure Track." *Campus-Wide Information Systems* 4 (2000): 113–19.

Whitman, M.E., A.R. Hendrickson, and A.M. Townsend. "Research Commentary. Academic Rewards for Teaching Research, and Service: Data and Discourse." *Information Systems Research* 10 (1999): 99–109.

Wiberley, Stephen E. "Habits of Humanists: Scholarly Behavior and New Information Technologies." *Library Hi Tech* 9 (1991): 17–21.

Wiberley, Stephen E., and William G. Jones. "Humanists Revisited: A Longitudinal Look at the Adoption of Information Technology." *College & Research Libraries* 55 (1994): 499–509.

William, David. "Well, They Say He's Published, but Only Electronically." *Chronicle of Higher Education*, November 26, 1999, B3.

Williams & Wilkins Co. v. United States. Supreme Court of the United States, 1974.

Wilson, Robin. "Computer Scientists Flee Academe for Industry's Greener Pastures." *Chronicle of Higher Education*, September 24, 1999, A16–A17.

Wittenberg, Kate. "Digital Technology and Historical Scholarship: A Publishing Experiment." *Perspectives* (May 2002). http://www.theaha.org/perspectives/issues/2002/0205/0205pub4.cfm.

Wolcott, Linda L. "Tenure, Promotion, and Distance Teaching: A Study of Faculty Rewards and Incentives." Arlington, VA: ERIC Document Reproduction Service, ED413861, 1997.

Wolstenholme, Eric F. *System Enquiry: A System Dynamics Approach*. New York: John Wiley & Sons, 1990.

Wyly, Brendan J. "Competition in Scholarly Publishing? What Publisher Profits Reveal." *ARL Newsletter* Issue 200, October 1998. www.arl.org/newsltr/200/wyly.html.

Yergin, Daniel, and Thane Gustafson. *Russia 2010, and What It Means for the World*. New York: Vintage Books, 1995.

Young, Jeffrey R. "Ever So Slowly, Colleges Start to Count Work with Technology in Tenure Decisions." *Chronicle of Higher Education*, February 22, 2002, A25–A28. chronicle.com/weekly/v48/i24/24a02501.htm (for registered Chronicle users).

About the Editor
and Contributors

Deborah Lines Andersen is an Assistant Professor of Information Science and Policy at the University at Albany, State University of New York. She teaches statistics, research methods, and information policy to graduate students interested in librarianship, archival administration, and records management and preservation, and serves as co-editor of the *Journal of the Association for History and Computing* (mcel.pacificu.edu/JAHC/ jahcindex.htm). Her research interests are policies and management for public libraries, and the use of electronic information access technologies by special-user populations, particularly by academic historians. dla@albany.edu

Ian G. Anderson is Lecturer in New Technologies for the Humanities Advanced Technology and Information Institute (HATII) at the University of Glasgow, Scotland. His research interests include user and needs analysis, interface and multimedia design, computer-based pedagogies, and digitization projects. He is currently working on a collaborative project (with Professor Helen Tibbo of the University of North Carolina at Chapel Hill) on historians' information retrieval strategies and electronic archival finding aids. Anderson is the local project manager for the Contemporary and Historic Census Collection Project, a national initiative between Glasgow, Essex, Manchester, and Leeds Universities to develop contemporary and historical census data into a major learning and teaching resource. He is the author of "Developing Multimedia Courseware for Teaching History: A U.K. Perspective," *Journal for MultiMedia History* 3 (2001) (www.albany.edu/jmmh). I.Anderson@hatii.arts.gla.ac.uk

Kathleen Carlisle Fountain, Political Science and Social Work Librarian, serves as a reference librarian at the Meriam Library, California State University, Chico. She maintains a directory of interest groups that lobby the U.S. Congress (www.csuchico.edu/~kcfount/), and serves as a specialist for faculty and students in the areas of American politics, international relations, law, criminal justice, and public administration. In 2002 she published "Lay-ing a Foundation for Comparing Departmental Structures Between Reference and Instructional Services: Analysis of a Nationwide Survey" (with Kristen Johnson) in *College & Research Libraries* 63, No. 3. kfountain@csuchico.edu

Ryan Johnson, Electronic Resources Librarian at the Holland/New Library of Washington State University, is Data Services Librarian, and the subject selector for and liaison to the Departments of Sociology, Human Development and Comparative American Cultures at the university. He is a 2002 Fellow of the Berglund Center for Internet Studies, Pacific University, and the 2002–2003 president of the American Association for History and Computing. Johnson is also co-editor of the *Journal of the Association for History and Computing.* (mcel.pacificu.edu/JAHC/jahcindex.htm). johnsor@wsu.edu

Daphne Jorgensen is an Adjunct Professor and PhD student in the School of Education, Department of Educational Theory and Practice, at the University at Albany where she teaches graduate courses on the use of media in teaching and learning, and educational Web site development. Her areas of specialization are instructional technology, distance education, and educational Web site evaluation. She has recently published, "The Challenges and Benefits of On-line Classrooms: The Cost, Collaboration and Community Building" in *Reference Librarian* 37, No. 77 (2002). daphne@nycap.rr.com

Rob Kling was Professor of Information Systems and Information Science, School of Library and Information Science at Indiana University, Bloomington. As Director of the Center for Social Informatics at Bloomington, Kling's area of specialization was the changing nature of communications in an increasingly information-centered and technology-mediated society. A Fellow of the American Association for the Advancement of Science (2001), his work includes "Not Just a Matter of Time: Field Differences in the Shaping of Electronic Media Supporting Scientific Communication" (with Geoffrey McKim) in the *Journal of the American Society for Information Science* 51, No. 14 (2000), and an edited volume, *Computerization and Controversy: Value Conflicts and Social Choices* (2d ed), San Diego Academic Press, 1996.

Jessica Lacher-Feldman is an Assistant Professor and the Public Outreach Services Coordinator for the W.S. Hoole Special Collections Library at the University of Alabama. She is past president of the American Association for History and Computing. Her interests include public service, exhibits, and outreach in special collections, as well as the use of digital technology in the special collections environment. She is the developer of the on-line exhibit, *Over There! and Back Again: Patriotic American Sheet Music from the First World War* (www.lib.ua.edu/libraries/hoole/digital/overthere/index.htm) and is involved in the development of a statewide project to digitize Alabama's historical and cultural resources. She contributes a column on Archives and the Web for the *Reference, Access, and Outreach Newsletter* for the Society of American Archivists, and is also a member of the RAO Steering Committee. jlfeldma@bama.ua.edu

Thomas P. Mackey is an Assistant Professor of Information Science and Policy at the University at Albany, State University of New York, and former Assistant Director of Instructional Technology at the Center for Excellence in Teaching and Learning at the University at Albany (www.albany.edu/cetl/). His teaching and research interests focus on student-centered Web development, Web accessibility, and information literacy, including a study on the impact of collaboration on student Web design. He is a member of the Advisory Panel on Information Literacy for the Middle States Commission on Higher Education. tmackey@uamail.albany.edu

Terrence Maxwell is Assistant Professor in the Graduate School of Information Science and Policy at the University at Albany. His PhD is from the School of Public Affairs and Policy at the University at Albany, where he specialized in policy analysis and organizational behavior. His research interests are information organization management and policy, particularly intellectual property, and government information use. Maxwell served as director of the New York State Forum for Information Resource Management (www.nysfirm.org/), and is a former Eastern Regional Director of the National Association of State Information Resource Executives (www.nascio.org). TAMaxwell@aol.com

Susan L. McCormick is the Associate Editor of the *Journal for MultiMedia History* (www.albany.edu/jmmh), a Co-Producer of *Talking History: Aural History Productions*, and the Co-Director of *Capital Voices—Capital Lives*, a project that seeks to locate, preserve, and disseminate the sounds and voices of the historic Capital Region of New York State. Working at the University at Albany, she specializes in U.S. Social History and the intersections of work, public policy, and gender; oral and video history; and the integration of new media into research and teaching in history. sm0712@albany.edu

Lisa B. Spector is Research Associate in the Center for Social Informatics, School of Library and Information Science at Indiana University, Bloomington. Her research interests are community change analysis and implementation. She has recently published "Locally Controlled Scholarly Publishing Via the Internet: The Guild Model" (with Rob Kling and Geoff McKim) in the *Journal of Electronic Publishing* 8, No. 1 (August 2002). lspector@indiana.edu

David J. Staley Assistant Professor of History and Director of Grants at Heidelberg College in Tiffin, Ohio, works in the areas of historical methodology, history and the future, and technology and society. He is the author of *Computers, Visualization, and History: How Technologies Will Transform Our Understanding of the Past*, Armonk, NY: M.E. Sharpe, 2002, and "A History of the Future," *History and Theory*, December 2002, as well as an editor for the American Association for History and Computing/ M.E. Sharpe series "History, the Humanities and New Technology." dstaley@heidelberg.edu

Dennis A. Trinkle is Associate Coordinator of Information Services and Technology, and Tenzer University Professor of Instructional Technology at DePauw University, Greencastle, Indiana. He serves as Executive Director of the American Association for History and Computing (www.theaahc.org). He has published widely in technology, teaching, and history. His books published by M.E. Sharpe include *The History Highway, A Guide to Internet Resources*; *Writing, Teaching, and Researching History in the Electronic Age*, 1997; and *History.edu: Essays on Teaching with Technology*, 2001. dtrinkle@depauw.edu

Lynn C. Hattendorf Westney is Associate Professor and Assistant Reference Librarian at the Richard J. Daley Library at the University of Illinois at Chicago. Editor of *Educational Rankings Annual*, her areas of research and interest include reference collection development, especially in the areas of business, careers, education and the social sciences, electronic and digital publishing, and teaching with technology. Recently appointed to the American Anthropological Association Library Advisory Board, she serves on committees for a wide variety of national associations, including the American Library Association and the American Association for History and Computing. lynnhatt@uic.edu

Gerald Zahavi, Professor of History at the University at Albany, State University of New York, is the co-founder and current editor of the *Journal for MultiMedia History* (www.albany.edu/jmmh), an on-line journal devoted to presenting and reviewing nonprint and electronic works of history. He is the founder and director of *Talking History* (talkinghistory.org), an aural history production center and radio program. Specializing in U.S. business and labor, local and regional, and oral history, as well as in quantitative data analysis, he is presently researching and writing *A Community of Capital: An Oral History of the General Electric Company*, as told by managers, engineers, scientists, and blue- and pink-collar workers. gz580@albany.edu

Index